Harvard Historical Studies, 106

Published under the auspices
of the Department of History
from the income of the
Paul Revere Frothingham Bequest
Robert Louis Stroock Fund
Henry Warren Torrey Fund

Fierce Communion

Family and Community in Early America

Helena M. Wall

Harvard University Press
Cambridge, Massachusetts
London, England

First Harvard University Press paperback edition, 1995

Library of Congress Cataloging-in-Publication Data

Wall, Helena M.
  Fierce communion : family and community in early America /
Helena M. Wall.
    p.   cm.—(Harvard historical studies)
    Includes bibliographical references.
    ISBN 0-674-29958-2 (cloth)
    ISBN 0-674-29959-0 (pbk.)
    I. United States—Social conditions—To 1865. 2. Family—United
States—History. 3. Community—History. 4. Interpersonal
relations—History. 5. United States—History—Colonial period,
ca. 1600-1775. I. Title. II. Series.
HN57.W27   1990
306.85'0973–dc20

89-26806
CIP

For Deena and Steve

Preface

Colonial society began by deferring to the needs of the community and ended by deferring to the rights of the individual. The shift in the relative importance of community and individual occurred so gradually and unevenly over the course of the colonial period, and has so fundamentally recast our subsequent values and behavior, that it requires some effort of imagination to recapture the primacy of community in colonial America. The community was the matrix of colonial life: it shaped society at every level from land distribution to personal relationships. Through formal actions and informal pressures, the community influenced most of the activities and relationships of daily life.

This book examines the conduct of private life in a culture dominated, in every region, by community values and expectations; it ends by sketching the shift to a culture based instead on the rights and values of individuals and autonomous families. The colonial community rested on an often unexamined tension between the requirements of social organization and the changing demands of private life. Ironically—but logically—that tension was exposed most sharply for those regions and groups with the strongest and most coherently organized community life. Equally ironic, many of the same features that benefited community life often bred problems that threatened it. The very expressions of community concern for family life undermined the integrity and autonomy of the family and hampered the development of affective relationships. Even outside the family, concessions to close-knit family life often carried great personal and psychological costs, which increasingly outweighed the benefits.

By the middle and late eighteenth century, Americans accorded far less importance to the prerogatives of community life and far more to those of private life. Of course, many assumptions and characteristics of colonial community life persisted into the nineteenth century; some persist even today. But the boundaries of community life were more clearly delineated and were drawn over a different alignment of cultural values and daily relationships and behavior. By the early nineteenth century, American community life found itself on firmer if more modest ground, a kind of middle ground between social goals and personal needs. Nineteenth-century American life—both private and public—was built on many tensions and conflicts, but they were not the same conflicts that had shaped colonial life.

It requires some suspension of disbelief to read a book about all of British North America throughout this period. Indeed, it has required some suspension of disbelief to write it. From the publication twenty-five years ago of Sumner Chilton Powell's *Puritan Village* through the generation of New England town studies by Greven, Demos, and Lockridge to the work of the "Chesapeake group" and studies based on the middle colonies, much of the most exciting and important work on colonial America has taken the form of community studies.

This body of scholarship has created our understanding of regional and religious diversity in the colonies and has made it impossible to speak of "the colonial community" as though it were a monolith. Even *within* regions we can see important differences of culture and patterns of historical change. Recent works by Stephen Innes, Christine Heyrman, and Edward Byers, among others, amply demonstrate that community studies have much more to teach us; many questions, in fact, will yield only to the kind of close analysis community studies offer.

But the community study has brought its own dangers to the field. Historians can barely conceive the most banal sentence about life in colonial America before burying it beneath a welter of regional qualification and counterexample. It is both possible and necessary, I believe, to build on and move beyond our reliance on the community study; and it is imperative if we are to give the field greater synthetic coherence. This is not to banish the profoundly important questions that arise from variations by region, religion, class, race, ethnicity, and gender. But surely we need a clearer picture of the whole in order to appreciate the significance of the parts. By its nature, the relationship between family and community permits such an approach. The structure of families, the nature of family life, the character and enforcement of community goals—all varied strikingly according to regional and religious patterns. Crucial differences in demographic patterns, if nothing else, were bound to create somewhat different forms of family life in the colonies. But in their understanding of community and family life, colonists from New England to the Carolinas remained more alike than different, and in their basic assumptions and attitudes they were closer to each other than to their nineteenth-century counterparts.

It is possible, then, to consider some (not all) differences in region and religion, and even class and gender, as variations on certain themes in the history of family and community. Although different communities defined their specific purposes and standards of behavior in their own ways, they all accepted the preeminent right of the community to regulate the lives of its members and to measure individual actions by their effect on the larger group. All communities prized stability and harmony, and they sought to achieve it in part through the regulation of individual, neighborhood, and family behavior. This reflected the assumption that appropriate personal and familial conduct was central to community order, and it encouraged the subordination of private life to community concerns throughout the country.

Although this is not a local study, it rests almost exclusively on local sources: town, church, and, most important, court records. Local court records are increasingly claiming the attention of historians, with good reason: they are an extraordinarily rich source, yielding concrete information and insights into the daily life and concerns of women and men whose history might otherwise be lost. Court records may be especially useful for colonial history because courts oversaw and intervened in a wide range of personal matters and held broad administrative as well as judicial powers. Colonial courts were a *presence* in daily life in a way that is difficult to imagine today. They not only expressed the values and judgments of the community but invited the active participation of many individuals. Court testimony reveals, often serendipitously, how colonial Americans thought and lived. This provides a necessary corrective to sources that address primarily the male, the literate, the upper class.

The most serious objection to court records is that they chart deviant behavior. This charge carries some obvious truth, but its importance can be overstated. Colonial courtrooms were not the cesspools of society, gathering places for a class of outcasts or sociopaths. On the contrary: colonial courts were much more like open forums for the community. Most of the parties to a case, witnesses as well as plaintiffs and defendants, were not "deviant" in any usual sense of the word; nor was it exceptional for anyone, in the highly litigious society of colonial America, to appear in court in one capacity or another. But there is an even simpler point to make about the use of court records: as for every source, the quality of the answers we get depends on the questions we ask. To infer the degree of conflict in colonial society from court cases would be foolish, but we can learn much about the nature of those conflicts and their treatment; divorce and separation records will not tell us what proportion of marriages were unhappy, but they will suggest what made marriages unhappy and what people's expectations of marriage were. All sources have disadvantages, but court records offer the historians of colonial society unique advantages.

One final word about the use of evidence here: I rely heavily—too heavily, many will think—on individual examples and observations. In working on this book I have often recalled, and been chastened by, the Talmud's observation that "for example is not proof." Rather than challenge this observation directly, I would maintain simply that a body of cases, examples, and stories from individual lives may not "prove" anything, but it does suggest a great deal. To explore some of the central concerns and conflicts of colonial life, to convey something of the texture, values, and limits of early Americans' lives, is, I think, a worthwhile endeavor. That has been my goal here.

Contents

Introduction: Family and Society in Early America

One of the many ironies of early American society is that the European colonists sought to reproduce, even to freeze in time, patterns of family and community life that were already beginning to erode in Europe. The community provided a cohesive force in early modern society, seeking and occasionally achieving stability, order, and cooperation. It enforced its prerogatives through both institutional and informal means: religious sanctions, guild regulations, folk rituals such as the charivari, even witch hunts.[1] But by the early seventeenth century a number of forces began to challenge the bases of "traditional" community life in Europe and especially in England. Population growth, geographic mobility, economic changes—all these and more promised to remake community life.[2]

But adjustments to these changes came slowly and raggedly. Traditional expectations of community and family life continued to exert a powerful influence, and perhaps nowhere more so than in early America. Highly conscious of their strange environment, fearful of departing too far from European society, the colonists clung to their received ideas about the community and the family's place in it. Indeed, these ideas may have drawn added urgency from the disorder of a new society and the colonists' apprehension of failure. By the end of the century, Cotton Mather was writing of the "Creolean Degeneracy" of colonial America, but the first generation of settlers had anticipated his complaint. The effects of this "degeneracy" appeared at many levels of colonial society, from the late seventeenth-century upheavals in politics to the apparent breakdown of family discipline. Courts complained of dependents who did not behave as they "ought to do, and usually did in our native country, being subject to there commands and discipline."[3]

New Englanders, in particular, expressed a sense of deep-seated threats to family life—and therefore to social order—in their new environment. Abundance of land, with its promise of freedom and economic independence, worked as a solvent on patriarchal authority; and scarcity of labor blurred the former lines of dependence, putting family heads in greater need of their children and apprentices.[4] New Englanders described these changes ruefully, conveying both confusion and sadness. One minister warned that it was "justly to be feared, to be too much our case in New England, where many of the youth grow so rude and profane, so regardless of Superiors, in the family, as masters, in the state, as Magistrates, in the Church as Elders . . . in a word, where is so little yet appearing of God, or good, in too many of them; I say it is justly to be feared, that children here are not honorous of Parents."[5] In the patriarchal world of the early modern West, such slippage in family authority threatened chaos in the larger social order as well.[6]

In this strangely unsettled society, colonists turned to traditional forms of family and community life with even more sharply felt needs for order and stability. New Englanders and New Netherlanders articulated this concern most fully and explicitly, and in many ways New England villages became the most powerful expression of community life; to see a New England town even today—with its clustered houses, village green, its church at the center—is to see a physical map of communal ideals. But it is one thing to recognize the strength of community life in these forms and quite another to define it solely by these forms. Much of colonial America promoted a sense of community without such specific markers. Barry Levy, for instance, has demonstrated how successfully the Quakers of the Delaware Valley sustained community life over wide areas and "sprawling" townships that might have seemed to work against such efforts.[7]

Settlement in the seventeenth-century Chesapeake region was far more dispersed than in New England, and its religious character far weaker than that of Puritan New England or the Quaker Delaware Valley. In addition, the recruitment and demographic conditions of the early Chesapeake created a population more receptive to the claims of individualism and materialism, more antipathetic to the demands of community, than any other group in the colonies. In this sense, Timothy Breen has suggested, early Virginia was an "aberrant" society, different not only from the rest of the colonies but from England as well.

This difference emerged in some unusual tensions between individualism and communalism. Throughout the seventeenth century, for instance, Virginians discussed the advantages of the New England town model (for economic as well as other reasons) and occasionally tried to impose it on their colony. Such clustered communities, though much discussed and apparently admired, never materialized in the Chesapeake.[8] Instead, as several historians have documented, Chesapeake communities came to cohere around other forms and rituals: court days, militia musters, even horseracing and cockfighting.[9] Even as these social dramas served purposes other than communal unity, notably the enforcement of distinctions in social status, their success rested on the participation and tacit approval of the group, a sense of shared values and social life.

In many ways, what is most remarkable about family and community life in the Chesapeake was not how different it was from New England but how similar it was in values and goals. As Darrett and Anita Rutman found in their study of one Virginia county, "dispersed as they were, those who ran the affairs of Middlesex consciously sought to order their lives around families and the neighborhood institutions with which they were familiar."[10] In the face of devastating mortality rates, an unstable population, dispersed settlement, and all of what Gloria Main calls the "centripetal forces of the tobacco economy,"[11] the Chesapeake developed its own vital forms of community life. Even its local government reveals how much Chesapeake settlers shared in and promoted traditional English values and protected community life just as colonists did in other regions. As Lois Green Carr wrote in an essay on local government in Maryland, " 'Order,' 'well ordering,' 'quiet rule'—these words often appear in Maryland court records of the seventeenth century. They were key words in the thoughts of English and Maryland rulers and ruled. Everyone was considered obligated to help the community maintain this order . . . participation of the whole community was the assumption that underlay the operations of local government and justice."[12] If they shared little else, Chesapeake settlers did share these assumptions and expectations with the settlers of other regions.

Throughout colonial America, settlers supported the preeminence of the community, relied on the family as a source of social order, and empowered local authorities to protect communal values and stability. Officials everywhere paid close attention to individual conduct and morality, although important differences in the definition of disorder and the level of official intrusiveness emerged. Not surprisingly, Puritan New Englanders set standards more stringently and enforced them more zealously than did other colonists. They punished not only such flagrant offenses as fornication, drunkenness, and sloth but also a host of lesser irregularities. Infractions ranged from unneighborly behavior—cursing, contentiousness, stubbornness, and fighting—to excessive conviviality in the form of dancing, gambling, and rowdiness. To prevent unseemly behavior required constant vigilance on the part of the authorities, but they proved equal to the task. Few details of everyday life escaped their notice. In Massachusetts the town of Cambridge, for example, appointed a committee "to have Inspection into families that there be no drinking nor any misdemenour," and Richard Norcross of Watertown was "complained of for negligence in his calling" and forced to give the selectmen "an account of his living from under family government and How he hath improved his time"; and in Maine William Towson was charged in court as "an Idle person, one not provideing for his family, and for given of Abuseive [language] to those who do reprove him."[13]

Although New England exercised the keenest moral oversight, all colonies enforced some standard of individual behavior. Even in the Chesapeake communities—the most lax of the moral watchdogs—personal conduct often became a matter of public concern. Robert Holt appeared before a Maryland court in 1662 because he "not haveing the feare of God before his eyes" lived with a woman who was not his wife.[14] Forty years later in Prince George's County a servant woman was given "on her bare back fifteen lashes well laid on" because she "did Suffer her Selfe to be begotten with Childe Commonly Called a Bastard, against all Sobriety and good manners."[15]

Colonial authorities condemned such transgressions first of all as violations of the collective moral code. In Maryland in 1700, for example, John Snugg's "keepeing Company" with a married woman was termed "a Great Scandall to Christian Religion" as well as "a Breach of his Majesties Peace."[16] One Quaker distinguished between the treatment of those who sinned privately against another person and those who sinned openly against the community. Neighbors should quietly attempt to reform a private sinner, William Shewen wrote: "But if any that is called a Brother, Sin openly, or is a Fornicator, is a profane Person, is an Idolator, Drunkard, Extortioner, etc., thou needs not go to such a one and tell him his Fault." Instead, Shewen explained, since "his wickedness" was "open and Manifest to all; he is to be denied and judged of all."[17]

Pragmatic as well as moral considerations prompted individual regulation. Just as one sin oiled the slide into a life of wickedness, so, in the eyes of colonial authorities, did one form of delinquency lead to others. Prodigality and dissipation, inherently wicked, particularly offended authorities when they threatened family life. Anxious New Amsterdam officials noted "daily complaints" against tavern keepers "who to keep their business going detain such persons, as for their own sake and advantage would better attend to their occupations and protect their families honorably with God's help." The tavern business was so brisk, in fact, that the customers "not only spend their daily earnings, but also when out of money pawn the goods serving to the necessities of their families and thereby obtain the means of continuing their usual drinking bouts."[18]

The community acted in cases of personal weakness or neglect of duty because it often suffered from their consequences. A wastrel or a drunkard affronted God and all right-thinking people; in addition, he and his family drained the finances of the community. In Ipswich, Massachusetts, Samuel Perkins was arrested "for withdrawing himself and not attending his duty as a husband, father and master of a family." Perkins had "threatened that he will, and indeed saith he hath alreadie disposed of his estate so that his wife shall not be the better for it, whereby his wife and family may come to ly upon the publique charge." The court's response showed how moral and practical considerations reinforced each other to define standards of conduct; since his intentions were "not agreeable to Christian rule and gives ground to suspect that the Towne may be Charged through his default," Perkins was released only after acknowledging his error.[19] In other cases the authorities explicitly stated their desire to avoid financial obligations. In 1709 a New York court ordered Vincent Delamontague to "allow his wife and Children to live in the great Room of his dwelling house ... in Order to prevent their becoming a Charge to the Parish," and in Gloucester County, Virginia, an orphan whose master had died was placed with another who pledged to support him as necessary "to keep the aforesaid parish ... from all manner of charges or [his] being anywayes burdensome to the said parish."[20]

Errant individuals further injured the community by setting a bad example. In 1622 Maryland punished Penelope Hall for bearing an illegitimate child "to the evell example of others," and when the Salem Quarterly Court in Massachusetts censured Eleanor Hollingworth for "many railing speeches and reproachful words" against a neighbor, she admitted acting "to the dishonor of God, the church and court and to the great reproach of the partys and evill example of others."[21] Authorities often turned the effect of individual example to their own advantage; a Delaware court considered the negligence of one of its own judges and deemed "itt fitt that hee for an Example to others be fyned."[22] The most resourceful officials even extracted explicit cautionary lessons from the culprits themselves. Eleanor Hollingworth, for example, ended her public apology by asking "all good people that may be ofended, to forgive me, and to take warning by me of such evil practices."[23] Another Massachusetts settler confessed to violating a marriage contract and hoped "that it may be a warning to all whom it may concerne, not to deale rashly in matters of such weight."[24]

Exemplary behavior was most incumbent upon those who professed strict moral beliefs. A Puritan writer warned that "when Women go idling and tatling abroad, neglecting their household affaires; the Apostle says, they give occasion to the adversary to speak reproachfully. They expose the profession of Christianity to reproach."[25] Furthermore, officials often considered the appearance of proper behavior as important as its reality. Mary Briggs of Scituate appeared before the Plymouth court for telling a lie. The court cleared her of the charge but "admonish[ed] her to bee wary of giveing occation of offence to others, by unnecessary talkeing to the occationing of others to complain or raise such aspersions."[26] The court told Goodwife Briggs, in effect, that it was not enough to be innocent: she should never have exposed herself to an accusation. Plymouth expected its citizens to be beyond suspicion as well as reproach.

Official regulation of neighborhood activity and entertainment also stressed the importance of example and the appearance of order. New England and New Amsterdam officials in particular moved against all forms of disorderliness, especially gambling, drunkenness, dancing, mischiefmaking at services, unchaperoned walking out, fighting, swearing, and threatening speeches. To stem the corruption of youth, especially young men and servants, authorities struck at the occasions of temptation. A New Amsterdam official vetoed a liquor license because "many Soldiers and Servants will, thereby, be led into debauchery and many irregularities will occur."[27] Massachusetts Bay complained of the "loose and sinfull custome" of men and women riding from town to town "upon pretence of going to lecture, but it appeares to be meerely to drincke and revell in ordinaryes and tavernes, which is itself scandalous, and it is to be feared a notable meanes to debauch our youth and hazard the chastity of such as are draune thereunto."[28]

The community sought to protect its own reputation as well as individual virtue. A Delaware court punished unwed mothers so that "this place may not serve and be counted a shelter for whoores."[29] Massachusetts Bay, "accounting it their duty by all due means to prevent appearance of sinn and wickedness in any kind," prevented women with absent husbands from taking in lodgers and stopped the extension of credit to spendthrift sons because the practice led to "the great greife of theire friends, dishonor of God and reproach of the country."[30] These laws drew their justification from the power of scandal in the seventeenth-century world view, the conviction that the knowledge or even the appearance of unpunished sin would gladden the enemies of goodness and would spread like dry rot through the foundations of society. Scandalous behavior corrupted the weak first, but ultimately destroyed the whole moral order.

The official response to disorder, moral and otherwise, often carried a powerful emotional charge, and the fact that it often seemed strangely out of proportion to the provocation testifies to the distinctive concerns of colonial culture. New England authorities reacted to the faintest signs of unruliness, even in physical appearance. One Massachusetts minister voiced what many felt when he despaired of the many young people who were "so new fangled in their fashions and ruffianly in their hair."[31] Such worries gained added force from the fears of degeneracy so prominent later in the century, and they found their way into the jeremiadical literature of the time. Massachusetts Bay pointed in a 1662 sumptuary law to "excesse in apparrell amongst us, unbecoming a wilderness condition, and the profession of the gospell, whereby the rising generation are in dainger to be corrupted and effeminated" and punished both the owners and the tailors of unsuitable garments.[32]

The reaction to children who disrupted church meetings was even more intense, indeed almost obsessive. In New Haven, for example, in 1660, "Great disorders amongst children in the meetinghouse in the time of divine worship was complained of." To combat this problem the town not only reordered the seating of the meetinghouse but also appointed special monitors "who, if they observe any disorders, the first time they are to complain to authority, that such disorders may be punished, that God be not provoked."[33]

This scene repeated itself up and down New England. Town meetings debated the question frequently and apparently fervently, mapping out strategy by which their children "may Be looked after that the sabbath be not profaned by them."[34] In 1674 the Ipswich Quarterly Court actually adjudged two girls "culpable of disturbance and disorder in the meetinghouse."[35] Unhappily, the problem defied these efforts: a generation later the New Haven town meeting continued to brood over the matter, with greater exasperation but to no better effect. Their frustration may be read in the adoption of more vigorous tactics. Monitors at meeting were henceforth to "have a stick or wand wherewith to smite such as are unruly or of uncouth behavior."[36] The job of keeping a roomful of children in their seats for a couple of hours so vexed these people that time and again in town after town they discussed it as a matter of public business and finally armed themselves for the task.

Far more common and significant in its effects, though, was the community's involvement in family life. Indeed, colonists conceived of the family almost entirely within the context of community. Nothing else so clearly demonstrates the subordination of private life to communal goals. Colonial communities expected families to be orderly in their own conduct and relied on them to promote order in society. "Families are the Nurseries of all Societies," Cotton Mather wrote, "and the First Combinations of mankind. Well-ordered Families naturally produce a Good Order in other Societies."[37] Since the well-ordered family was a microcosm of society, built on the same lines of authority and responsibility, English and colonial writers believed that "a conscionable performance of domesticall and household duties, tend[s] to the good ordering of Church and commonwealth, as being meanes to fit and prepare men thereunto."[38] Conversely, "where no wisedome is used in governing families, there all goeth to wracke, and there many enormities are to be found."[39] In ill-ordered families "begins all Apostacy and degeneration; the ruine of Churches and Country springs from thence: *Ruine Families, and ruine all.*"[40] Puritan writers expressed the community's expectations of family life most explicitly, but all colonial authorities tacitly accepted the view that "To Serve the Families of our Neighborhood, will be a Service to all our Interest."[41] In colonial life the lines between family and community interests were blurred, when they existed at all. One sign of this is how often family members defined their relationship to one another in terms of social obligation.

The family's first duty was to train children properly. The education of children was broadly defined, profoundly important, and sweeping in its consequences. "This Care is highly prudent, and incumbent Duty, in Families, in Schools, and in Societies; for in general it may be said and expected, That the Morals and Principles which are first imprinted will be of Duration, and if good, of great Advantage, since in the Course of Providence, the Children of this Age are to be the People of the next."[42] Children should be taught not only to read and write but also "in some course, trade or other estate," and "not only our Sons but our Daughters also should be taught such things as will afterwards make them Useful in their places."[43] The ideal product of the well-ordered family was a literate, thrifty, sober, self-supporting, God-fearing adult, one who recognized authority and submitted to it, who knew his duty and performed it.

Religious training was particularly important for many writers: "it is evident, that Religion must be stirring in Christian families, and that good government looketh to bring godly behavior into families, as well as thrift and husbandrie. For want of this care, many parents leave their children faire faces and foul mindes; full coffers and empty hearts."[44] To neglect family prayer was a "shameful grievous crime" and "Prayerless Families" were the "great Nurseries of Ignorance and Wickedness in the World . . . The Nests that produce Serpents; The Dens that will probably nourish very Dragons of Malignity against the ways of God."[45] Many writers tried to impress upon parents the happy effects of proper childrearing and especially religious education. Cotton Mather predicted, "You will certainly find your Families the more Tractable, and Orderly, and Obedient, for your Catechising of them. The more you do your Duty to them, the more Dut[iful] they will be to you." Mather ended a tirade against irreligous families on an even more practical note: "O who will venture to put out a Son or Daughter to live in such a Family?"[46]

But most writers saved their ink to describe the disastrous consequences of disorderly families. Slackards in childrearing were "most worthy to be esteemed rather Monsters than Parents . . . who are not sollicitous to give their Children an Agreeable Education."[47] Children thus badly brought up showed a "crooked, perverse, stubborn, churlish, doggish disposition" and were "worse than Infidels, yea worse than the brute beasts."[48] The neglect of family obligations opened a permanent fault line at the base of the social order because the defect passed through generations: "O you parents, you are either the making or the marring of the world: for if your children learn no good condition at your hands, how should they be good fathers after you?"[49]

Quakers, according to Barry Levy's recent work, placed even more emphasis than Puritans on parental responsibility and decried the evil consequences of indulgence or passivity.[50] Philadelphia Quakers called it "apparent, that much of the Disorder complained of, is owing to the great Neglect in well governing and restraining of Apprentices and Servants, as well as Children; and probably more so, by the unreasonable liberties they take, and the ill example they shew to Children."[51] New Amsterdam officials underlined a similar point by punishing parents who did not punish their own children for stealing lumber, "whereby they grow up in their wickedness and finally cannot give up their daily habits."[52] New England officials, as usual, set the highest standards. Each town appointed tithing men "to inspect the manners of all disorderly persons" and to report "the course or practice of any person or persons whatsoever tending to debauchery, irreligion, prophaness, and atheisme among us, wherein by omission of family government, nurture, and religious duties, and instruction of children and servants, or idleness, profligat, uncivill, or rude practises of any sort."[53]

The relationship between husband and wife carried a heavy social burden as well. Even as writers granted that spouses "should have a very great and tender love and affection to one another," they tied connubial bliss to family duty.[54] The first duty of a wife was to obey her husband, since this relationship was understood to parallel that of king and subject. Husbands also had obligations, like all superiors to dependents, and they were expected to care for and protect their wives. Seventeenth-century writers emphasized elements of reciprocity and partnership as well as hierarchy and authority in marriage. The Puritan writer William Gouge noted, "A loving mutual affection must passe betwixt husband and wife, or else no dutie will be well performed: this is the ground of all the rest."[55] Benjamin Wadsworth, the author of another tract on family life, added details: "They should (out of Conscience to God) study and strive to render each others life, easy, quiet and comfortable; to please, gratifie and oblige one another, as far as lawfully they can." Quarreling couples "do the Devil's work . . . such contention provokes God, it dishonours him." Moreover, "it's a *vile example* before Inferiours in the Family; it tends to prevent *Family Prayer* . . . tends to obstruct almost all *Duties and Comforts;* tis a very extensive mischief, and draws innumerable sins and sorrows after it."[56] Such ideas, as Keith Wrightson has noted, were not confined to Puritans: "they were part of the Christian mainstream."[57] As Puritans emphasized the need for mutual affection and responsibility *within* marriage, they also reminded couples of their responsibilities to the community at large. In the eyes of these writers—and of colonial society—family disorder or disharmony of any sort rippled through the rest of society. As a result, all aspects of family life deserved and received careful scrutiny by the community.

The community expected propriety in personal relationships outside the family as well. "To live or dwell together in Love, Unity, Peace and heavenly Concord or Agreement," William Shewen wrote, was "the Glory, Strength and Crown of a People; and the contrary their Weakness, Shame, and Reproach, Confusion and Destruction also."[58] Comity and cooperation were much more than paper-thin ideals: they assumed great practical importance in colonial America since people necessarily depended on neighborly goodwill in the many informal arrangements and understandings that held together their communities. Necessity could bind groups as well as religion. Some communities demanded special efforts of truly good neighbors. One Bostonian argued logically that "if we love our Neighbors as we ought to love ourselves, we must, above all, seek, in our Capacity, to be helpful to their Souls good; for this is the greatest kindness we can (in Truth) desire from our Neighbour . . . to save him from Hell."[59] Others concentrated on preventing earthly torments. Maine courts, for example, set in the stocks or whipped women "that shall abuse their husband or neighbors or any others by approbrius language," and they punished men for the same offense.[60] As Dod and Clever noted simply, "Hee that would have no enemies must make himself none, by unjust, unkinde, or unneighborly dealing; but he must rather by courteousness of speech, helpfulness, and good neighborhood, win the love and liking of men."[61] Christian charity might begin at home but it could not end there.

Thus the community sought, as a legitimate part of its responsibility, to organize and determine the conduct of private life in colonial America. Individual desires, personal relationships, family life: all gave way to the demands of the community. The colonists valued order, stability, harmony, and Christian cooperation. They strove to create communities that would uphold these values and that would be powerful enough to enforce them in the face of resistance and weakness. To a remarkable degree, colonial Americans achieved their ambitions for family and community life—and they suffered the consequences of their success.

CHAPTER 1 The Force of Community

Jane Austen said of the English villages she described that everyone in them lived in a neighborhood of voluntary spies. The same might be said for much of colonial America. Most neighbors felt not only a right but a duty to oversee and intervene in the lives of people around them—"to keep a holy watchfulness" was how the church charters phrased it. "Neighborliness" in its richest sense sustained these communities and rested on ideals of comity and cooperation. But many elements that supported community goals carried heavy personal and psychological costs. Steady oversight by neighbors both exploited and exacerbated the nearly obsessive concern of colonial Americans with reputation and good name, their sensitivity to issues of shame and public humiliation. These concerns protected the community in many ways: fear of discovery and public scorn undoubtedly deterred many from transgression and richly punished those who were not deterred. But such controls, such open nerves, also sparked tensions that threatened community life. Communities that prized harmony were often riven by personal conflicts. Witchcraft accusations and malicious lawsuits revealed the strain of close neighborhood bonds. The church not only failed to stop much of this conflict but often served as a lightning rod for community tensions. The expectations of neighborhood life and the pervasiveness of neighborhood influence bred pressures that encouraged people eventually to establish boundaries between private and public life.

There was no escaping neighbors in colonial America. They seemed to be there always, to go everywhere and know everything. What a neighbor did not see for herself she could easily surmise or hear from someone else. It was impossible to sustain privacy within households: the houses were too small, the rooms too cramped, the walls too thin.[1]

It was almost as difficult to protect houses from friendly invasions and few people expected otherwise. Mary Sollas of Massachusetts stumbled across a couple engaged in "lascivious carriages" in 1674 when she entered the house "without knocking. the door being open, she being a neighbour."[2] When Ephraim Tinkham of Plymouth found no one home at Joseph Churchill's, he nevertheless "went in and stayed a while in the outward roome."[3]

Neighbors enjoyed this kind of freedom most commonly and most predictably in the closely settled villages of New England and New Netherland, but they were an imposing presence even in the more dispersed settlements of the Chesapeake. Brigid Johnson of Talbot County, Maryland, testified in 1672 that when she went to fetch Elizabeth Madberie, she opened the door, though it was "Shutt and made fast with the Pestle," there to find her own fiancé in bed with the married Madberie.[4] Considering a disputed land transfer in 1737, the Maryland Chancery Court asked each witness if he lived "in the Neighborhood so as to be often at the House or Visitor in the . . . Family" involved. The court went on to ask if any witness had heard rumors in the neighborhood that bore on the case.[5] New England courts too relied on the local grapevine. In 1664 Robert Bradford of Massachusetts said that he believed Samuel Walton was innocent of the charge of withholding property; if Walton had done what he was accused of, Bradford insisted, he "was sure he would have heard of it, because they were neighbors, always going between each other's houses."[6]

Close neighborhood bonds were encouraged for their usefulness to the community. In New Netherland in 1682, the child of two French immigrants died of respiratory trouble. The parents, confused and frightened, failed to notify anyone of the child's death. When the court asked them why they had not asked their next-door neighbor for help, they explained "that they had troubled him about so many things that they were ashamed," though now they agreed "that they made a mistake in not doing so."[7] In Maryland in the 1730s, Mary Mobberly, Catherine Ryley, and Mary Street all attested that they had survived hard times only through the "charity of neighbors."[8] In the absence of more formal institutions, colonial Americans cared for their poor, sick, disabled, aged, even their prisoners, by boarding them in the homes of families or neighbors. When such institutions as jails and almshouses did develop, their designers initially—and quite deliberately—emulated this familial model.[9]

Private individuals as well as officials relied on neighborhood bonds for different kinds of help. In Plymouth in 1651, nine-year-old John Slocum strayed in the woods. His father, unable to find him, "raised the towne, and with a considerable companie the whole night following" and for three more days searched for him unsuccessfully.[10] Elizabeth Hutcheson of New Jersey and Mary Rolf of Massachusetts asked neighbors to stay with them while their husbands were away so that they would not be alone.[11] And Henry Darnall's testimony suggests the usefulness of neighborhood ties in business. In Maryland in 1742, Darnall complained that a London merchant, William Black, had defrauded him. Knowing that Darnall was "Universally esteemed and Respected by all that knew him," Black used Darnall "as an Instrument to establish his . . . own Interest" with Darnall's friends in order to "greatly advance his Reputation and Business."[12] Unfortunately for Darnall, his large acquaintance proved more profitable to William Black than to himself.

Neighbors asked each other for advice as well as practical help, even in close family matters. New Englanders in particular deferred to the wishes and preferences of their neighbors in arranging their own affairs. Mr. Gibbard of New Haven, for example, agreed in 1656 to part with a troublesome apprentice when he learned that "some of his neighbours are not willing that he should have the boy to dwell with him againe."[13] Dense settlement and communitarian values bolstered the influence of neighbors most effectively in New England, but other regions showed the same spirit. In Delaware in 1680, Maria Block's neighbors attended the resurveying of her land "that soe noe person may bee Injured and that all future stryfes and Contentions may bee avoyded."[14]

The good opinion of neighbors was a valuable prize in colonial communities, as significant as it was intangible. It established a person's standing in the community, secured happiness in daily life and personal dealings, and eased many individuals through difficulties with the authorities. Embroiled in a dispute in 1726, Alexander Molliston of Pennsylvania helped his cause by contending "that he was neither Rogue nor Rascal any more than [his opponent], but was as honest a Man as himself, and so esteemed among my Neighbours."[15] Among other things, character references aided petitions for poor relief.[16] In Boston Thomas Trott was partially acquitted of fathering an illegitimate child in 1673 after he presented an "Attest of severall of his neighbourhood of his good conversation"; a few years later a Plymouth man, convicted of selling cider to the Indians, had half his fine remitted because he was poor and "his neighbours generally thinke he hath not been used to transgress in such kind."[17] By contrast, William Brereton of Maryland suffered in 1733 when his neighbors testified that he was "of aloose and ill Character all his Days and has not agood Name like his Neighbors"; Brereton was, according to neighbors questioned by the court, "Meane from his Youth."[18]

The tacit rules that governed daily intercourse among neighbors developed through custom or experience or simple necessity; but however they grew, and however unspoken they remained, these rules strongly molded community relationships. Some communities, notably in New England, sought to make such rules into law. Plymouth, for example, ordered in 1636 and reaffirmed ten years later that "all such misdemeanours of any person or persons as tend to the hurt and detriment of society Civility peace and neighborhood be enquired into by the grand Enquest," so that those at fault could be "punished and the peace and welfare of the subject comfortably preserved."[19] More concretely, New Haven ordered landmarkers set up in 1660 so "that righteousness and peace may be preserved, and differences among neighboures may be prevented."[20]

Officials promoted the influence of neighbors in matters more intimate than boundary lines. Because Joseph Ramsden had lived "in an uncivell way, in the woods with his wife alone, whereby great inconveniences have followed," the Plymouth court ordered him in 1656 to move "downe to sume naigborhood" or else see his house pulled down.[21] John Littleale of Haverhill was advised in 1672 to move in with some orderly family instead of living alone "contrary to the law of the country, whereby he is subject to much sin and iniquity, which ordinarily are the companions and consequences of a solitary life."[22] Littleale thus joined the ranks of many "solitary livers" returned to the fold by New England law. New Englanders, in fact, were forced not only to live under their neighbors' scrutiny but even to listen to their advice without grumbling. Maine authorities rebuked John Bonighton in 1656 for "abuseing his Neighbours when they advized him" to pay his taxes and William Towson in 1673 for offering "Abuseive Landuidge to those who do reprove him" for idleness.[23]

Authorities everywhere condemned discord and disciplined quarrelsome folk. Jacob Vander Veer of Delaware, "a Troublesome mutinous person and one of a turbulent spirritt," was banished from his town, "his lyfe and Living resembling more that of an Indian than of a Christian Sence our tyme hee has ben in Continuall stryfe with his neighbours."[24] Massachusetts fined two women in 1649 "for scolding and speaking opprobrious words" to their neighbors, and ordered Isabel Pudeator whipped in 1676 for drinking and unruliness after neighbors swore "they knew her to be a brawling and contentious woman."[25] New Englanders always displayed the highest, perhaps even the most desperate, hopes for communal harmony, and they reacted most strongly and bitterly in the face of disagreements and squabbling. But even Chesapeake authorities—who were neither fueled by the religious zeal of New Englanders nor so utopian in their social ambitions nor so clustered as to enforce easily the demands of community—even Chesapeake authorities dealt sharply with contentious neighbors. In order "to prevent the many scurrilous reproachfull and unneighborly differences and Languages" between Mr. John Gibbs and Captain John Frome, a Virginia court ordered in 1655 that the first one to begin a quarrel would pay the other £1500 in tobacco.[26] Another Virginia court threatened Katherine Reiver with a similar punishment a few years later if she provoked James Mulliken's wife "or any others of her neighborhood."[27]

As such cases demonstrate, community expectations of neighborhood behavior were so great that they often proved impossible to meet. Especially in New England, the influence of neighbors, upheld by authorities, was bound to breed resentment and conflict. Only occasionally did colonial Americans address these resentments directly, and in those cases the responses usually seemed deviant. When Mary Grant of Massachusetts offered Richard Holmes advice on mending fences, he told her that she deserved "a rope around her neck for meddling with such things," perhaps because she was a woman.[28] Maritie Jacobs of Albany raised a more readily understandable objection in 1676. When Roeloff Carstenz, who had impregnated her, came to discuss marriage he brought along two neighbors. "'What have these other people to do with us?' she asked. "'What we do with each other is between God and us.'"[29] But such reasoning was out of place in colonial communities. Seventeenth-century assumptions made such autonomy and privacy hard to ask for, and the workings of these communities would have made them even harder to keep.

As a result, individuals in the early colonial period rarely questioned explicitly the legitimacy of neighborhood involvement in their lives or challenged their lack of privacy.[30] Instead these strains found expression in other forms or exploded in personal conflicts. Verbal attacks were one way to lash out at excessive neighborliness, and the more cohesive the community, the greater the temptation to revile its norms. Hence New Englanders frequently appeared in court for such offenses as "abusing neighbors in an unseemly manner with bad words" and "endeavoring to make discord among neighbors" and "making and reporting sundrey pernitious lys which tends to the Causing of discord between men and their wifes and breach of peace amongst Neighbours."[31] One New Englander vented his fury at claustrophobic village life by threatening to "set his house on fire and run away by the light" because "he would live no longer among such a company of hell hounds."[32] Town organizations as well as individuals watched their hopes for harmony founder on petty disagreements. The training company of Amesbury, Massachusetts, for example, endeavored "to live in piety peace and unity" and so could only be "grieved, and cannot but dislike the designes of any person whoever that shall by any meanes perturb our peace"; to protect their peace, the members of the company complained against Samuel Foot in 1671 as a person "unquiat and factious in word and deed."[33]

In New England bickering often focused on the church. Puritan doctrine itself offered fertile ground for disagreement, often less in differences of interpretation than in its "inherent radicalism." As Philip Gura has suggested, nonseparating Congregationalism required only a slight shift in emphasis to unleash the religious individualism of a Williams or a Hutchinson. In addition to facing challenges from a number of sources and strains of religious thought, Puritan authorities in New England were forced to contain or even to deny the logic of their own assumptions.[34]

As a social unit too the church often proved an unwieldy instrument of communalism. Disagreements of all sorts flourished: where to put a new meetinghouse, who should pay for it, which minister to hire, what to pay him. New Englanders did not have to wait for the controversy over the Halfway Covenant to learn how easily a church could be splintered. Paul Lucas has found that in the towns of the Connecticut River Valley, struggling to define church order and to control church government, "the Puritans made dissension a way of life."[35] Church conflicts sometimes festered for years and seemed always to mock hopes for a godly life in the new Canaan. In the course of an extended controversy in Newbury, Massachusetts, one of the factions of the church, which included the minister, lamented that the "manifold contentions that have been among us for sundry years have bin matter of continuall griefe and ought to be of continuall humiliation, that such things should arise among people whose beauty consists in their union to christ and one with another."[36] In another typical case, the General Court of Massachusetts Bay dispatched mediators to Salisbury in 1677 to heal differences, which had brought "great disturbance to the church and place."[37]

One reason church strife was so often long and bitter was that it frequently tapped into deeper fissures in the community. In Salem, for instance, the same dynamic of church conflict that ended in the witch trials erupted in the church first. In the 1670s and 1680s, grievances between Salem Town and Salem Village helped make three ministers' terms nasty and short; one of them, George Burroughs, was later brought back to Salem to be tried and executed as a witch; and the town crisis peaked after the Villagers fixed, with eerie precision, on a new minister who shared and articulated their deepest anxieties.[38]

Salem was extreme in the outcome, but not at all unusual in its experience of church conflict. Despite mediations and injunctions to peace, church disputes not only continued through the colonial period but may even have intensified. David Konig has found, for instance, that after 1660 Essex County, Massachusetts, ministers were increasingly forced to rely on the courts to answer challenges to their authority.[39] New Englanders were by no means alone in experiencing problems with church and community. The established Anglican church in Virginia suffered from a number of institutional and social weaknesses: inadequate revenues, poorly trained ministers, the lack of a resident episcopate, uncertain social influence, and the power of the lay vestry.[40] Michael Kammen has described the variety of problems that shaped the impact of establishment and sectarianism on provincial New York: "Regardless of which denomination is examined, the story is roughly the same: slow growth, insufficient clergy, inadequate funds, conflicts with the governor and Assembly, theological conservatism, internal schism over pietism, fluidity across congregational lines, and, ultimately, the emergence of toleration and a kind of ecumenical 'civil religion.'"[41] Throughout colonial America, well before the upheavals of the Great Awakening, the power of churches and ministers and their relationship to their communities were often problematic. The irony of New England's church problems was that so many tensions stemmed from the centrality of religion to that society and from the strength of the church as an institution. It was a galling irony for New Englanders, who believed, as one writer put it, that "if there be Sickness in the Church, there will be little health in the Commonwealth."[42] For many

New Englanders, in fact, there was no point to the commonwealth if the church were amiss.

Church disputes were one indirect expression of local tensions, and there were many others: colonial Americans, especially New Englanders, were almost as reluctant to acknowledge conflict as to legitimate it. New Englanders at odds with their neighbors often found themselves suspected of witchcraft. In some cases, witchcraft accusations fit into broad patterns of social change and conflict. Boyer and Nissenbaum locate the origins of the Salem hysteria in the complex of tensions arising from the commercial development and political ascendancy of Salem Town. For Salem Villagers, economically and politically cramped, fearful of commercialism and threats to traditional communal life, embittered by their own diminishing prospects, the witchcraft trials were a rearguard action in a war they knew they were losing. Stephen Innes has also noted the frequency of witchcraft cases in the relatively commercialized communities of the Connecticut River Valley. David Konig analyzes the Salem trials from a different angle, suggesting that Salem, indeed Essex County accusers in general, were defending traditional forms of authority and legalistic means of enforcement and control. Christine Heyrman links witchcraft in Essex County to still another set of tensions, those bred by religious dissent, particularly Quakerism.[43] In each case, whatever the particular cause of tension, witchcraft accusations testify to the presence of bitter conflicts within colonial communities.

John Demos and Carol Karlsen, in very different ways, have also shown how witchcraft stemmed from and rechanneled personal fears and hostilities in New England communities.[44] The case of Ann Hibbens illustrates the point. Evidently a strong-willed woman and, significantly, a well-off widow, Ann Hibbens was condemned to die for witchcraft in 1656. Years before she had been excommunicated by Boston's First Church, and the excommunication proceedings suggest the reasons for Hibbens' isolation within the community and her subsequent vulnerability to witchcraft charges. Hibbens quarreled with a carpenter over some work and refused to settle the matter. The church excommunicated her for this, as well as for her "Causeless uncharitable Jelosies and suspicions against him and sundry of the brethren that are joyners." Just as unacceptable in the eyes of the church, she had ignored the admonitions of fellow church members to make peace, remaining "Impenitent and obstinate."[45] New Englanders themselves drew the connection between neighborhood conflict and witchcraft.

Grumblings about Mary Corey of Salem drove her husband to press a defamation suit to protect her reputation and led one of the neighbors to note in her defense that she was "civil and orderly" and that "it was out of mere prejudice that she was now molested."[46]

Outside New England, witchcraft accusations were comparatively rare. But throughout colonial America individuals who were angry with their neighbors and weary of their obligations turned to malicious lawsuits to vent spleen. In Virginia in 1664, the "scurrilous brawles and mutual objurgacions" of their wives moved George Spencer and David Goodale to file "reciprocall frivilous litigious suites contrary to the Lawes for quiett and peaceable rule, government and neighbor-hood of the people." The women were ducked at the next full tide "for punishment of their past disturbances and their better reconcelment and correspondency hereafter."[47] One legal scholar concludes that in Massachusetts "trivial, unfounded, or vexatious suits were apparently common," common enough to elicit prescribed penalties for common barratry.[48] A barrator is defined as a cheat, trickster, or quarrelsome person or, in this sense, as "one who vexatiously raises or incites to litigation; a mover or maintainer of law-suits; one who from maliciousness, or for the sake of gain, raises discord between neighbors."[49]

Barratry caused complaints throughout the colonies. In Massachusetts Joseph Armitage was denounced in 1674 as a "common barrator, one who vexes his neighbors with unnecessary suits,"[50] and in 1669 Maryland authorities castigated Henry Mitchell at least as severely as those in Massachusetts Bay could have done. Mitchell appeared as a "Common Barretor, a dayly and publique disturber of the peace . . . a common and turbulent Calumniator, a Reproacher, a fighter, a sower of striffes and discords amongst his neighbours so that he hath moved procured and stirred up divers strifes brawlings and fightings then and there and at other places elsewhere amongst the good people" of Maryland.[51] The vehemence of this language as well as the specific charges reveal how closely colonial Americans associated the law with discord. Antilegalism flowed naturally from their social vision, a vision of unity and corporatism, a vision always vulnerable and easily shattered. It was typical too of the ironies of colonial society that this highly litigious people condemned litigiousness in ferocious terms.

Fearing conflict and finding themselves unable to escape it, colonial Americans tried to defuse tensions as much as possible. Arbitration was one of the primary means by which they sought to contain conflict, and its application reveals much about the ideals of communalism and the limits of its success.[52] Arbitration appeared as a means of extralegal dispute settlement in all the colonies. Despite some differences in detail, the same general features obtained everywhere. Parties who disagreed submitted their case to arbitrators, almost always a committee of two or three men. Commonly each side chose one arbitrator, and the court appointed the third member. No arbitrator was expected to be an advocate for the party who chose him: all were to be "indifferent men." Not surprisingly, arbitrators were usually men who enjoyed the respect of the community; they were commonly addressed by the honorific "Mr." or a military title, and local officials, magistrates, and ministers often served as arbitrators. The disputants normally agreed beforehand to abide by the arbitrators' decision and posted a bond as proof of their good faith; courts usually enforced the forfeiture of the bond. This typical arbitration agreement dates from 1670 and appears in the files of the Essex County Court: "Know all men by these presents that wee Thomas Knowlton and William Knowlton of Ipswich in the county of Essex do bind ourselves . . . each to other in the sum of twenty pounds to stand by the award of Mr. William Hubbard and Sergeant Jacob about all differences between us from the beginning of the world to this day."[53]

Courts or town officials frequently advised litigants to submit their cases to arbitration, and some even required it. In 1635 the Boston town meeting prohibited church members from litigating unless they had tried arbitration first, and the town government of Providence agreed in 1637 that they knew "no way so suitable to our Condition as government by way of arbitration." With no apparent sense of irony, they decided that "if men refuse that which is but common humanity betweene man and man," arbitrators should be empowered to "compel such unreasonable persons to a reasonable way."[54] Far more often, however, the persuasion of the court sufficed, and in still other cases parties turned to arbitration without any prompting. People often wrote into their wills a provision that disagreements over their estates and arguments among executors and relatives be settled by arbitration; similar provisions appeared in business agreements.[55]

The form and degree of formality of arbitration hearings varied considerably. Relative informality was one of the advantages of arbitration, although this occasionally led to confusion. One bewildered litigant in Maryland asked the court in 1650 if a paper signed by the appointed arbitrators constituted their award, "in respect there were no parties named therein nor anything awarded to bee paid nor noe end put to any difference." The court concluded that the arbitrators had indeed intended the document to represent their award, though they conceded "there was some want of forme in the said paper writing."[56]

Fortunately, most arbitrators proceeded along more clearly established lines. They interviewed witnesses as well as the disputants in private,[57] and when relevant the arbitrators themselves went to view the land or work in question. Arbitrators almost always presented their determination or award in writing to the court; the court recorded the decision and sometimes officially adopted it.[58] Arbitrators were expected to act quickly; in a case in North Carolina they were ordered to decide "as soon as possible," in Virginia within thirty days, and in Oyster Bay, New York, one award would be voided if not rendered by the time the sun set two days later.[59] Arbitrators were almost never paid, but since they often deliberated at a local inn, the disputants defrayed the cost of their refreshments. Maryland made an exception to this general practice in 1718. After Samuel Young Esq. complained that he was obliged to referee too many cases, the Maryland Chancery Court ordered that arbitrators receive twenty shillings from the party in whose favor they ruled.[60]

Most arbitration hearings concerned differences between individuals and addressed both business and personal matters. Cases involving larger groups and authorities went to arbitration as well. In 1700 arbitrators settled Jon Euwatse's complaint against the city of New York; in 1708 the vestry of Charles Parish, Virginia, submitted its differences with a neighboring parish to arbitration; and the town of Huntington, Long Island, turned to arbitration when plans for a new church divided the residents of two parts of the town.[61] Arbitration within families was more unusual and generally involved quarreling spouses. Arbitrators in New York, for example, handled a property dispute between Nicasius de Sille and his wife; and after failing to reconcile Susan Cannaday and her husband in 1656, arbitrators in Maryland settled the financial terms of their separation.[62]

A combination of pragmatic and ideological considerations underlay arbitration. Courts and officials turned to arbitration in order to lighten their workloads. The Connecticut General Court noted in 1645 that unnecessary jury trials could be avoided by more frequent recourse to arbitration, and in judicial instructions in 1676, Sir Edmund Andros urged the referral to arbitration "of as many matters, (Particularly under the vallue of five pounds) as may properly be determined that way."[63] After finding his complaint against John Smith to "bee of frivilous nature," the Plymouth court sent George Bonum to arbitrators, and when Thomas Humphreys of Warwick, Rhode Island, filed a defamation suit, "the neibourhood perceiving it to be an immateryall rangling business" persuaded him to refer the matter instead to arbitration.[64]

Courts freed themselves not only of trivial suits but also of those poorly prepared for adjudication, cases in which witnesses were missing or crucial evidence lacking or the issues too confusing. Plymouth called in arbitrators for the cross-actions of Joseph Beadle and Edwin Dowty, "their matters being raw and imperfect," and so did a Maryland court when the cases of Manners versus Pheypo and Keeting and Keeting versus Manners proved "imperfect and not fitt for the determination of the Court at present."[65] New Haven found Mitchell versus Tuttill, "a darke case," suitable for arbitration, and northern New York authorities, after considering Dareth versus Withart, found "the case on both sides somewhat doubtful and put the matter into the hands of two referees."[66] And officials gladly turned over to arbitrators cases that promised to be too much trouble. In 1685 a Virginia court sent Woodson versus Charles to arbitration because the case seemed "a troublesome business which will take up much time"; and fifty years later a Georgia official advised arbitration for a matter which he found "a long intricate, and tedious Piece of Work."[67]

Disputants themselves found arbitration a practical alternative to the courts; in particular they viewed arbitration as a way to save time, money, and annoyance. Frustration with the law leaked from John Watts, a New York merchant, when he accepted an arbitration in 1762 "as the most speedy and just determination, rather than be put to the expence of two or three lingering Law suits, that may be spun out for Years in the way the Law is here."[68] Generations of Americans had voiced the same complaints before him. In 1678 John Giffard and John Lee of Massachusetts noted the "grat disbursements and truble" they had incurred before agreeing to arbitration; in Maryland in 1684, John Watson and the executors of Robert Graham's estate submitted their disagreement to arbitration "thereby to Save Charges, Trouble and greater Expence"; and in 1727, two litigants in Maine settled out of court to avoid "the grievous burden of leaving their buisiness, travelling to, and attendance at the Sessions."[69]

A powerful current of antilegalism also steered disputants away from the courts and into arbitration. Colonial Americans mistrusted the law and they hated lawyers. Lawyers represented mischief, conflict, and contempt for the truth. In 1674, the Puritan Samuel Arnold called for the suppression of lawyers who "for their own ends espouse any Case right or wrong, and by their wits put a fair Cloak upon a foul Case, and create needless Suits, and be *incendiaries* in places, and maintain Contention that Contention may maintain them, such as care not who looses, so they may gain."[70] William Byrd counted lawyers among the "great Scourges of Mankind," and evangelical religion only reinforced this opinion.[71] Later Alexis de Tocqueville would rank lawyers as the American aristocracy, "the highest political class and the most cultivated portion of society," but throughout the colonial period American lawyers remained poorly trained, popularly resented, and socially unprestigious.[72] Antilegalism was a way of life for many. Quakers disowned members who rejected arbitration and went to court, in part because this necessitated swearing an oath; one Maryland man, who was not a Quaker, threatened to disinherit any of his relatives who sued each other instead of submitting to arbitration.[73]

Antilegalistic attitudes drew much of their force from the colonists' abhorrence of conflict. The notion that two well-meaning persons might agree to disagree would have seemed to them not only alien but dangerous. They would have regarded the intellectual ambiguity of such a stance as a species of moral cowardice. Above all, they could not have accommodated conflict so readily. In their view, conflict of almost any sort and in almost any degree soured relationships and divided communities. Simply to acknowledge conflict was difficult, to tolerate it was perilous, and to formalize it in a lawsuit was pernicious. As a Rhode Island plaintiff wrote in urging the defendant to accept arbitration, "such Continewall strife" as arose from their case "will not amounte to any Christiane acounte."[74] Far from resolving disagreements, lawsuits seemed to harden the lines of conflict and embitter the participants. Dod and Clever warned in 1612: "Be not hastie to goe to Law, no not in a right cause, but agree at home. For besides that a man doth seldom escape without great losses, (in which respect it is also to be avoided, as an enemie to thrift) thy neighbour is openly put to reproch, he becommeth thy mortall enemie and will alwaies watch to doe thee hurt."[75] Two Providence residents echoed this desire for peace mixed with practicality. Related by marriage, Rebekah Whipple and John Whipple agreed to arbitration because to "bring their difference

into a Course of law . . . would be greately troublesome to all partyes
. . . and great charge would Ensue upon it . . . and would cause Anni-
mossityes of spirits, and Alination in affection amongst Relations."[76]

This intolerance of conflict, the striving for consensus and harmony,
shaped the practice of arbitration in colonial America more powerfully
than any other element. Arbitration was expected not only to settle the
immediate disagreement but also to restore genuine peace. The informality of the proceeding, its privacy, the force of impartial mediation
and friendly persuasion, the emphasis on compromise rather than absolute victory: all aimed at personal reconciliation far more than a
quasi-legal determination. Injunctions to fellowship and peace run like
a refrain through arbitration records, a refrain joining the hope that
arbitration would heal differences to the conviction that it must if orderly community life were to survive. Arbitrators acted "in accordance
with the spirit of love in all amity and friendship."[77] They were asked
to ensure "that peace and truth may be continued," to "settle all things
in peace," and "to Endeavour a friendly Composure."[78] Arbitration
hearings were undertaken for "the settling of peace amongst the neig-
borhood," and so that "matters [might be] ended in a loving way," and
in order that "mutuall peace and love maybe preserved amongst us."[79]

Religious and communitarian values strongly influenced colonial attitudes toward conflict and in turn encouraged arbitration. One writer
announced that those who "are Peace-makers, counter-work Satan,
they oppose him in his great design."[80] Puritans in New England,
Dutch Calvinists in New York, and Quakers everywhere pursued harmony most assiduously and used arbitration emphatically to that end.
But even settlements where communal zeal seemed faint by comparison, or where it appeared primarily as a "community of profit," promoted arbitration as a way to keep peace.[81] In the Chesapeake, for
example, arbitration was used to heal divisions from the very beginning. In 1619 a member of the Virginia Company agreed to arbitration,
"That so all cause of scandall and discord amongst the Company might
have an end."[82] A full century later the practice retained its appeal; in
Maryland in 1727 arbitrators brought two quarreling parties to "a final peace, unity and concord."[83] Throughout the colonies the primary
purpose of arbitration was to defuse conflict and to promote peace in
the community. At the end of arbitration hearings, disputants were
commonly urged "to walke in love and peace" or to "live together in
good friendship and Neighbourhood" or to affirm their reconciliation

"by the friendly shaking of hands, all differences being cast into the fire of love."[84]

Arbitration seemed to answer many of the needs and goals of colonial culture. But the informality and voluntary character of arbitration proved a weakness. Courts encouraged but almost never compelled arbitration, and many litigants flatly refused to submit to it.[85] In one Maryland case, two hotheads agreed to arbitrate their case but then fell out over the wording of the arbitration bond and so ended up in court anyway.[86] Ironically, arbitrators themselves sometimes failed to agree. In Connecticut the settlement of Blackleech versus Hoadleye failed "through the disagreement of the arbitrators"; in 1718 three arbitrators in Pennsylvania returned their case to the court when they could not agree; and New Amsterdam officials were forced to appoint new arbitrators in Jans versus Clazen in 1660 when the original referees "set off one against the other."[87] Then too the losing party could challenge the arbitrators' decision. John Woodcoke of Massachusetts and Thomas Fairman of Pennsylvania both complained of "errors" in their settlements; one plaintiff in Connecticut considered his award "unjust" and another in Maryland termed his "prejudiciall"; and in 1680 John Sharpe of New York asked for new arbitrators and another hearing because he did "not well Like . . . the said Award."[88]

Appeals of this kind expose the central myth of arbitration in colonial society: arbitration did not, could not, heal all differences. Worrying their grievances like a sore tooth, parties who appealed decisions revealed the failure of arbitration—it represented not a resolution of differences but one step in a potentially open-ended process. What literary theorists now call indeterminacy was in fact a disturbing social problem for colonial Americans. It was precisely this condition of ambiguity and latent conflict that arbitration was designed, in vain, to avoid.

Once courts stepped in to enforce the forfeiture of the bond or to adjudicate the case, it was obvious that arbitration hearings had failed. But some attempts at arbitration seemed doomed from the outset. It is doubtful that the most resourceful and persistent arbitrators could have reconciled Captain James Smith of Massachusetts and his brother-in-law Richard Rowland. Their case not only tried the patience of their referees but also reveals the limits of arbitration in the presence of unbridgeable differences. As early as 1661, Rowland was charged with "many abuses" of his mother-in-law Mary Smith. In the next court session Mary Smith was cited for "passionate distempers in difference" with Rowland. In December 1666 James Smith sued Rowland for unlawfully holding his land, trespass, "making waste of timber, cutting his grass and molesting his tenant," removing from his house "money, bedding, clothing etc," and debt. Rowland in turn sued Smith for debt and slander.

In March of the following year they submitted "all their differences" to arbitration. The arbitrators' award did not favor either man but seemed instead a carefully designed compromise. Even so, Rowland sued Smith for the arbitration bond of £500 three months later when Smith failed to abide by the award. Rowland won the verdict, but Smith managed to have the bond lowered to £50—another compromise engineered by the court, it seems. Not surprisingly, the men continued to argue during this period, and the quarrel spread through their families. One witness later deposed that she had seen Smith and his sister, who was Rowland's wife, "talking loudly." Smith called his sister "vile names and said she came home drunk from Salem and could not tell whether she went upon her head or her feet."

The conflict continued, with no sign of abating, for many more months. In January 1668 Smith called Rowland a "thievish Welch rogue, etc," lacing ethnic jealousies into the family tensions.[89] By January 1669 they were again willing to submit to arbitration, but the results still proved unsatisfactory. Smith immediately sued Rowland for forfeiture of the bond, debt, and the charges he had first brought in 1666. Even worse, this episode embroiled not only Rowland, his wife, and her brother, but also his mother-in-law, brothers, sisters, other brothers-in-law, and friends and servants on both sides of the family. A year later, in August 1670, "upon mediation of friends," Smith and Rowland posted a £40 bond "that they would live peaceably and quietly."

This resolve lasted longer than might be expected, but two years later they were at it again. Smith sued Rowland in June 1672 "for intermeddling with his dealings and perrisciously suggesting misapprehensions to people's minds in his dealings." Smith elaborated on his sentiments in November of 1672 when he struck Rowland. Rowland sued, but the court dismissed the charge as unproved. In March 1673 Smith and Rowland had another argument in the course of which, according to a neighbor who probably told time by the regularity of the arguments, Smith "made provoking speeches not becoming a brother or a neighbor."[90] This was not the last court appearance of the Smith-Rowland clan, but after ten years of squabbling, the pattern is clear. Arbitration could not heal the profound enmity of this family group; it may even have worsened the situation by adding the forfeited bonds and disputed settlements to the store of grievances.

The purposes and limits of arbitration reflect some of the contradictions of community in colonial America. Arbitration sought to resolve conflict without acknowledging its presence, to bridge irreconcilable differences with fragile compromises and conciliatory rhetoric, and to cement conclusions through friendly and informal methods. Arbitration worked best when the courts formalized and enforced it—in other words, arbitration was most likely to succeed when it abandoned its own assumptions and strategies. But if arbitration often seemed quixotic or ineffective in early America, by the end of the period it seemed irrelevant.[91] The persistence of tensions in community life, and the failure of means such as arbitration to lessen them, fueled questions about the nature of community and the sacrifices it demanded.

CHAPTER 2 The Tyranny of Neighbors:
Slander

In Kingston, New York, in 1665 Hendrick Jochemsen sued Ariaen
Gerretson for abusing his wife and calling her a "Manglestick." After
some heated discussion in court, it emerged that neither party—indeed
no one present—could explain the meaning of manglestick or the nature of the insult. The baffled judges ended the case by ordering both
sides "to hold their children under better discipline, so as to call people
by their proper names."[1] In fact, a *manglestok* or mangle was a ma-
chine used to press clothing and in England carried associations of poverty.[2] The residents of Kingston spoke Dutch, however, and they seem
to have accepted the spirit of the English insult without learning its
meaning. Only a culture that placed an extraordinarily high value on
good name would encourage a plaintiff to take legal action against an
insult no one understood.

Such cases suggest the importance of reputation and the fear of disgrace throughout colonial America. One had always to propitiate the
community, to force it to recognize one's value and virtue. No one
could ignore community opinion because it mattered so much for an
individual's well-being. In 1682, for example, John Teney of Massachusetts refused to forgive a man who had publicly slighted him, even
after the man's brother apologized. That was not good enough, Teney
insisted: unless "the plaister be as big as the sore it will not doe for he
disgrast us openly in the face of the cuntry and we canot beare to be
disgraced by him but what we doe we doe to humble him."[3] Even in
the more dispersed settlements of the Chesapeake, colonists went to
great lengths to safeguard their reputations in order to maintain the
community's good will. In 1752 William Govane of Maryland explained to the Chancery Court that his wife was unusually jealous. Because it was "his Constant Study and Endeavour" to "preserve her

Character and his Own," he avoided all occasions that might arouse his wife's ready suspicions. But his wife, according to Govane's story, proved less constant. She took up with their overseer. Govane was wounded; not only was this dalliance the talk of the neighborhood, but he had little imagined that "she would have Condescended to Such freedoms with a Servant." He fired the overseer "for the Sake of both their Characters and in order to Remove any Ground for Such discourse in the Neighborhood for the time to come." Even more telling, Govane decided that, since it would be some time before the scandal subsided, they would move to Rhode Island or some other place in order to be "out of the way of the aforesaid Scandall." But his wife preferred disgrace to Rhode Island, and she moved in with the overseer.[4]

Legal actions for slander or oral defamation further demonstrate the power of public opinion. These cases are striking in their numbers alone. In Accomack County, Virginia, slander was the second most common action before the county court—second only to debt—by the 1630s, and in colonial Massachusetts it was second only to fornication.[5] The incidence of slander actions also rose in England throughout this period and the increase stemmed in part from the expanding definition of slander. Slander fell originally under the authority of medieval ecclesiastical courts. Ecclesiastical law recognized as slander only imputations of criminal action, that is, conduct for which the victim would be liable to prosecution. At least one definition of "crime" within the canon law, however, was broad enough "to embrace all sins whether venial or mortal, whether intentional or accidental."[6] Although a statute of 1275 recognized a criminal form of defamation, the ineffectiveness of the common law in remedying defamation led eventually to the enforcement of the statute by the Star Chamber. Star Chamber addressed primarily cases of written defamation about officials, but it came to view even nonpolitical libels as breaches of the peace. In the late sixteenth century, Star Chamber responded to a rising tide of slander actions by limiting the causes to actionable words that were "published" or uttered before a third party.

But by the early seventeenth century, the common-law definition of slander had broadened to include accusations that brought damage to the plaintiff even if they did not charge him with a prosecutable crime. The common law recognized three types of slander per se. The first remained the charge of an indictab'e crime. The second was the allegation of a loathsome, contagious disease, usually leprosy or venereal disease. The third category was the suggestion of financial impropriety or professional incompetence.[7] Even this broader definition was not applied strictly. The legal requirements of defamation as well as the allowable remedy were interpreted loosely, expanding the scope of defamation suits still further. As R. H. Helmholz notes, "Defamation has had a way of breaking out of its boundaries, even when they are sensible boundaries."[8]

One other legal element shaped the social importance of slander. As it developed, the law of defamation came to distinguish between written libel and spoken slander. Libel, which was essentially seditious libel, remained the far more serious offense. The proven truth of a seditious statement offered no defense against the charge. On the contrary: according to English authorities, the greater the truth of a seditious statement, the greater the threat to the government. In America, despite the Zenger case, truth was not accepted as a defense against libel until the Sedition Act of 1798. But truth *was* a defense against slander. For different reasons, both ecclesiastical law and common law considered truth a pertinent issue; in ecclesiastical courts the truth of a charge signified that the plaintiff had sinned, and in common law courts the fact prevented the plaintiff from proving damages.[9] As a result, slander trials often examined in detail the character, conduct, and history of the parties. Plaintiffs and defendants and even witnesses opened themselves to the scrutiny of the community, and neighborhood relationships and pressures often influenced the proceedings more than the stated charges.

The broader definition of slander opened the way to a wide range of slander actions in colonial America, especially since so many matters of personal conduct and morality were regulated by law and so could be actionable. Indeed, colonists often pressed the limits of legal definition and used slander suits to rebut name calling and angry words. New Amsterdam authorities more than once lost patience and reprimanded parties for troubling them "about such trifles" as cross words and chronic bickering.[10] By 1662 Virginia had had enough of the "many vexatious persons [who] doe very much trouble the courts, and their neighbors for babbling words," and they limited slander causes to actionable words.[11] Still slander suits answered a number of purposes. Officials pressed suits to protect their authority, tradesmen to protect their profits, and ordinary people to protect their good name. Through a mixture of vehemence and fear, all of them showed that reputation was as vital as it was intangible, and as vulnerable as it was irreplaceable.

Even cases in which slander seems to be secondary suggest the power of speech in colonial America. The colonists shared the English concern with attacks on public officials. In punishing such attacks as challenges to the public peace, colonial governments acted on their sense of the force of community opinion and the tenuousness of their own authority. A Maryland official complained in 1664 that scandalous speeches left him bereft of his good name and "disenabled to execute" his office.[12] When a New Netherland official sued Hendrick Jansen for slander in 1642, the court maintained explicitly that it was "a matter of grave and dangerous consequences which cannot be tolerated or suffered in countries where it is customary to maintain justice."[13] In 1678 the assembled court of New Castle, Delaware, had its hands full with John Andries and his wife. The couple abused the court as "Cheating Rogues" and with many other unflattering expressions before being charged with slander, contempt of authority, assault, and breach of the peace. The court explained that these offenses violated colonial as well as English laws and were "of a bad Consequence and an Extreme ill pr[e]sident to others" in deriding the king's authority. "Noe well Settled Government," they emphasized, "can bee Established and maintayned where such notorious offences are past by." Ironically, the Andries first pleaded not guilty to the charges but then surrendered to the mercy of the court, rogues and all.[14]

New Englanders were particularly sensitive to slanderous attacks on the clergy. Richard Gibson of Maine sued a slanderer in 1640 in part because he was "much disparaged in his ministery," and when Nathaniel Soule admitted vilifying the minister of Duxbury, Massachusetts, in 1668, he publicly acknowledged that his "wickedness in soe speaking of soe godly men is greatly aggravated in that it hath a tendency to the hinderance of the efficacye of that great and honorable worke of the preaching of the gospell."[15] In other regions, the socially privileged often turned to slander suits to defuse attacks. Tryntje Slecht of Kingston, New York, explained in 1663 that she had called the "Noble Lord de Decker" a bloodsucker only because she was "depressed and discouraged because of the many misfortunes that had befallen her through the savages." The Kingston court was sufficiently softened by this tale that they let Slecht go with a fine; seventy-five years later in North Carolina, Joseph Jenoure was released after publicly confessing that he had cast "certain scandalous Reflections touching the Reputation of Sir Richard Everard['s] Lady and Daughters."[16] Richard Brown did not fare so well in Virginia. In 1649 he was given twenty lashes well laid on for fueling an evil report about Mr. Robert Willys, "a gentleman of good descent."[17]

Colonists used slander charges to support personal legal interests as well as rank and authority. Plaintiffs often filed slander suits in combination with lawsuits they regarded as more important. In these instances the testimony usually included at least implicit recognition that slander was the secondary issue. When Thomas Woodbridge of Massachusetts defaulted on a business deal with Captain William Gerrish, Gerrish filed a slander suit along with his business complaint; he threw his primary worry into relief by withdrawing the slander suit after receiving a monetary settlement.[18] Several other Massachusetts settlers acted in the same spirit. William Bowditch sued John Pilgrim for debt and defamation, John Rodes sued Alexander Gold for slander and for killing his dog, and Henry Roby added defamation to a list of complaints against Edward Colcord that already included molestation and "troubling him with many vexatious suits."[19] In these cases, slander charges were apparently used to strengthen the plaintiff's position. By piling charge upon charge, a plaintiff might hope to overwhelm the defendant and make it difficult for him to respond to all the charges. He could also portray himself as the victim of the defendant's sustained malicious attacks.

In other cases slander proved a ready tool for revenge and spite. In 1653 a Virginia court could find no evidence to support Richard Flynt's claim that Sarah Bowyer had defamed him; instead, the court felt, his suit seemed "evident more of malice . . . being grounded upon a former differance."[20] Certainly people filed slander suits on impulses of retaliation as well as indignation. After losing one suit to his brother-in-law in March 1669 and another in June, Captain James Smith of Massachusetts countered with a suit of his own that month.[21] Michael Iver of Massachusetts, sued for slander separately by Thomas Tuck and George Dill in 1639, replied to both with slander suits in the same session.[22] For these plaintiffs, at least, slander suits provided a response in kind to other litigation.

More subtly, a person accused of criminal action could attempt to forestall prosecution by lashing back at his accuser with a slander suit, hoping to unleash the community's condemnation of his opponent. Some plaintiffs may have acted in the belief that failure to refute suspicions could be received as an admission of guilt. In accordance with the legal definition of slander, many cases sprang from informal charges of illegal conduct. Plaintiffs in these cases often identified the threat of prosecution or incarceration already suffered as a rankling concern. Lieutenant Anthony Collimore of Plymouth Colony complained against Humphrey Johnson in 1686 for implicating him in a crime, "by reason of which unjust and false information" Collimore was "carried before authority, exposed to disparagement of creditt, to loss of time, and expence of mony."[23] In Maryland Thomas Bushell sued Michael Harker in 1644 for suggesting that he was a Roman Catholic "to the damage of the plaintiff and the questioning of his life," and Joseph Jordan of North Carolina complained in 1714 that William Wilson had falsely accused him of burglary in order "to Take away and destroy [his] good name fame Creditt Estamation and repute" and to bring him "Innocently into Danger of forfeiting all and Singular his Chattles Lands and Tenements and Loseing of his life."[24]

It is difficult to separate the plaintiffs who protested too much from the numbers who sincerely sought to clear their names. In any event, pressing a slander charge did not save everyone from prosecution. Christopher Collins of Massachusetts sued Enoch Coldam in March 1653 for calling his wife a witch; but in June 1654 Collins again sought redress against Coldam, this time for defamation and for "being the occasion of Jane Collins lying two weeks and upward in prison and calling her witch and arraigning her at the bar."[25] Some plaintiffs who sued for slander may even have precipitated their prosecution for another offense. That was apparently the experience of John Bartoll of Massachusetts Bay. In July 1645 he sued Alice Peach for defamation for charging that his wife, Parnell Bartoll, had four years earlier committed adultery with the boatswain of the *Sampson*. The record indicates that Peach "proved the truth of her assertion," and later in the same court session Parnell Bartoll was presented "for her miscarriages on the ship Sampson."[26] Similarly, in 1669 in Massachusetts George Martin sued William Sargent for calling his wife a witch. Though the judges did not concur in the verdict, the jury found for the defendant—and in the same session Susannah Martin was ordered committed to prison unless she posted a £10 bond for her appearance at the next Court of Assistants "upon suspicion of witchcraft."[27]

Slander suits fit not only into such webs of litigation but also into networks of neighborhood relations and personal conflict. In Connecticut in 1654, Walter Gray admitted concocting a tale of adultery featuring two neighbors, provoked, he said, "by some conceaved Injuries." "Yet," he conceded, "these imagined injuries were not a suffitient ground for him to raise up those false and scandalous reports."[28] A church controversy in Lynn, Massachusetts spawned two slander suits in June 1659. Thomas Newell sued George Keyser for words apparently spoken in the course of that dispute, while Thomas Wheeler prosecuted Matthew Farrington for saying that he had "venomously, wickedly and mischievously plotted, with others, against Thomas Newell to damage him, concerning the matter that was before the church" between Keyser and Newell.[29] In this case the focus shifted from the original disagreement to the slander charges. Indeed, that may have been the unconscious point: by directing attention to slander, the parties to the church controversy avoided the more troublesome issues at hand.

Slander appeared conspicuously in so many neighborhood conflicts because it directly tapped deep-lying concerns about reputation. One man impugned another's honor because he knew it would wound, because he knew where to find a sore spot; plaintiffs sued because they were eager to keep their neighbors' good opinion. New Amsterdam authorities noted the motives of both sides in slander suits. In 1662 they affirmed a plaintiff's need to vindicate his honor, which they termed "a tender plant"; they punished the defendant "as an example to all other slanderers, who for trifles and insignificancies have constantly in their mouths curses and abuse of other honourable people, whenever things do not go just according to their fancy."[30]

The personal experience of John Godfrey of Andover, Massachusetts, further suggests that many slander suits should be considered against a backdrop of neighborhood friction. Godfrey was probably a crotchety, discontented character, but he was in any case on notoriously bad terms with his neighbors. In addition to being sued six times in seven years for slander or defamation, he was variously accused of stealing oxen, stealing and selling ammunition to Indians, attempting to bribe witnesses, and, most often, of being a witch. Apparently his favorite form of counterattack was the slander suit, which he used with increasing frequency. The slander suit became for Godfrey as much a defense against harassment as a defense of his reputation. More than that perhaps: given Godfrey's quirky, contentious ways, his slander suits may have been acts of aggression, expressions of hostility as well as means of self-protection.[31]

Godfrey's experience also hints at ways in which slander actions ad-

vanced general community purposes: slander suits seem in some instances to have offered forums for people to air grievances and to resolve lingering disputes. When John Devorex of Massachusetts sued
Peter Pittford for defamation in 1651, he complained that Pittford
"often threatened him, whereby he went in fear of him." Devorex
seems little concerned with his reputation here, though he experienced
some anxiety about his personal safety. He may have breathed easier
after the court censured Pittford and bound him to good behavior.[32]
Prompted by slander suits, courts offered mediation as well as protection. In the defamation case of Hobs versus Palmer in 1647, the Essex
County Court of Massachusetts urged that "all differences" between
the parties be ended, and when two women appeared before a New
Amsterdam court in 1656 for slander and quarreling on Broadway, the
court "imposed silence on parties and ordered them to live henceforth
quiet and in peace and order as good neighbors ought to do."[33]

Although a variety of personal and community concerns could influence slander suits, the central issue in most cases remained good name
and its loss. Here too practical considerations entered in. Threats to
livelihood prompted many slander suits, and people whose financial
success rested on a clear reputation may have feared diminished income as much as diminished standing in the community. It was clearly
bad for business if neighbors gossiped that William Beale, a miller, gave
short weight, or that William Browne, a merchant, kept false accounts,
or that Robert Cross was "a cheating knave and that he should have as
good trading with the devil as with him, and better, too."[34] A good
reputation on all counts, not only in business matters, was critical to
many economic relationships in colonial America, relationships that
remained deeply personal. When Anthony Wyatt of Virginia sued for
slander in 1665, he asked the court "to consider that the transaccons
and dealings of Virginia depend (most) upon creditt and reputacon,
wch once stayned as the petitioner is by this unjust and opprobrious
calumny (if not vindicated) inferrs damages beyond expression."[35] Re-
sponding to a loose charge of fornication in 1664, a doctor in Massachusetts appraised the business value of his good name. "You have
abused me and taken away my Reputation, which I vallew at a thousand pound," Mr. Richard Cording maintained, "for I am a Gentleman
and live by my practice."[36]
    Time and again plaintiffs explained how their fortunes were tied to

the esteem of their neighbors. In 1679 George Tyte of Maryland expected slander "to bring him into trouble vexation scandall and infamy, by which he should be rendred a person not fitt to be imployed or intrusted as aforesaid, nor to trade and traffique"; in 1701 a Pennsylvania couple complained that they had suffered "much in their Reputation, and by that means in their Trade."[37] Merchants and craftsmen could measure their losses, could almost name the customers who took their business elsewhere because they listened to scurrilous rumors. John Bell, a carpenter in New York City, claimed in 1720 that "divers Merchants and Others good men" who used to employ him "have refused and dayly more and more do refuse to Employ him" after Cornelius Tiebout suggested that one of Bell's workers was paid for more labor than he performed.[38] Some men lost workers as well as customers—at least, so Samuel Legg, a ship's master in Boston, contended. In 1678 Legg charged that "severall men . . . were discouraged from his Service" after James Flood impugned his treatment of employees.[39] Still others claimed to have lost political preferments. Richard Whitehead of Virginia had "been imployed, invested with and put into places and offices of Greate Truste, to his Espetyall advantage and Livelihood"; but all that, he said in 1660, was lost in the wake of slander.[40]

Some plaintiffs went so far as to plead extreme economic hardship as a result of slurs against them. Nehemiah Blakiston of Maryland anticipated in 1679 that he and "his whole family must in a short tyme come to penury and want."[41] Thirty years later in New York, John Webb feared that he and his wife would sink into "poverty and beggary" after he was tagged as a slave trader.[42] These plaintiffs may well have exaggerated their plight; they were after all suing for damages. Still more than enough credible evidence remains to suggest that persons attacked in their reputations could well suffer in their livelihoods. As Julian Pitt-Rivers has observed, in communities built on face-to-face relationships, "a good name is the most valuable of assets."[43] That fact alone suggests the power of neighborhood opinion in colonial communities. But the full weight of neighbors' influence emerges even more clearly in slander cases that did not address fears of financial loss, in cases where a besmirched reputation inflicted instead deep personal pain.

Colonial Americans stood ever ready to rebut charges that undermined their standing in the community. The charges themselves ranged widely in content—everything from personal misconduct to unneighborly behavior to simple name calling surfaced in slander suits. Jan

Perie of New Amsterdam filed to defend himself from a charge of cowardice, and George Dill of Massachusetts, Hester Rickard of Plymouth, and Richard Bennett of Long Island all answered charges of drunkenness with suits.[44] Broader charges of misbehavior were even more likely to spark suits. Richard Manship of Maryland sued when neighbors accused his wife of witchcraft, Solomon La Clair of New Amsterdam sued when he was called "a rogue, a thief, a beast," and in Massachusetts Richard Stackhouse appeared in court for calling Francis Skerry's wife "a blot and reproach to the church and a rotten member and a scandal to the Gospel."[45] Suspicions of bad faith or malice in particular required some answer from the subject if fences were to be mended in the neighborhood. New Englanders were especially quick to defend themselves from charges of lying, since this called their integrity into question in all their dealings. Who, for example, would trust Samuel Bennet again if he failed to answer Henry Greenland's accusation that he was "the verryest Rascal in New England and that he would not take his word for a groat"?[46]

Lying may have been an especially sensitive issue for New Englanders, but charges of financial and sexual misdeeds hit raw nerves throughout the land. In North Carolina Matthew Winn sued John Jenins for directing these words at him: "you are a perjured Rogue you are a Hogstealing Rogue and Ile prove it."[47] Farther north, Ariaen Cornelissen of New Amsterdam sued when Wolfert Webber called him a corn and cattle thief, and in Massachusetts Thomas Chandler sued Job Tyler for saying that Chandler was "a base, lying cheating knave and that he had gotten all his estate by cheating, etc."[48] Sexual innuendo started just as many suits. Men and women went to court to clear themselves of all sorts of slurs; typically women protested suggestions of promiscuity, and men charges of unlawful seduction and paternity.[49] Interestingly, Mary Beth Norton has found that, in seventeenth-century Maryland, at least, men were far more likely to sue in response to remarks about sexual behavior when they came from women; women were equally likely to sue whether their accusers were male or female. In addition, *married* women were far more likely than single women to resort to a suit to defend their honor. They were more likely to win too, if their husbands appeared for them or sued on their behalf; Norton found that 91 percent of the women plaintiffs whose husbands appeared for them won their cases.[50] The charge of promiscuity, though not confined to women, carried deeper meaning for them and usually worse consequences. John Gould of Maryland spoke for a whole culture when he sued Giles Glover for calling his wife a whore. This was, Gould explained, "the greatest infamy that a malitious toung Can Cast upon a woman seeing that 'Shee lives for ever in eternall shame / that lives to see the death of her good name.'"[51]

The fulfillment of sexual roles as well as morality prompted slander suits. In 1637 John Waltham of Virginia defended his virility by suing two neighboring women who had sneered that he "hade his Mounthly Courses as Women have, and . . . that John Waltham was not able to gett a child."[52] A few years later in Maine, Francis Rayns sued on behalf of his wife when neighbors said, among other things, that "twas the pride of her hart to weare her husbands hatte about and a waskoat."[53] This presumably challenged her husband's authority as well as the constraints of her prescribed role. The subtle regulation of sexual behavior, especially for women, reveals the effectiveness of slander and gossip as a "normative restriction" in early modern culture. In fact, Roger Thompson terms slander "the literary equivalent of more physical forms of folk ridicule such as rough music or the charivari."[54] Slander, like these other forms of local discipline, established community standards of behavior, guided personal conduct, checked deviance, and prodded reform. These measures succeeded by exploiting the value of good name and the power of shame in the community.

How deeply colonial Americans feared the loss of their neighbors' respect may appear further in their reaction to insults and name calling. Today parents advise small children to ignore such things as trifles. But colonial Americans did not ignore them—they sued. Job Chandler of Maryland sued Thomas Baker for calling him a "spindel shanke Doge," and in New Haven Robert Sinclair sued John Ludman for calling him "dogg and runnagado."[55] William Kelsey of Connecticut mused that a neighbor's "language and looks were such as if he came out of the bottomless pitt," and wound up in court.[56] So did William Perkins of Massachusetts for saying that John Holgrave "was a plague to the town and now the plague was going away."[57] "Rogue" was a particularly cutting and versatile insult: Jacob Varrevanger of New Amsterdam was called "a rogue of rogues and murderer of murderers," while Erasmus James of Massachusetts was labeled a "cheating rogue, one-eyed rogue, one-eyed dog."[58]

Some cases turned on the definition of the insult. In 1645 Mr. Brewster of New Haven called Hannah Marsh a "Billingsgate slut," and he stood by the charge in court. But after the governor explained "the ordynary acceptation of Billingsgate slut, namely that some that were soe called were convicted scolds and punished at the [ducking] stoole for it, and some of them chardged with incontinency," Brewster conceded that he could not prove these particular charges and so he apologized.[59] Of course many insults that seem obscure or quaint or even silly now carried much deeper meaning—and pain—within colonial culture. To be called a dog today would be unflattering, but to be called a dog in the seventeenth century, as Robert St. George has noted, was to be called "servile and dependent." In fact, to be called by any animal name was to be reduced to the level of a creature that had no soul and hence no hope for redemption.[60]

The proper context helps explain the prominence of certain epithets and their effect on colonial Americans. But the contemporary meanings of insults do not go far enough in explaining the *strength* of plaintiffs' reactions to them. Their outrage—so easy to provoke and so difficult to assuage—drew its underlying force from a different feature of the social context. In case after case, the plaintiff pleaded his wish to protect his reputation for its own sake and to refute slurs that poisoned his relationship to the community. One New Yorker confronted his slanderer as a "robber of reputations" in 1662; another maintained that, as amenable as he was, "under no circumstances" could "he suffer his reputation, name and fame to be in the least injured"; and in Massachusetts Henry Collins sued for slander in the hope that "gods glory and my suffering name may be vindicated."[61]

Many plaintiffs must have postured a good bit in their court appearances, and no doubt many exaggerated the extent of their sufferings. But plaintiffs would not emphasize the grief of a damaged reputation if that were not a credible claim, if they did not hope to elicit sympathy from the audience. And even allowing for the extravagance of plaintiffs' claims, genuine pain and fear of disgrace emerge from behind the formulaic wording of complaints. In 1692 Francis Foxcraft of Virginia petitioned that through slander his "fame creditt and reputation," which were "much dearer to him than his life," were "impaired, Lessened and much blasted . . . in the face of the whole Countrey."[62] In 1663 a Maryland woman called her reputation and honor "far dearer than life," and twenty years later still another lamented that she had been brought into "Contempt, Scorne and Publique Disgrace . . . amongst her said Neighbours."[63]

The cries of such plaintiffs were believable because slander cases were rooted in colonial Americans' cast-iron faith in the power of gossip to shape and even ruin people's lives. Loose talk, thoughtless words, malicious lies—all worked subtly, perniciously, and relentlessly. Plaintiffs in slander suits were not all prickly, overly sensitive individuals. They reflected accurately the values and fears of their culture, as official pronouncements on the subject reveal. In 1647 Rhode Island, echoing Ecclesiastes, justified its slander law by observing that "a good name is better than precious ointment, and Slanderers are worser than dead flies to corrupt and alter the savour thereof."[64]

Many plaintiffs expressed more than a general sense of public disgrace as proof of their pain; they offered specific examples of how slander affected their everyday lives. Some complained that slander hurt their marriages. This would be predictable in cases based on charges of adultery or promiscuity, but it happened in other cases as well and seems attributable to the strain generated by the suit rather than the specific charge. In Massachusetts in 1640, William Stidson's wife accused Jane Moulton of lodging a false accusation of rape against John Treble; Stidson claimed that Moulton owed Treble money and hoped to escape the debt by disgracing him. In suing, the Moultons maintained that the slander not only hurt Jane Moulton's reputation but also caused "much disquiet and contention between the Plaintiffs."[65] Even marriage prospects could suffer. Robert Bryan explained to a Maryland court in 1673 that he was "at present a Single person"—and likely to remain one, it seemed, since he found his hopes "to Attaine a Wife and to live soberly" blasted by defamation and scandal.[66] The threat to women's marriage prospects was even more serious since, as Cornelia Dayton observes, "the level of prosperity and social prestige a woman could hope to achieve in the rest of her life was determined by the man she married in her youth."[67]

By far the most common cause for grief, according to plaintiffs, lay in the coldness and opprobrium of their neighbors. Plaintiffs received daily proof of their neighbors' distrust; north and south, rural and urban, they felt ostracized and humiliated. In Massachusetts in 1678, Elizabeth Hamons reported that slander "Did hinder [her] from the charitable benevolence of many Christian people."[68] Elinor Clinton of Maryland found herself in 1715 "not only much the worse in her good name, fame, Credit and Estimation . . . brought into Great Infamy and discredit amongst her Neighbours"; she also found that "divers of her Neighbours . . . from the Company of the said Eleanor do altogeather withdraw themselves and . . . the said Eleanor any wise to Intermeddle or Employ do altogether refuse."[69] Even New York City neighbors refused "to keep Company as before they were wont to do" with John and Margaret Clark after a scandal in 1717.[70] Slander victims experienced more than a collective cold shoulder. After scandalous reports circulated about him, John Mitchell of Maryland was stoned by a neighbor's servant as he walked to church; "for any thing that I know," he said, "his master might set him on to Mischefe me."[71] Some plaintiffs feared that neighborhood contempt would cross generations. When Benjamin Price and his wife called Goodwife Edwards a "base, lying woman" in Easthampton, New York, William Edwards regarded it as "a great Defamation to him and his postirity in that it may bee sayd hereafter here goe the bratts of a base lier."[72]

The more public the slander, the greater the plaintiff's fears. Plaintiffs frequently emphasized the forum of the slander rather than the content; what was said often seemed to matter less than how many heard it. Joseph Jordan of North Carolina complained that he was slandered in the "presence and hearing of divers of his neighbours and other faithfull and Credible persons."[73] Mary Bloch of Delaware suffered before "a full and knowne Company," Pieter Tonneman of New Amsterdam before more than twenty persons by his count, John Acie of Massachusetts in a public town meeting, and Francis Foxcraft of Virginia before "a Crowd of People."[74] Plaintiffs worried most of all when their immediate neighbors witnessed their shame. Richard Boughton of Maryland despaired when he was slandered before several persons, but "more especially Certaine of his Neighbours among whome for any man to live in Credit and Good repute" was essential. "The Damage Inconvenience discommodity and detriment That may ensue on the Contrary is altogether inexpressible," he said.[75] Even when the original slander did not occur before large gatherings, plaintiffs anticipated the same result. They expected slander to proliferate, to spread quickly and insidiously. In Massachusetts Walter Taylor claimed that one man's remark "caused him to be reproached and derided up and down the country," and after some gossip indirectly touched them, a Virginia woman warned her husband "that if these things be suffered people will report that our house is a Bawdy house."[76]

Restoring good name and reestablishing public esteem were not only the goals of slander suits—a good reputation was itself an asset in the suits, just as a bad name was a liability. Plaintiffs explicitly relied on previously untarnished reputations to defend themselves against slander. In 1680 Henry Henley boasted that since coming to Maryland he had lived in "unblemished honesty and reputation . . . unspotted of any such wicked crime or of any other hurtfull crime whatsoever."[77] Arthur Browne of Maryland similarly reported that he had lived among his neighbors "in good reputation and credit without scandalous reproach of false or injurious dealeing."[78] But other plaintiffs found themselves undermined by public opinion; as one defendant in Massachusetts put it, "if common fame be credited 'it is not a very easy matter to slander the plaintiff.'"[79] The defendant could find his history at issue too. When Thomas Baker slandered John Nevill's wife in Maryland in 1662, Nevill successfully countered with a suit and the charge that Baker had been "a Common defamor of most of all his neighbours and profers to prove it and particularly by the neighbourhood who can tes-tifie hee [Baker] never lived in any good fame since thay knew him."[80] Even the reputation of witnesses entered the calculus. In a Maryland case in 1663, the defendant argued that the plaintiff's witnesses were all men "of very slender repute, in comparison of the persons present whose oaths if need be I can produce."[81]

After filing suit, most plaintiffs remained more interested in clearing their names than in punishing their accusers. They often settled for an apology as the quickest route to vindication, even when it entailed a lighter sentence for the defendant. In New Netherland, for example, Pieter Andriessen was satisfied when his slanderer begged his forgive-ness in court, "acknowledging and holding him to be an honest and honorable man."[82] Elizabeth Jago of Massachusetts withdrew her slander complaint "upon a public confession of the wrong done her," as did Martha Lamson when John Sady and his wife confessed that "through misinformation or their own misconjectures . . . they had wronged her and were sorry for it."[83] Their honor restored, these plain-tiffs saw no reason to pursue the matter—they had regained what was most important to them.

Defendants who did not confess their error so obligingly, either to assuage their conscience or to mitigate their punishment, almost al-ways found themselves forced to do so after conviction. Colonial courts uniformly included a public acknowledgment of guilt in a slan-derer's punishment. These acknowledgments are strikingly similar in pattern. First, defendants made their apologies in the most public forum available. New Englanders typically confessed at church or town meetings, other colonists in court.[84] It was crucial to the proceed-ing that the entire community be able to witness the plaintiff's vindi-cation. By their presence, neighbors signified their acceptance of the plaintiff on his former terms of good standing; the plaintiff, in theory at least, need not fear lingering doubts of his innocence. To complete the circle, the courts in some cases assembled the witnesses to the original slander to witness the victim's exculpation. In New Haven in 1649, Francis Newman's wife apologized privately for maligning Lancelot Fuller's wife, but Goodwife Fuller considered it "not sufficient except she clered her where it had been spoken."[85] A New Netherland court ordered in 1642 that "the persons who were present when Dirck Cornelisz slandered the daughter of Hendrick Jansen shall be assembled here and that he shall declare before them that he has nothing to say about the daughter nor about her bridegroom that reflects in any way on their honor or virtue."[86]

Second, acknowledgments of guilt were usually required within a specified time period that was as short as possible. In Massachusetts John Broadstreet was to receive satisfaction within three days and Jeremiah Watts within one month; Elsie Gerrits of New Amsterdam was ordered to acknowledge her fault "at the next Court day"; and Benjamin Salisbury of Virginia had to repent "Immediately."[87] The purpose here is clear enough: the sooner the cloud over the plaintiff's reputation was dissipated, the sooner he could resume without anxiety his place in the community.

Finally, these acknowledgments were closely detailed and specific, amounting at times to verbatim retractions. Daniel Hutchins of Massachusetts was ordered in 1668 to confess that he "did sinfully in slanderously and falsely saying to Mrs. Giffard that shee was abase lying woeman and that I would not beleeve a word shee said and that I would bring forty witnesses more to Justifie what I had said and for which saying I am Hartily sory and doe desire Mrs. Giffard to forgive me."[88] The reason for such specificity is also evident: the plaintiff wanted to have his innocence made absolutely clear, with no ambiguity or hairsplitting or hint of unanswered questions.

Courts deviated from this pattern of enforced acknowledgment only in ways that humiliated the defeated defendant still more. In Maryland Thomas Baker in 1662 and John Wickes in 1673 had to beg forgiveness on bended knees; in New Netherland Hendrick Jansen was condemned "to declare before the door of [the plaintiff] with uncovered head, after the ringing of the bell, that these infamous words were falsely and scandalously spoken by him, and then there to pray God, justice and his opponent for forgiveness."[89] Mordecai Bowden of West New Jersey had not only to make a public acknowledgment but also to sign a confession posted for two weeks in the center of town; when John Wolstonecraft was ordered to make public satisfaction, the "manner and measure" of it were left to the pleasure of the plaintiff; in Massachusetts John Smith publicly vowed that he would henceforth "endeavour to vindicate and cleare [the plaintiff's] creditt and reputation in what I may"; and in Virginia Robert Wyard had to "stand three severall Sundayes in the tyme of devine service before the face of the whole Congragation in a white sheete with a white wan[d] in his hand" and ask for forgiveness.[90]

From principle or obduracy, some defendants refused to soothe plaintiffs with acknowledgments and had to be coerced to do so. The Essex County Court ordered Daniel Hutchins to confess the slander of John Giffard's wife in June 1668. By November, Giffard felt obliged to ask the court to compel Hutchins to apologize; Hutchins had refused, saying that "he would rather spend a hundred pounds."[91] John Atkinson of Massachusetts proved more subtle. Ordered to confess slander against James Mirik at a house raising, Atkinson testified "that whereas he had agreed to make acknowledgement for slander in saying that James Mirik had told a hundred lies," he confessed that he was wrong in being "so surten As to the nomber of lies I know not how many [lies] that he hus tould."[92]

But such recalcitrance was exceptional. Most convicted slanderers found the alternatives to public acknowledgment even more unpalatable. Pennsylvania ordered in 1682 that slanderers be "severely punished, as enemies to the peace and concord of this province," and Connecticut was typical in specifying heavy fines and whippings for slander and related crimes.[93] In addition, courts frequently sentenced slanderers to sit in the stocks. In West New Jersey, Mary Allan was set on a pillory with a sign identifying her as a "falce perjured infamous woman," and in Massachusetts Elizabeth Due was "to be whipped twenty stripes on some lecture day, and a paper to be pinned upon her forehead with this inscription in capital letters: 'A Slanderer of Mr. Zerobabell Endicott.'"[94]

Although men as well as women received such punishments, and men were at least as likely to be tried for slander,[95] women were particularly identified with slander and offenses such as malicious gossip, opprobrious language, and verbal abuse of neighbors. One Puritan writer complained of women who went "idling and tatling abroad," and in 1662 Virginia authorities framed their slander legislation with specific reference to the "many brabling women [who] often slander and scandalize their neighbours for which their poore husbands are often brought into chargeable and vexatious suits."[96] Women who bad-mouthed their neighbors not only disrupted the community and sowed discord; their unruliness constituted a kind of domestic insubordination. Excluded from authority in so many ways, women used the one power still available to them. As Mary Beth Norton notes, "For men, gossip was an available option; for women, it was an essential tool, perhaps the most valuable and reliable means of advancing or protecting their own interests."[97]

The view that women are more likely to gossip and that their gossip is generally more destructive is common in other cultures as well. A modern cultural anthropologist has observed that in Valloire, a village in the French Alps, women seen conversing are immediately assumed to be "indulging in *mauvaise langue*—gossip, malice, 'character assassination.'" To deflect such suspicions the women deliberately avoid being seen together; if necessary, they stay indoors.[98] For colonial women who took less care than the women of Valloire to avoid the occasions of gossip, authorities reserved special sanctions. The "brabling women" of Virginia suffered duckings as well as fines; and to make sure that no one missed the point, Massachusetts authorities condemned Elizabeth Applegate in 1636 "to stand with her tongue in a Cleft stick for swearing, railing and revileing."[99]

These punishments—both the acknowledgments and the public humiliations—were a psychological eye for an eye: the defendants incurred shame for having inflicted it on others. Plaintiffs rebuilt their reputations on the ruins of the defendant's name, and they hoped to emerge from slander trials cleansed, their places in society reaffirmed. It did not always work out that way. All plaintiffs who demanded reparation of honor invited the judgment of the community, and not all benefited from the attention. Hannah Marsh of New Haven, for example, barely won her slander suit in 1645 when the court found that the defendant could not prove against her everything that the term "Billingsgate slut" implied. Narrowly saved by the dictionary, Marsh was then chastised by the court for her "forward disposition." The court reminded her that "meekness is a chojse ornament for weoman, and wished her to take it as a rebucke from God, and to keepe a better watch over her sperit herafter, least the Lord proceede to manifest his displeasure further agaynst her."[100] This was in a case Hannah Marsh *won*.

A more fundamental—and intractable—problem for plaintiffs lay in the very elusiveness of reputation. Reputation was inevitably important in colonial communities. As J. G. Peristiany has noted, "Honour and shame are the constant preoccupation of individuals in small-scale, exclusive societies."[101] These concerns could help unify the community by supporting its norms and deterring transgression.[102] But individuals paid a high price for consensus, trading peace of mind for the order of the group. Public esteem seemed always much easier lost than won, and it was never secure. One of John Winthrop's correspondents justly feared that no matter what lies a slanderous tongue "soe unjustlye cast out, yett [it] never fayles to leave some spots in the Aprehentions of some behinde."[103] Reputations may be lost anywhere, but in colonial America the pressures to sustain a good name were so great, and the consequences of disrepute so grievous, as to be almost unbearable. The strains of community life emerged in many ways in colonial America, in religious controversies and malicious lawsuits and witchcraft accusations—and in a concern for reputation that bordered on the obsessive. This remained true until the late eighteenth century, when traditional community life lost much of its coherence and community ridicule lost much of its sting.

CHAPTER 3

The Contradictions of Family:
Marriage

In colonial America husbands and wives were bound as closely to the community as to each other. From courtship to death, through informal pressures and official sanctions, by meddlesome in-laws as well as local authorities, the community influenced every aspect of married life. The goal was to protect stable and peaceful marriages in general and to aid the victims of love gone awry: jilted brides, cuckolded husbands, beaten wives. But the many benefits of community protection could not overcome its contradictory purposes and often painful consequences. Community influence tended to give greater weight to social obligations than to emotional needs, to the reinforcement of expected roles within marriage, and to maintaining the appearance of a happy marriage while sacrificing hopes for its achievement. Marriages bore the burden of community expectations as well as personal demands and suffered from their cross-purposes.

Parents naturally influenced their children's marriages in significant ways, most clearly in the matter of consent. Minors needed parental consent to marry, but most adult children sought it just as fervently, to preserve hopes for inheritance as well as filial affection. Indeed, some couples sought the approval of more than their own parents. In Warwick, Rhode Island, Gabriel Hike announced in his banns that he had "obtained the good will and approbation of Mr. William Arnold together with the neighbors of patuxit" in order to marry Mary Percy, "they being in stead of parents unto her."[1] Most people, though, contented themselves with parental consent, and for many that was trouble enough. In 1690, after "som discorse about this busines" Joseph Whitman of Long Island won Henry Whitney's consent to marry his daughter if he could support her. Unluckily for Whitman, Whitney changed his mind and sued him "for steling of his da[ugh]ters afetions contrary to her mothars mind and using unlaful menes to obtayne his da[ugh]ters love."[2] Other parents were equally capricious. John Hopkinson of Massachusetts "laboured to Gaine" his mother's consent to marry Hannah Palmer "but she still remained opposite." Mrs. Hopkinson complained that they were "Childish: and our beginnings was Contrary to the way that gods people went in," but she finally conceded that she objected chiefly to her prospective in-laws: "she would not be soe near related to the Acies." Though "much dejected," John Hopkinson and Hannah Palmer broke off their engagement, at least for a time.[3]

But many children were more persuasive, or more stubborn, than the quiescent John Hopkinson. In Ipswich in 1664, Martha Cross found herself unmarried and pregnant. When this circumstance alone did not melt her father's resistance to a marriage, she asked a neighbor to speak to her father on her behalf. She also went to her sister "in sore destresse of mind in the Considoration as shee Conseved she had binn cast out of her fathers favor: and familie." The sister, in turn "much afected lamenten with teares," visited another neighbor who agreed to help her reconcile the father to the marriage. They proceeded to Robert Cross's house "and there found them in a sad and sorrofull Condition verie much horrified in there sperite not knowing which way to turen or what to say." The neighbor found it easy to take charge of this sorry group and pressed Martha's case. Finally Robert Cross agreed. The parties to this complicated affair then discovered, no doubt to their considerable dismay, that the expected bridegroom, William Durkee, was in no hurry to marry, saying "that he had rather keep the child than keep her." But he too relented, tendering the unenthusiastic proposal that "if he kept one he would keep the other." He proved as good as his word; when Robert Cross withdrew his consent, Durkee sued for and won the right to marry his daughter.[4]

Occasional successes notwithstanding, defiance of parental wishes was a perilous course. Wayward children risked estrangement from their parents, a heavy burden in a patriarchal society. Furthermore, the threat of disinheritance ran just beneath the surface of these disagreements.[5] Chesapeake suitors in the seventeenth century, both men and women, enjoyed more freedom in marrying than did most colonists, primarily because Chesapeake parents were more likely to die before their children reached marriageable age. But, as Lorena Walsh notes, parents who did live to see their children marry asserted their influence just as New Englanders did, especially when the marriage affected significant property holdings.[6] Quaker meetings went so far as to enjoin their members to cut off children who married non-Quakers. When John Elliott informed a Baltimore meeting in 1688 that his daughter had married "against his mind to a man of the world," they urged all parents of such errant children "not to give them any part of their Estate but to let Such Suffer," and in 1704 the same meeting reaffirmed that parents "should disown their action and them in it."[7] This offense, "marriage out of unity," remained the most frequent cause for disownment by Quaker meetings throughout the colonial period.[8]

Local law as well as custom bolstered parental authority, especially in the seventeenth century and particularly in New England. The required publication of banns reinforced rules of parental consent by smoking out irregularly formed engagements. Lacking sufficient clergy and means of enforcement, Chesapeake authorities commonly tolerated lapses in formal marriage proceedings during the seventeenth century, but they remained exceptional.[9] Most colonies fined transgressors of these laws; Plymouth authorized a "fine or corporal punishment or both"; and in a law "Touching Menstealers," Rhode Island ordered "that the taking away, deflouring or contracting in marriage a maid under sixteen years of age, against the will of, or unknown to the Father or Mother of the Maid, is a kind of stealing of her," punishable by five years' imprisonment or "satisfaction of her parents."[10] By the end of the seventeenth century, even Maryland authorities had grown weary of their region's reputation as a haven for eloping Virginia couples and were increasingly concerned about the evils of improper marriages (especially "the utter ruin of many heirs and heiresses"); in 1696 Maryland acted to oppose clandestine marriages and enforce banns.[11]

These laws were applied rigorously enough to buttress the parents' control.[12] Masters also enjoyed legal protection of their rights. In 1652 Plymouth presented Jonathan Coventry "for makeing a mocion of marriage with Katheren Bradberey, servant unto Dr. Burne . . . without her master's consent," and a Connecticut judge found in 1654 that Will Chapman "hath trespassed against the Saide order [on consent] in an high nature goinge aboute to gaine the affectyons by way of marraidge of one Elizabeth Bateman Servant to Cap: John Cullick."[13] In Virginia servants could not marry without a certificate of their masters' consent; Maryland and North Carolina fined ministers for marrying servants without their masters' consent.[14] Courts often punished not only those who married or published banns without consent but also the individuals who helped them or performed the ceremony.[15] New Netherland authorities were particularly incensed by a case in 1648, when William Harck not only married a couple without their parents' consent "but also provided them instantaneously in his house with bed and room to consummate the marriage."[16]

Parents' influence did not end when their children married, and some managed to separate couples even then. Charged with living apart from their wives, one Massachusetts man answered in 1643 that "his mother was not willing to let his wyfe come," and another explained in 1648 "that he married her without consent of her friends, who would not suffer her to live with him and kept her from him with her consent."[17] Usually, however, parents and their married offspring settled into a stable relationship, often drawn together by financial and living arrangements as well as affection.[18] Most of the personal and emotional ways in which parents influenced married children remain difficult to trace, but one tangible form of support parents offered was a refuge from troubled marriages. Elizabeth Wildey told the court in Northumberland, Virginia, in 1700 that she left her husband because "he mistreated her, and that she is now living with her Mother."[19] Daniel Lawrence of Flushing formalized such an agreement in 1755 by providing in his will for his "daughter Mary, wife of James Thorne, a sufficient maintenance during such time as she lives separate from her husband."[20] But a haven for one spouse could well look like excessive interference to the other. Thomas Davidtse of Albany sued his father-in-law in 1681 "to let him have his wife and children and the effects belonging to him," and asked the court to order the father-in-law "to commit no further trespass . . . but rather to incline his daughter toward the idea of a permanent union and an irrevocable marriage tie."[21]

Disagreements with in-laws surfaced in other ways as well. In 1691 the Baltimore Friends' meeting agreed "to assist and stand by" a Quaker woman whose "dead husbands Relations Endeavour to make her Marriage voyd and not according to Law" in order to block her inheritance.[22] Reversing the usual roles, a Massachusetts woman so disliked the man with whom her mother "had long kept company" that she brought them before a judge, who "ordered them to separate upon pain of punishment, but they continued as before, to the daughter's great grief, and were seeking means to be married."[23] Others acted more directly. In 1650 Mary Pray stood convicted in Essex County, Massachusetts, "for that shee should say to her mother-in-lawe get you whome [home] you old hogge get you whome and withall threw stones at her," and in Kingston, New York, Jan Jansen Van Amersfoort was charged by his mother-in-law with calling her "an old hog and a beast" and with mistreating her daughter, his wife.[24] Such tensions arose naturally as parents remained a presence in their children's marriages, and friction with in-laws could be expected. But colonial Americans accepted parental influence in marriage, and they expected families to live together in harmony. So they sought to ease the tensions rather than alter the relationship, and on that fall day in 1665 the Kingston court did not tell Jan Van Amersfoort's mother-in-law to mind her own business, but instead ordered him "to quietly and decently hold himself against his wife and mother-in-law, so that no further complaints for heavier punishment may be brought against him."[25]

Neighbors and friends drew their influence in other people's marriages less from law than from custom and proximity. Neighbors clearly knew a great deal about and freely discussed marital affairs in their community. In 1648 Thomas Lyon of Stamford, Connecticut, complained of his mother-in-law's behavior, especially "several carages betwene the felow she now hath to bee her Husband and she," adding that "the people allsoe tooke notis of it which was to her disgrace which greved me verie much."[26] Some neighbors were as well informed as the principals. When "some difference" arose between Margaret Gifford of Lynn and her fiancé in 1673, one of the neighbors told her mother about it. The mother questioned the apparently reticent Margaret about the matter, guessed at the cause of the disagreement, and added for good measure that the "neighbors would be apt to think so too."[27] Matrimonial goings-on so intrigued neighbors that some even bet on their outcome, including two Virginia men who laid odds in 1634 that "mr. william Burditt should never mach in wedlocke with the widdow Sanders while they lived in Virginia."[28]

Not everyone welcomed so much neighborly interest. In 1674 rumors and neighbors' talk alerted Susannah Martin to the possibility that "one Thomas Tukesberry," through frequent visits, was causing trouble between her son and his wife. Martin, as she told the Essex County Court, asked another relative to help prevent Tukesberry's visits, if only "to stop the mouths of people, for their mouths were open." But the relative was made of sterner, or at least more prickly, stuff and replied, "let them shut againe, for he should come in spite of your teeth or any bodys els."[29] As little as they may have wished to, though, most colonists resigned themselves to sharing much of their lives with their neighbors. Colonial courts not only recognized but exploited this fact, relying heavily on the testimony of neighbors in judgments. The disposition of Nicholas Wyatt's estate in 1675 turned entirely on the opinion of his Maryland neighbors that he had been "very Loving and kinde to his wife."[30] In 1670 Hannah Huitt of Stonington, Connecticut, received a divorce from her husband, whom she presumed dead, when "the neighbors allsoe [testified] that the said Huitt hath been so long absent and that they have not heard of him or of the vessell or company he went with since their departure."[31]

Neighbors' testimony in court often revealed years of close observation. In Maryland in 1736, Jane Pattison sued her second husband for a separation and financial support. Her neighbor, Hannah Clare, testified that she had known Pattison since her former marriage and that she "bore the character of being a good and dutiful wife." In the present marriage Clare "had often seen the Defendant beat with his Fists kick and Stamp upon the Complainant and beat her with sticks in a Cruel Manner insomuch that this deponent has thought he would have killed her." Furthermore, he "used to Pick Quarrels" with his wife "and Abuse her in the manner aforesaid without having received any Provocation." Clare's testimony, which others corroborated, guided the court toward its judgment for the wife.[32]

The natural fruit of so much neighborly watchfulness was much free advice. When Sarah Taylor of Maryland discovered that the man who had been courting her "did privately abuse her, by reporting that he had had uncivell doeings with her . . . by the advice of her freinds she did strive to wean her selfe from her former Childish Love"; she completed the weaning process by suing him for defamation in 1662.[33] Andrew Scott, on the other hand, resisted "the Repeated Advices of his saide Neighbours" to separate from his wife until 1746, when his wife "brought a Desease upon him for which for Decency and the Shamefullness of it, he forbears to give a name to."[34] Neighbors reproved as well as advised, and sometimes to a refractory audience. In June 1673 Mary Woodbury saw bruises that Mary Harris carried from a beating by her husband. A few days later Samuel Harris came to Woodbury's house "to inquire for his wife, and when told that she was not there, he began to complain of her for running abroad so much." Woodbury told him that his wife "had little encouragement to stay at home because he beat her so. He replied, 'Well, what if I doe, If I doe she shall have more of it.'"[35] In Maryland in 1657 William Marshall told Robert

Robins "that it was a pityfull thing for him and his wife to live Soe, whereupon the said Robins made reply; what would you have me doe, for She is a Common whore, and I have Good Wittness that William Herde, rid her from Stump to Stump."[36] Marshall had no answer.

Neighbors who offered practical help usually met with a warmer reception; they often found themselves more deeply involved as well. Mary Jones told a Maryland court in 1678 that "she should ere this have perished" but for the "charitable assistance and reliefe of her good neighbours" when she left her abusive husband.[37] Andrew Scott found life with his wife "so indecent, Disordely Abusefull and Turbulent, occasioned by her common and frequent Drunkenness that he could not live in the house or Cohabit with her with any Degree of Comfort or Satisfaction and was often Obliged for Peace and Quietness to himself to Leave his own house and go to some neighbours to be out of her way." At the same time, his wife complained that he behaved "with so much Cruilty and Inhumanity" that she could not live with him "without running a Manifest hazard of her life and an utter loss of all peace and Quiet"; she finally was "Driven out of Doores almost naked and quite Dis[ti]tute of all the Necessaries of Life and forced to fly for Refuge and a Subsistence to her friends by her said husband."[38] The Scotts' separation in 1746 may have brought as much peace to their neighbors' lives as to their own.

Neighbors served as intermediaries from the beginning to the end of married life. In 1652 Cornelis van Tienhoven confessed to his Dutch landlady that he was not married to the New Netherland woman who shared his room, explaining "that friends were employed to obtain her parents' consent, and that then he should marry her."[39] When Mary Codd's husband left her after twenty years of marriage in 1729, she told the Maryland court that she had enlisted friends to help bring him home. Ledger Codd meanwhile claimed that she had rejected his attempts at reconciliation and, giving up, he had asked "his Eldest Daughter and some of [Mary Codd's] Friends and relations to acquaint her that he would no longer endure such Treatment" and to ask her to take separate lodgings for which he would pay.[40] Through testamentary provisions, some ingenious spouses enlisted the aid of friends to support their wishes even after death. Husbands took a special interest in their possible successors. John Green of South Carolina provided in 1723 that if his wife remarried "against consent of executors, she will forfeit all willed to her."[41] Another South Carolinian was even fussier;

in 1736 John McGilvery of St. Helena's Parish left his widow the "residue of all estate if she does not marry an Irishman, if she does, then only one-third estate."[42]

In many cases neighbors considered it not only natural to intervene in romantic affairs but their duty to do so. They grew particularly bold in defending community standards of morality. John Everett of Massachusetts Bay confessed in 1665 to a "wanton and shamefull dalliance with Elizabeth Frost, his wives neece," which would have reached "even to the committing of the act of uncleanes, had not some immediately come in to prevent it"; and in Essex County in 1670, in a case that calls to mind the European custom of the charivari, Thomas Gatchell and Henry Conder attacked William Beale's house, "besetting it with clubs, saying 'come out you cuckolly curr: we are come to beatt thee: thou livest in adultery.'"[43] Community officials explicitly sanctioned neighbors' involvement in such matters and even censured them for negligence. In 1660 the New Haven General Court did not stop at punishing Jacob Murline and Sarah Tuttle for improprieties in their courtship. It declared that by countenancing such behavior Jacob Murline's sister, Maria, had committed "a very great evil"; to perform her duty she "should have shewed her indignation against [them] and have told her mother that shee [Sarah Tuttle] might have beene shut out of doores."[44]

The expectations of neighbors' influence at work here, endorsed by authorities, lent neighbors' opinions and interventions a power that mere proximity and meddlesomeness could not. And though some colonists, especially those in New England and New Netherland, felt a special moral obligation—and justification—to oversee matrimonial behavior in the neighborhood, neighbors in other colonies were also observant and influential. Communities up and down the Atlantic coast accepted and even encouraged such involvement, sometimes in remarkable ways. In 1657, for example, the Maryland Provincial Court permitted Robert Harwood to renew his courtship of Elizabeth Gary despite the objections of her parents. The court set conditions for the courtship that testify to the breadth and legitimacy of neighbors' involvement, conditions that did not seem extraordinary to individuals long accustomed to the presence of neighbors in their private lives:

that the said Elizabeth Gary shall within fifteen dayes after the date hereof, be Conveyed to the house of mr. Thomas Davis at the Cliftes and there She is to remaine for the Space of Six weekes . . . And the Said Robert Harwood is to have during all the Said Time, full free and perfect Liberty (bringing one or more of the Neighbours with him) to have all freedom of discourse with the said Elizabeth Gary and to use all faire and Lawfull Endeavours with her to Marry or Contract Marriage . . . one or more of the Neighbours being always present . . . when they are in Company together.[45]

The actions of local authorities reveal even more forcefully the extent of community influence in marital life. Unlike parents and neighbors, community officials could usually enforce their advice to couples, but they did not always find it necessary to do so. In 1640 William Wake "was councelled" by the Massachusetts authorities to go home to his wife and was discharged when he agreed.[46] Summoned by a Maryland church in 1737, Robert Collins promised "to turn Anne Sylby away and to have no Society with her in any Respect"; Bartholomew Brown of Kent County similarly renounced Sara Hollis in 1714.[47] In some cases of marital difficulty, officials offered specific practical advice. In 1651 Thomas Rolinson of Massachusetts "proven impotent, on complaint of his wife, was to take counsel of physicians forthwith, follow their advice, and report to court."[48] In other instances authorities urged a broader course of personal reformation. In 1682 Jan Roeloffse promised a court in northern New York to "live in a Christian and decent manner with my wife and not maltreat her any more, nor hereafter give her any occasion to complain about me if she does not give me any occasion to do so; also [to] avoid drunkenness and lead a sober and decent life as a Christian man should."[49]

Authorities, particularly in the northern colonies, frequently counseled and mediated between quarreling spouses. When William Hallet petitioned in 1674 to annul his marital separation agreement, the Council of New Netherland recommended the commission of "some persons to hear the complaints of the Petitioner and the answer of his wife, and to use all possible efforts to reconcile the parties."[50] Rachel Davenport of New Amsterdam wished to separate from her husband in 1671, "alleadging that for many yeares together she hath undergone a bitter and wearisome life by Reason of her husbands Inhumane usage Blowes, and Cruel Carriages towards her." Although she was able to prove several of her charges, the court could see no legal reason for a divorce and urged both parties to seek "a frindly Composure, and that all former differances should Remaine in Oblivion." When the Davenports "for the present could not be perswaded," the Mayor's Court appointed two men "to use all possible meanes and perswations for a Composure betwixt the said parties." Only when these two arbitrators reported "that they could not see any probability of making up the difference between them" did the court concede defeat and allow a separation.[51]

A New Jersey court had more success, albeit briefly. In 1694 Thomas Peachee appeared before the Grand Jury to explain why he and his wife lived separately. He said that "because Shee abuses and Scandalizes him and therefor in regard they could not live in any Peace or Comfort togeather," they had agreed to separate. The court then admonished them "to come to a Reconciliation and live togeather as husband and wife ought to doe." Mary Peachee expressed herself "heartily willing and desireous thereto," and Thomas Peachee was "also willing they should be reconcyled togeather Provided Shee will acknowledge shee hath Scandalized him wrongfully." His wife agreed. The Peachees' facade of amicability promptly cracked over the exact wording of her acknowledgment, but "after some good admonitions from the Bench" harmony seemed restored. "They both promise they will forgett and never mention what unkind speeches or Actions have formerly past betweene them or Concerning each other . . . And they are againe reconciled togeather, and Hee said Thomas promisses shee behaveing her selfe with tendernesse and love to him, hee will remaine as a Loveing and Carefull Husband to her." Their reconciliation did not last long. The Peachees soon appeared again before the court and agreed that "Mary with her Sonne will depart this Province for England . . . And soe not be further chargeable to the said Doctor Thomas Peachee."[52]

Try as they might to rely on tactics of persuasion, colonial authorities could and often did coerce couples into observing their marriage vows. New England authorities intervened in all sorts of matters, whereas Chesapeake authorities addressed primarily cases of adultery and fornication. Chesapeake vestries referred to the courts the cases of individuals who ignored their warnings.[53] As always, though, New England authorities displayed the most force. When reported by his father-in-law for living apart from his wife, Richard Pryer "not appearing but making escape, court ordered an attachment to apprehend him and put him into the house of correction, there to remain until he give security to live with his wife." In addition, "all persons were pro-

hibited from entertaining him with either victuals, lodging or employment."[54] In 1650 the Essex County Court ordered "that Mr. Bacheler
and Mary his wife shall live together, as they publicly agreed to do, and
if either desert the other, the marshal to take them to Boston to be kept
until next quarter Court of Assistants, to consider a divorce."[55]

Official interest in New England comprehended many practical details. In 1670 Lawrence Clenton was "severely whipped with twenty
stripes well laid on" for improper advances to a woman. He was then
"ordered to allow his wife 2 s. per week toward her maintenance, to
carry it himself to her, to live with her, as duty binds him, and at least
to lodge with her one night a week." Clenton was to obtain from his
wife or the constable a certificate that he met these conditions or else
"be sent to the house of correction."[56] This light touch failed to unite
the Clentons, however. Each appeared subsequently for living apart
from the other; in 1677 Rachel Clenton requested, in vain, a divorce,
while confessing to "unlawful familiarity" with John Ford; and in
1678 Lawrence Clenton was reported as the father of an illegitimate
child.[57]

Colonists everywhere not only tended to accept community intervention; many encouraged it by asking for assistance or airing their
marital problems in public. In 1661 Geertruyt Wyngaert asked the
New Amsterdam court to compel Geleyn Verplanck to marry her, "inasmuch as he had so far seduced her, with fair words and promises,
that he had carnal conversation with her, and she is pregnant with child
by him"; but she added, in somewhat startling testimony to the high
price of virginity, that she would settle for his paying her "for the de-
floration, a sum of six hundred guilders in beavers, one hundred guilders for her lying in, and one hundred guilders a year for the child's
aliment."[58] Others sought to protect more conventional forms of property, commonly by publicly disclaiming debts contracted by errant
spouses.[59]

Spouses sought official aid most often in cases of adultery and cruelty,[60] but they also turned to the authorities with more general marital
problems. In 1658 Nicholas Boot complained of his wife's behavior to
the president of the New Amsterdam Court, who laid the matter before
the whole court. Boot hoped that the judges would "reprimand" his
wife "for her irregular life, and if she will not amend, that they separate
one from the other." Sending for the wife immediately, the court ordered them "to live in peace."[61] Thomas Brackett explained in 1680

that "the greate affliction that he groanes under, by reason of his wife's cruel carriage towards him" compelled him to petition the Salem court. Through "cunning and fraudulent dealing", he claimed, his wife had inveigled him, "a poore simple man," into signing away his property. He further pointed to his wife's "unchristian and inhumane carriage to me when at any Tyme I am in the house with her; which christian modesty forbids me to speak of; although," his reticence slipping a little, "it be not hid from my neighbors, who are able to give full evidence for me." And indeed one of the neighbors, untrammeled by Christian modesty, testified to no one's surprise that the Bracketts "did not live orderly as man and wife ought to do."[62]

Still other spouses brought before the community differences that might just as easily have been settled privately, apparently hoping that the very openness and formality of the forum would ease their resolution—and hoping too, it would seem, to vindicate their own actions. In 1667 Ann Gray voluntarily appeared before Justice Edmond Scarborough of the Accomack County Court and acknowledged before three witnesses that she had committed adultery. Scarborough cautioned her to consider the gravity of the offense. Gray answered that "her owne guilty Conscience and desire to ask her husbands forgiveness did occasion this her confession of Adultery." Gray's action suggests a striking need to seek public acquittal, forgiveness by the community as well as by her husband; it may also have been an attempt to enlist the support of the community in her negotiations with her husband.[63] In another case, in 1669 George Potter submitted an agreement to the town of Providence. He observed that "there has been some differences of late" between him and his wife which had caused her "with my Consent and in hope of More peaceable liveing" to move to Boston. Potter now, however, "finding it uncomfortable so to live, and I being desireous to Come together againe doe here for her further in Couragement and to prevent after Strifes and Alinations propose these following things," published for the town to read, "as Artickles of our Agreement."[64] Perhaps the case of Thomas Davidste of New York illustrates most strikingly the willingness of colonial Americans to open their marital lives to the community. Reconciling with his wife in 1681, "for better assurance of his real Intention and good resolution to observe the same, he requests that two good men be named to oversee his conduct at New York towards his wife . . . subjecting himself willingly to the rule and censure of the said men."[65] Here the community becomes the guarantor of marital conduct, a form of group insurance against the potential weakness of the individual parties.

If the very extent of community influence was significant, so too were its effects. The specific areas of regulation, the values promoted, the kinds of behavior validated and censured—all reveal more clearly what the colonial community expected of married life. In particular, the community pursued order and harmony in both the form and conduct of marriage; unstable marriages threatened society in practical ways and also in powerful emotional and symbolic terms. The community upheld these values and exerted its influence even when its own goals were contradictory or when they ran contrary to the needs and desires of couples.

Community regulation began even before marriage, with the engagement or contract to marry. Colonial authorities formalized this event in order to keep the parties mindful of its gravity; their means ranged from published banns to posted bonds to investigations of conduct.[66] An engagement was often even harder to break than to begin, especially if one of the parties resisted. In 1654 Anna van Vorst explained that she no longer wanted to marry Pieter Kock because of "certain misbehavior" and demonstrated that he had agreed, promising her "a written acquittal to that effect." But when Kock sued to hold her to the engagement, the New Amsterdam court decided "that the promise of marriage having been made and given before the Eyes of God, shall remain in force." Each was barred from marrying someone else without the approval of the magistrates as well as the other party, and Anna van Vorst was to keep the gifts Peter Kock had given her "until parties with the pleasure, good will, contentment and inclination of both, shall marry together, or with the knowledge of the Magistracy shall release and set each other free."[67] Mary Russell fared better. Convicted by a jury in 1661 of breaking an engagement to John Sutton, the court cleared her in 1663 and instead blamed her father for reporting "such thinges concerning the said Sutton as might justly discurrage her." The court vindicated Mary Russell's intentions rather than her judgment, since "the truth of such reports" about Sutton "wee see not cause to determine."[68]

Propriety often weighed more heavily than good intentions, however. When James Wakely of Connecticut sued the Widow Boosy in

1650, the court found that the evidence of an engagement, though not a contract, between the two rendered "her proceedings with another before a Cleare dissingagement . . . from the former [Wakely] . . . at least dissorderly."[69] In clearer cases of disorder, courts acted more forcefully. When Robert Cocker "betrothed himself too securely to one maiden, and then contracted with another woman" in 1642, the Essex County Court sentenced him "to be severely whipped, and to pay to Thomas Kinge, who subsequently married the first maiden, five pounds."[70] In other cases, a guilty conscience proved punishment enough. In 1640 Nicholas Pacy confessed to knowing that his wife was already engaged when he married her and admitted that his action had grieved "the harts not only of my wife and [the former fiancé], whom I have wronged, but also . . . other godly christians." His wife further testified that she had been so "troubled in her conscience about it since her marriage" that she "had sinned in denying conjugal respects unto her husband because of her scruples."[71]

Broken promises were not the only worry for colonial authorities, and some problems in courtship outweighed the integrity of contract. Johannes van Beeck contracted to marry in 1654 "not only without his father's knowledge, but contrary to his express prohibition to marry abroad." Despite this clear irregularity, the New Amsterdam authorities permitted the marriage, in part because of "the danger that in such circumstances matters by long delay might come to be disclosed between these aforesaid young people, which would bring disgrace on both families."[72] In 1686 New Haven authorities complained "that much sin hath been committed against God, and much inconvenience hath growen to some members of this Jurisdiction by the irregular and disorderly carriage of young persons of both Sexes, upon purpose or pretence of Marriage." It then forbade anyone to "indeavour to inveagle, or draw the affections" of any woman without consent, "whether it be by speech, writing, message, company keeping, unnecessary familiarity, disorderly night meetings, sinful dalliance, gifts, or any other way, directly or indirectly."[73]

Fears of prenuptial pregnancy prompted much of the community's scrutiny of engaged couples. When pregnancy did occur, the authorities often hastened the marriage to assure legitimacy and financial support for the child. They sometimes had to act in the face of new resistance from the expectant father. John Coague proposed to Elizabeth Coale, published the banns three times, and fathered her child before backing away from his engagement in 1680. The New York City Mayor's Court, however, held him in custody "untill the mayor and Aldermen shall Seriously weigh wherefore hee Should not marry her."[74] But colonial authorities did not condone all the steps individuals took to legitimize children. Massachusetts Bay sentenced Seaborne Batchilor to be whipped with twenty stripes "for committing folly with Ezekiall Everill, being with child by him and marrying with John Cromwell and not discovering the same to him."[75]

Courts aided those deceived in other ways during courtship. A servant, Mary Manning, asked the court of New Castle, Delaware, in 1677 to "Cleare hur from the threats and future scandall" of Jeremy Farrington, explaining that he had "deluded her from [her employer] making her beleeve he had a good estate att St. Maries, and telling the Peticoner hee would carry hur there and marry hur butt all that prooved a meere t' cheat" and he did not marry her.[76] Others proved rather too eager to marry. In Boston in 1678 John Tipping was charged with "making Sute to some maids or women in order to marriage, hee having a wife in London"; William Norman of Maine acknowledged in 1651 that he had done Margery Randall "much wrong" in marrying her without divorcing his wife in England; and a Delaware church warden presented Evert Hendriks in 1679 "for having two wyves both now alive att Crainhoeck."[77] The Maryland Provincial Court pardoned Robert Holt for marrying Christine Bonnefield in 1658—"his owne lawfull wife Dorothy being still liveing"—but presented him again in 1662 because he "not haveing the feare of God before his eyes" continued to live with Bonnefield.[78]

After clearing the contract hurdle, couples published their banns. This step invited public scrutiny and theoretically ensured the discovery of any irregularity. Authorities took this matter very seriously; as one historian puts it, "strictures in regard to marriage were as much in the interest of the state as for the satisfaction of the parents."[79] In 1701 Rhode Island ordered persons who married without appropriate publication to pay five pounds "or be imprisoned three months in the common jail, or suffer corporal punishments not exceeding thirty-nine stripes on his naked back, at the publick whipping-post."[80] New Amsterdam authorities paid particular attention to properly executed banns; their regulations reflect profound concern even as they hint at ineffective enforcement. Finding in 1654 that a couple had not published banns in their home town, an action "contrary to the style and laws of our Fatherland," New Amsterdam asked to be informed of such lapses in the future in order to prevent "all improprieties."[81] In

1658 they noticed that some couples delayed marriage after publishing banns, "contrary to good order," and they imposed a time limit "to prevent the irregularities arising from such delays."[82]

Some couples redeemed the irregularity of their courtship by the soundness of their married life. In 1661 Plymouth fined Robert Whetcombe and Mary Cudworth ten pounds "for disorderly coming together without consent of theire parents and lawful marriage" and imprisoned them "during the pleasure of the Court." A year later, however, the court decided to remit half the fine because of the couple's "having since been orderly married, and living orderly together, and following theire callings industriously, and attending the worship of God dilligently, as is testified by some of their neighbors of good report."[83] But most courts dealt justice rather than mercy to such couples, and to their accomplices as well. Elizabeth Basnett, a New Jersey innkeeper, was fined in 1700 for allowing a clandestine marriage to be both performed and consummated in her house, "to the great damage grief and affliction of the [bride's] parents, the Reproach of the Province, and Scandal to the Christian proffession and Civil Society and Neighborhood."[84]

In particular, courts punished those who performed illegal ceremonies. The Maryland Provincial Court fined Thomas Manning £5000 in tobacco for marrying a couple without a license or publishing banns.[85] When the same court charged Robert Holt with a bigamous marriage in 1658, it also censured the double-dyed error of William Wilkinson "in contryving and Counselling the said marriage, after hee had divorced" Holt illegally from his first wife.[86] The Georgia Common Council noted the practical evils of such negligence; in 1738 it considered a complaint against a chaplain for marrying all kinds of people illegally, including "servants to different masters, which may prove of ill consequence to those masters."[87]

A Delaware case in 1678 sounded fears of deeper threats to the community. New Castle authorities hoped that by punishing William Wharton for presiding over his own marriage ceremony "the Reproach may bee taken away from the River and that such notorious Breatches of the Lawes and disorders may for the future not passe unpunnished Especially in persons of Lesser qualitys." The court emphasized that Wharton, a justice of the peace, "ought to give good examples to others" and that for him to go unpunished would set a dangerous precedent.[88] Propriety and established procedures in engagements and wedding ceremonies meant more than bureaucratic tidiness to colonial authorities. Their keen attention to so many details and their sharp reaction to violated standards sprang from their belief—or their hope—that order in personal affairs benefited the community while disorder imperiled it.

Communities regulated conduct as well as procedural forms to promote marital stability, including some conduct outside the bounds of marriage. Authorities punished fornication not only because of its immorality and its frequently troublesome consequences, but also because such illicit relationships challenged the integrity of marriage and its place in society. Illegitimate children represented the principal concern as well as the clearest evidence of fornication, although authorities did not always wait for an illicit pregnancy in order to act.[89] Whereas authorities decried the "evil example" of unwed mothers,[90] they sought above all else to ensure financial support for the child. When Elizabeth Lowe of Plymouth, for example, named Philip Leonard as the father of her child, Leonard was immediately required to provide a weekly allowance until the child reached the age of seven.[91] With unwed mothers more reticent than Elizabeth Lowe, authorities commonly asked midwives to extract the name of the father during childbirth.[92] If necessary to guarantee support, they forced a marriage. A northern New York court reasoned in 1654 that when people "live together like man and wife one can never know when the woman will again be pregnant by him." They then ordered Klaes Ripse to marry the woman who carried his child as quickly as possible "in order to avoid all scandal, to prevent further mischief, to promote good order, to maintain justice and finally to fulfill our bounden duty."[93]

Convincing displays of remorse sometimes bleached the sin of fornication. Maryland judges softened toward Thomas Hynson in 1664 when he appeared "very sorrowful," and the Plymouth church admonished Susanna Clarke but then dropped her case after "she manifested much sorrow and heavynesse by words and teares."[94] Couples charged with fornication before marriage—who generally appeared in court after the suspiciously early arrival of their first child—also received some special consideration: Quaker meetings punished fornication far more leniently when the couple was affianced, and Plymouth routinely lessened the fine for couples who could prove that they had sinned "before marriage, but after contract."[95] Courts sympathized less with couples who fornicated after the end of their marriage. In 1678 Philip

Wharton and Mary Gridley of Boston were bound "to answer for theire disorderly and offensive cohabiting together having Sued out a divorce" and were ordered "to refrain the Company of each other."[96]

If fornication threatened disorder by flouting community morality and mocking the conventions of marriage, those who made light of their crime erred even more. Public acknowledgments and punishments aimed in part to impress upon the sinner—and potential sinners in the audience—the seriousness of the matter, to show that people accepted community standards even when they found them difficult to meet. As a result authorities commonly imposed public acts of contrition when they were not volunteered. John Pope of Virginia was ordered in 1638 to be whipped and "to acknowledge his fault" in church, and in Boston William and Elizabeth Middleton had to make "a satisfactory acknowledgement in the publique congregation where they usually heare."[97] By contrast, in 1684 when William Shirtliffe "shewed little sense of sin," the Plymouth church admonished him not only for fornication but also "for the pride and hardnesse of his heart."[98]

In fact, playful snickering could offend the community as much as outright contempt for its norms. In the spring of 1671 the Hampshire County Court in western Massachusetts, "being sensible of disorders growing more and more upon us," punished Richard Barnard and Sarah Clarke for fornication. The couple, who were expecting a child, then married and the court was content. But a mischievous neighbor, Thomas Stebbing, posted an unauthorized announcement of their wedding which was "underwrit in smaler Letters with a foolish and reprochful Rime castin reproch upon the Towne and the Maides in Towne." Stebbing not only sinned "against God abusing the Parents, the Partys, profaning the Sabath," and speaking disrespectfully of Hampshire and its "Maids," but he compounded his offenses by appearing "alittle saucy" in court before repenting and promising "to be more watchfull against such like disorder." The Hampshire court thus found itself in the same ironic position as Faulkner's Gavin Stevens, who upheld "the principle that chastity and virtue in women shall be defended whether they exist or not."[99]

The community influenced marriage more directly and more forcefully than by punishing ancillary crimes such as fornication. The community enjoined spouses to fulfill their duties to each other and sought to spare itself the ill effects of marital instability. Ironically, their emphasis on family stability led Connecticut and Massachusetts to pass the most liberal divorce laws in the colonies. In a departure from English practice, and influenced by the post-Reformation view of marriage as a civil contract, Connecticut and Massachusetts—and no other colonies— allowed absolute divorce for adultery, desertion, "continued absence without word, and uncontrollable enmity or cruelty."[100] Formal divorce remained extremely rare, however, and even in New England such provisions, while apparently liberal, by no means engendered greater freedom or equality within marriage. As Mary Beth Norton has noted, the "civil code of the New England colonies embodied a concept of marital unity striking in its expression of the patriarchal ideal that women's private interests had to be subordinated to the greater familial whole."[101] Authorities clearly expected couples to stay together, and they punished those who did not.[102] New England officials were particularly troubled by separated spouses. Their first recourse was always to send the wanderer home, frequently in the face of dim prospects for a happy reunion. A Maine court, for example, ordered Mary Weare to return quickly to her husband, even though she explained that while she would like to live with him, "her husband was not willing to have [her] Company, neither did hee provide helpe or necessary Accommodations for her Convenient reception."[103] Massachusetts usually fined those who refused to return to their spouses, which often meant returning to England, twenty pounds.

Some recalcitrants, particularly women, fared worse. In 1682 Boston refused to let Ann Tilige reside in town unless she agreed to join her husband in Nevis—the paradox of this order did not disturb the authorities—while Essex County ordered Goodwife Magiligan whipped "for absenting herself from her husband, night and day."[104] Authorities sometimes relented when the party proved that sincere and repeated efforts to reunite had failed. Essex County reprieved Thomas Rowell, whose wife was at present too sick to make the journey from England, and dismissed its case against John Leach when he explained that "he often sent and wrote to [his wife], but she was unwilling to come, and he was not able to live in Old England."[105] Some excuses were better than others. When Richard Windoe appeared in court in 1649 for living apart from his wife, he said that "he sent for her and learned she was dead."[106]

Authorities were sometimes obliged to recognize clear cases of desertion, but they did so reluctantly and only on very strong evidence. Massachusetts Bay granted a divorce to William Palmer, whose wife had "wholy deserted him, and marryed herselfe" to someone in England and "had children by him," in 1650; in an extreme case, Mary Bishop petitioned for divorce in Massachusetts in 1679 after her husband Job had "absented himself from hir seventeen yeares and since married to another woman in the Barbadoes."[107] On the other hand, the Plymouth court did not grant Mary Hacke a divorce from her husband, despite three years without word from him and some evidence that he was dead.[108] As distasteful as divorce was, authorities also feared the consequences of trapping people in marital limbo. In response to several petitions from deserted wives, Rhode Island officials agreed in 1685 to declare spouses legally dead after five years' absence. The General Assembly complained that the absence of these husbands "may give occasions for persons to break forth to the committing of folly, who otherwise might live honestly amongst their neighbors."[109]

Much of this official concern sprang directly from the fear that abandoned wives and children would require poor relief. Significantly, it was the Philadelphia Overseers of the Poor who sued Michael Brown in 1746 until he "agreed to take his Wife Sarah Home and to treat her as a Husband ought to do," and when John Luffe and his wife were presented for living apart in 1649, the Essex County Court ordered their town selectmen "to find work for said Luffe" and if he refused he was to go to jail.[110] Ironically, authorities sometimes accepted a separation or freed a woman to remarry precisely in order to assure financial support. When Grace Ramsay's husband refused to live with her in 1704, the Prince George's County Court ordered him to provide an annual allowance; Connecticut granted Sarah Towle, who had been left "without any care or provision made for supply of her or her child's maintenance by her husband," the "oppertunity to joyne herselfe in marriage with another man" in 1676; and Massachusetts set Dorcas Smith "at liberty to marry with another man" in 1681, seven years after her husband left her without "at all in that time sending to hir for hir or hir child's reliefe."[111]

Many petitions for official intervention focused explicitly on nonsupport or financial mismanagement as wives presented their husbands as wastrels and ne'er-do-wells.[112] Their stories teem with details of irresponsibility, neglect, and prodigality, and many expose all kinds of problematic family relationships. In Massachusetts William Daliver's wife and father-in-law complained that before deserting the family in 1683 "he had lived in a course of idleness, neglecting his family and taking no care to provide for them, but bringing them to suffering."

According to John Higginson, the father-in-law, Daliver after marrying a year earlier "hath the most part of his time since lived in such an Idle course as to do nothing towards a livelyhood for himselfe and Family but hath spent much of his Wives portion." Even when this feckless son-in-law "began to be in some employment, he hath so carried him-selfe as to cut himselfe from it: nor will he hearken to the Counsell of any of his friends." He left his family without any provision so that "his wife and child will either be in a perishing way, or be a charge to the town or"—Higginson gritted his teeth—"have their totall (and for ought I see perpetuall) dependence upon me for their maintenance, which I am not able to bear."[113]

In such cases the community explicitly sought to protect itself as well as neglected women and children. When Mary Booth of Virginia asked for support in 1712, the sheriff took her husband into custody until he could post a bond "with good security to save the parish harmles" from the charge of his wife and child, and the Pennsylvania Supreme Court ordered in 1741 that John Ross "ought to allow his wife a reasonable Maintenance, And thereby Indemnify the Towneship."[114] The greater the economic threat to the community, the more energetic the official response.[115] If necessary, authorities secured or seized the property of negligent husbands.[116] Indeed, authorities did not always wait for hus-bands to abandon their obligations before bringing out the safety net. When Ephraim Pierce and his wife quarreled in 1691, Providence offi-cials feared that their "family and Estate is like to fall to Ruin and thereby the Towne is like to have charge fall upon them." For both the family's sake "and for the securitye of the Towne of Providence," they forbade Pierce to sell or pledge his house or lands in any way "without the advice and full Consent" of delegated officials.[117]

Adultery was another clear breach of conjugal duty, condemned as an affront to the state of marriage and for its effects on the wronged spouses.[118] In fact, in punishing adultery authorities often deferred to the rights or wishes of spouses. In 1670, for example, a Rhode Island court agreed to suspend Mary Stock's sentence if she would leave the colony to join her husband, and in 1674 the Essex County Court told Sarah Roe to appear "unless she be reconciled to her husband and go to him before that time."[119] Furthermore, adultery constituted the most successful grounds for divorce, especially when men complained against their wives.[120] Some adulterers might have preferred divorce to the punishments they received in defense of their spouses' rights. Ruth Read left her husband in Massachusetts, lived with another man in

England for four years, adopted his name, and bore his child. When in 1673 she "Impudently return[ed] to these parts Imposing the said child on hir husband," the court ordered that if she did not leave the colony within two months she would stand "in the markett place on a stoole for one hower with a paper on hir breast with this Inscription THUS I STAND FOR MY ADULTEROUS AND WHORISH CARRIAGE . . . and then be severely whipt with thirty stripes."[121] Virginia authorities could be equally severe. In 1668 a Virginia court presented Elizabeth Moore for planning with Thomas Smith to run away and take with them "several goods" of her husband's estate. Edward Moore asked the court to protect his life and estate, "which hee dayly feared through the impious and impudent actions of his wanton wife, who hee delivered to the law for justice." The court obliged him. Elizabeth Moore was ordered to be taken into custody, given thirty lashes, and "put into Bridewell to [be] whipe[d] and worke till her Husband desire her out."[122]

But colonial authorities did not punish adultery simply on behalf of injured spouses. In fact, some officials fretted more than many spouses did about the possibility of infidelity. In 1700 a Maryland court indicted Richard Pile for incontinence with the wife of Mareen Devall. Devall then came to court to say that his wife was ill and Pile was a doctor "and should for the Same Reason aforesaid be allways for the fowture wellcom to vissett his wife."[123] A Boston woman charged with adultery in 1645 claimed that while the man had indeed made an advance, she had dissuaded him. The jury acquitted them of adultery—which was a capital crime in Massachusetts Bay until 1692—but convicted them of adulterous behavior. The court sentenced them "to stand upon the ladder at the place of execution with halters about their necks one hour, and then to be whipped, or each of them to pay 20 pounds." Through all this the woman's husband, "although he condemned his wife's immodest behavior, yet was so confident of her innocency in point of adultery" that he was willing to pay the fine rather than see his wife whipped. He could ill afford the twenty pounds, however, and she chose the punishment so that her husband would not "suffer so much for her folly," after which "he received her again. and they lived lovingly together."[124]

Some authorities exhorted spouses to guard more diligently against adultery. In 1663 the Plymouth court told Joseph Rogers to stay away from the wife of William Tubbs, and then "strictly charged" Tubbs himself "not to tollerate [Rogers] to come to his house att any time, as he will answare the same att his perill."[125] Even more significant, courts held some husbands at least partially responsible for their wives' adultery. After convicting William Paule and Katherine Anis of "unclean and filthy behavior" in 1657, the Plymouth court then charged Alexander Anis "for his leaveing his family, and exposing his wife to such temtations, and being as baud to her therin" and sentenced him to sit in the stocks while his wife and Paule were whipped; in 1666 Plymouth convicted Jonathan Hatch for suspicious behavior with Frances Crippin and then convicted Thomas Crippin "of lacivious speeches tending to the upholding of and being as a pandor of his wife in lightnes and laciviousness."[126] In these cases, a wife's adultery implied a husband's misconduct as well as the failure of his authority.

New Haven authorities revealed in a 1646 case how clearly they regarded adultery as a matter of concern to the whole community and how far their role extended beyond protecting deceived spouses. William Fancy's wife testified that, over the preceding two years, Thomas Robinson had made several forceful sexual advances to her. She resisted and told her husband, even asking him to complain to the governor. But since his wife had been punished once for theft, William Fancy feared that she might not be believed and so "desired it might be concealed." When Robinson was ordered whipped for lewd behavior, so were William Fancy and his wife for concealment, and Fancy was further censured "for his being as it were a pander . . . who should have been her protector."[127] This case suggests the duty of husbands to protect their wives, even as it shows that proper conduct within marriage was an obligation to the community as well as to the spouse.

Adultery particularly affronted the whole community by its immorality. Presentments for adultery commonly used such phrases as the "debauched and Lacivious life," "the horrible sinn of adultery," and a "Notorious and Scandalous Course of Life tending to Adultery and fornication."[128] To awaken the suspicions of the community, justified or not, was in itself a breach of good order. A Maine court charged Mary Daly in 1655 for "daly frequenting" a man's company "in such a suspicious manner as caused the neighbours to suspect them [of] incontinency," and in Maryland in 1741 Oliver Lee and Susannah Hendrick, while not convicted of adultery, were admonished because they had not "cleared up The great Suspicion which has been had of them."[129] Sensitive to even a taint of wrongdoing, authorities boasted long memories as well. In 1650 Plymouth punished Mary Norman for unchaste behavior and warned her "to take heed of such cariages for the future, lest her former cariage come in remembrance against her to make her punishment the greater."[130] Community officials were not alone in their vigilance. In New York in 1683 Ysebrant Ellis complained about "the ungodly life led by his daughter" with her husband's partner and vowed to present them to authorities, "as it had gone far enough and everyone knew about it." A friend advised him that "the complaint of a father about his child is very serious" and that his daughter "might be hanged." Ellis replied that "God's command is higher than the law and I should not be sorry if I saw them both going to the [whipping] post."[131]

Adulterous behavior hinted at corruption and disorder in the society that allowed it to continue. In 1723 the Reverend Hugh Henry of Scarborough, Maine, asked the authorities to separate a couple who cohabited "to the scandal of mankind and of the gospel . . . as if there were no order among us to restrain them." A few months later he renewed his plea for "assistance to suppress avowed abomination now for so long a time suffered in this place as if it were an heathen country where there non[e] fearing God to take course with it."[132] Sometimes authorities even found adultery easier to forgive than defiance. In 1658 Westchester County had Amos Turner's wife whipped because she "dis[o]bayed our Aturoyty in not attending" an order to stop seeing Robert Roose but instead "hath caryed herselfe lisiveously with him . . . and hath vilified the names of those in Atorety."[133]

Community regulation of marital life comprehended more than such flagrant offenses as adultery. Authorities watched the daily conduct of couples for any signs of disharmony or disorderliness, and as they enforced spouses' obligations to each other they also defined their joint obligation to the community. Authorities readily identified behavior they did not like. Maine presented Edward Waymouth in 1669 "for curesing and swaring and wecked wisheis to his wife"; in Massachusetts James Davies was summoned in 1640 for "his unquietnes with his wife," and Henry Flood appeared in 1674 for "bad carriages towards his wife abuseing her in ill words calling her whore and cursing of her."[134] Two New Yorkers testified in 1675 that Helmer Otte did "not live with his wife as he should, being often drunk and using much abusive language in speaking to her, leading therefore a scandalous life," and another witness agreed that Otte "at different times has not treated his wife well."[135]

Many cases focused solely on the husband's misconduct. Gerald O'Caine of Maryland, for example, was called in 1699 "to answer such things as Shall be Objected against him by Lidia his Wife."[136] For many men, mistreatment of their wives formed only part of a pattern of family neglect and unacceptable behavior, and many wives shrewdly strengthened complaints against husbands by tarring them as godless, drunken, violent, and quarrelsome.[137] Wives faced punishment for similar miscarriages, although their offenses were additionally colored by the sin of disobedience. Courts censured wives for such offenses as "unnecessary gadding from home," neglect of duty, "having walked disorderly," and abusive words to husband and neighbors. [138] Several wives appeared for using physical violence against their husbands, including a Plymouth woman brought to court in 1645 "for beating and reviling her husband, and egging her children to healp her, biding them knock him in the head, and wishing his victials might choke him." [139]

Like husbands, wives worsened their position by general misbehavior or disregard of authority.[140] Goodwife Line of New Haven managed a clean sweep, deeply offending her husband, her neighbors, and town officials. In 1655 she was charged with lying, petty thieving, assaulting a neighbor's child, and "much Athyisticall impudent" blasphemy. Edward Camp, the neighbor whose son she had beaten, testified that "to her husband her cariage hath bine verey gross and unsufferable," and said one example would suffice. She and her husband disagreed once about correcting their son for some misbehavior. According to Camp, "she fell into a rage and called him very bad names, and up with a stick and struck him on the head." When Camp and his wife came to see what the ruckus was, Line said "his wife abused him so as never man was abused, not onely in words, calling him devill, but in striking him also." An exasperated Camp asked her, "Will you never leave these courses?"—to which she replied, "he is a devill, he is a devill, two or three times, poynting to her husband." In court Goodwife Line confessed to these particulars, "onely she remembers not that she repeated the word devill so often."[141]

In still other marital troubles, authorities found both parties culpable, but sharing the blame did not ease the consequences. Such joint contentiousness often drew sharp punishment, extending in New England to public humiliations and whippings.[142] At the very least, authorities enjoined couples to live together peaceably in the future. A New York court warned Aelbert Andriesz in 1670 "that he must live properly with his wife as a good citizen ought to and is bound to do."[143] Charged in 1664 "for their disorderly living," Samuel and Hannah Hutcheson were discharged "upon condition that they live together orderly," and in 1669 Robert Ransom and his wife, summoned in Plymouth "to answere for theire contensions and unworthy carryages each to other in theire walkeing in marriage condition," were released "on theire engagement to live better in that behalfe."[144] Officials meant these warnings. The Essex County Court advised the Hutchesons, for example, that if they caused trouble again, they would be sent to the house of correction.

Authorities sometimes fleshed out these injunctions to amicability with detailed prescriptions for the couple's way of life. After sentencing Daniel and Faith Black to sit in the stocks for an hour, the Essex County Court told them in 1664 that henceforward Black "was not to threaten his wife or miscall her and to live peaceably with her, and she was to be orderly and not to gad abroad." Faith Black was also "ordered not to be in company with John How or Judah Trumble nor come to the house of John How unless her husband sent her on business." The Blacks were to be whipped "if either of them offended against this order."[145]

In 1672 Grace Miller of Maine charged her husband with "severall abusive speeches and behaviors towards his wife per great provocations and by throwing of her over board out of a Conow [canoe] and Calling of her hoore diverse tymes, whereby she is deeply provoaked," as well as "pulling off her Cloaths and stripping of her Naked, threatening to pull her child out of her body, etc." The court agreed that Richard Miller's behavior did not promote connubial bliss and ordered him to post a bond "for good behavior towards all persons espetially towards his wife" and to maintain her properly. Though far from excusing Richard Miller's actions, the court also decided that Grace Miller "hath given two much cause of suspition of neglect of her family and want of Industry therein, with other imprudent carages which may administer Jelocys to her husband," and so ordered her to "bee more carefull to avoyd all appearances of offence towards her husband and Attend the care and occasions of her husband and family with more carefullness and diligence."[146] A New York City court highlighted its own practical concerns in the course it dictated for the quarreling Mortimers. Deciding in 1735 that Samuel and Ann Mortimer were "in Health and able by their Labour to maintain their two Children," the court ordered them to live together and threatened them with further punishment if they did not care properly for their children.[147]

Colonial authorities so dreaded strife-ridden marriages that they often struggled heroically to restore peace, even at some cost to the principals. John Williams, for example, kept the Plymouth court busy for months with his marital problems. Claiming that his wife Elizabeth had borne a child who was not his, Williams refused to sleep with her and generally mistreated her. In June 1665 the court, after hearing "severall thinges to and frow betwixt them," decided that Williams could not prove his charges, admonished the couple "to apply themselves to such waies as might make for the recovering of peace and Love betwixt them," and appointed a neighbor to counsel them. Four months later, Williams continued to abuse and deride his wife. Again the court, "being earnestly desirous of a renewed closure of his hart and affections to his wife, and that his future conversation with her might bee better then his former," wished to show leniency and so released him "with exhortation to him to amend his wayes." A disappointed Elizabeth Williams asked that at least her name should be cleared. The court agreed, proclaiming that she had been "openly traduced and scandulised in her name, and by false reports and reproaches rendered as if shee were a dishonest woman" before sending her home to rekindle affection for her traducer. But in June 1666 the court finally admitted what the Williamses had known a year earlier, that they could not live together happily. John Williams was convicted of abusive carriages and neglect and for behaving "bitterly towards her in many respects; and whereas hee should have bine a shelter and a protection unto her, hath endeavoured to reproach, insnare and betray her." The court granted a separation, punished him for defamation, and fined him twenty pounds "inasmuch as these his wicked carryages have bine contrary to the lawes of God and man, and alsoe very disturbing and expensive to this government."[148]

Some peacemaking neighbors were equally slow to recognize irreconcilability. In 1651 Rose Smith of Maryland testified that during a visit with Robert and Dorothy Holt, Robert told her that his wife was going to kill him. Smith tried to allay his fears only to have Dorothy chime in that "she were as good kill him as live as She did." Smith then turned her attention to Dorothy Holt, warning that she would be hanged. Holt replied unworriedly, if a little murkily, that "then there was an end of two." But Smith persisted. When the Holts later separated, she advised Dorothy to return to her husband, "again telling her, what a Covenant She made at their Marriage that thereby She could not with Safe Conscience go from her husband." Holt answered flatly "that her heart was Soe hardened against him, that She would never darken his door again."

The Maryland authorities proved easier to convince. They listened to Robert Holt's complaints, evidence of Dorothy Holt's adultery, and one witness who heard her "cry for many Curses to God against her husband, that he might rott limb from limbe, and that She would daily pray to God that such Casualties might fall upon him, and likewise that her son Richard might end his days upon the gallows." The court ordered that she be whipped and that she live at a safe distance in order "to prevent any Mischief [that] may happen by their Comeing together otherwise." But even in this case the court cherished some small hope for a reconciliation; they emphasized that they did not intend by the separation order "at all to restrain" the Holts "from liveing together as man and wife ought to doe" if at any time they agreed to do so.[149]

In other cases too, authorities agreed that an unhappy couple might cause less trouble for themselves and the community if they separated. In 1668 Catrina Matthisen petitioned a New York court that she was "no longer able to keep house with her husband" because he daily beat and abused her and her children. He often threatened to kill her and because of his profligacy, she said, "there are scarcely victuals in the house." The court, recalling several earlier complaints and fruitless attempts to reform him, "finds itself obliged, for the purpose of preventing greater difficulties and the ruin of [the] wife and there children, to interfere." It ordered the husband arrested until he could be sent away for the period of one year and six weeks "to be separated from his wife."[150] And in some cases—rare as they were—authorities simply accepted a couple's own sense that a separation was inevitable or at least desirable. In Albany Maria Goosens and Steven Janssz met no objection in 1663 when they filed separation articles, "making known that on account of diver disputes and differences (God help them) they . . . now for more than eight years have kept apart . . . and as there is no likelihood that [they] will again unite to live together in quietness, peace and godliness, therefore, in order to prevent further strife and mischief," they freed each other to remarry.[151]

Authorities viewed some marital problems more sympathetically than they did a couple's plea that they could not get along. Impotence, for example, was often enough to justify a divorce. In these cases, courts responded both to the prevailing sense that children were the "true end of matrimony" and to the pleas of unhappy wives; Katherine Ellenwood of Massachusetts noted in her 1682 petition that "she was very young and would rather die than live with this man."[152] Still a divorce was by no means automatic in cases of impotence. When Dorothy Clark complained in 1686 that her husband was "always unable to perform the act of generation," the Plymouth court ordered that "his body be viewed by some persons skilfull and judicious." In the end the court "did not see cause" to grant a divorce, although they did provide for a partially separate living arrangement.[153] Charged by his wife in 1661, Elias White admitted his impotence and said he was "fully Contented to be separated if it please this Authority." Despite White's statement and his wife's plea, the Massachusetts Court of Assistants "did not see sufficient ground to separate them but advised them to a more loving and suitable Cohabitation one with the other and that all due phisicall meanes may be used."[154]

Courts showed some of the same unevenness in cases of wife beating, although in general the colonial community did much to protect wives from extreme cruelty. Interestingly, many women in the southern colonies who complained of abusive husbands emphasized that they themselves had properly discharged their responsibilities as dutiful wives. These women underscored the undeserved, unprovoked nature of their treatment; their emphasis suggests that physical cruelty by itself merited less attention. Grace Grey of Virginia explained in 1665 that in twenty-four years of marriage she had "not failed in the least requisite in a Loveing and obedient wife, but hath diligently served him with all possible care paines love loyall and true obedience." Her husband had nevertheless "most egregiously abused [her] by private and unspeakeable devices, by the worst of words, by desperate and unmercifull blowes, and by Cutting her eares and keeping her under the quality of a most contemptible slave 'n the hands of an Imperious tyrant."[155] Northern women, by contrast, were more likely to stress their husbands' breach of marital duty or, in Puritan terms, the covenant of marriage. Ann Warner of Rhode Island, for example, accused her husband in 1683 of "violating the marriage covenant, and abusing her by laying violent hands upon her."[156] One New Hampshire woman offered a simple but very rare explanation; after her husband threatened to poison and beat her, Sarah Pearce petitioned for help in 1681, saying that "the laws of nature . . . teacheth me to seek my own preservation."[157]

Whatever the wife's explanation, courts sometimes treated cruel husbands quite harshly. Boston ordered William Carpenter in 1672 and Richard Cowley in 1677 whipped for beating their wives, and in Plymouth Richard Marshall sat in the stocks at the court's pleasure "for abusing his wife by kicking her of[f] from a stoole into the fier."[158]

More practically, courts required bonds of good behavior in order to protect wives for the future, or at least for the duration of the bond.[159] In cases of extreme or habitual cruelty, many courts separated the couple. In 1707 the Maryland Chancery Court "Thought fitt for preservation" of Margaret McNamara's life to grant her a separation after she appeared before them "so battered, bruised and Inhumanly beaten in most parts of her body that had she not been of a Constitution more than ordinary Strong She could hardly have recovered."[160]

Not all courts showed such care in protecting wives. The Maine authorities judged it "meet to pass by" abuse charges against John Barrett in 1668 when he "acknowledg[ed] his falt and promis[ed] amendment"; when Henry Brody, accused of "beating of his wife grossly," claimed in court that "hee accidentally cutt his wife's hand and intended no further hurt to her," they discharged him with an admonition.[161] Maryland authorities repeatedly rejected Mary Sterling's petition for a separate maintenance, even though her husband forfeited his bond of good behavior and failed to appear in court in 1722, and in the same year they rejected as "Causeless and Malicious" Sarah Norton's claim that her husband had "several times very lately beat her most Immoderately without any provocation or cause att all and threatened to be the death of her."[162] In 1674 Jacob Pudeator was brought to court in Massachusetts "for striking and kicking his wife." A neighbor testified that she had seen Pudeator "strike his wife three or four times, throw her down and kick her" on the road that ran by her house. The court, "being informed that the woman 'is of great provocation,' had his sentence moderated."[163]

Decisions such as these necessarily raise the question of how differently men and women were treated in these cases and what the effects of those differences were. Despite the inconsistencies and vagaries of courts and other officials, it is difficult to escape the conclusion that women generally fared worse than men, and that courts served the cause of patriarchy more forcefully than the cause of justice or compassion. This bias may emerge most starkly in cases of domestic violence; Elizabeth Pleck, for one, has found that even the remarkable coherence of "Puritan communal vigilance" tended to evaporate in the face of wife beating and child beating.[164] Many other areas of colonial life testify to the pervasiveness of women's subordination and the determination to uphold patriarchy. Colonial law, with some notable exceptions in equity law, ratified these cultural expectations in a myriad of ways: by defining *femme covert* status; by restricting women's control over property; by creating a class of crimes, such as witchcraft and infanticide, all but limited to women; and by prosecuting women more vigorously for still other crimes, notably sexual offenses such as fornication.[165]

At the same time, many realities of colonial life undermined patriarchy to at least some degree. Seventeenth-century marriage and death patterns in the Chesapeake, for instance, made many women independent by making them widows and often cushioned their widowhood with property. Throughout the colonial period, religion offered some women, especially Quakers, greater authority in family life, if not always in larger institutions.[166] And of course the dynamics of individual marriages and families must often have rewritten larger social rules. But if the ideal of patriarchy and the subordination of women do not describe all women and all marriages, they do accurately describe the social position of women and the social institution of marriage. Exceptions and challenges do not mean that colonial society did not support patriarchy; it means simply that it was not always an easy job. In fact, it seems likely that it was precisely when established gender roles were most fluid or most vulnerable to attack that efforts to entrench them became most forceful. Carol Karlsen has argued recently that in Massachusetts witchcraft accusations were likely to focus not on weak, marginal women but on women who were potentially powerful, women independent of male influence (or protection) who stood to inherit substantial property. Karlsen's interpretation provides for the first time a satisfactory historical explanation for the prominence of women in witchcraft cases; and it suggests as well how thoroughly challenges to patriarchy were feared and guarded against.[167]

It is not surprising, then, to find that community officials and courts identified patriarchy with stability and perceived women who defied their restrictions as threats to the social order. Officials upheld patriarchy as an ideal and sought to preserve it in the administration of justice; these authorities, after all, *were* the patriarchy. It is less clear that in practice they upheld it any more effectively than they supported other ideals such as harmony. The inconsistent and sometimes contradictory actions of community officials suggest neither that they always intervened in family life on the side of patriarchy nor that they always succeeded when they did. Cross-currents and exceptions and quiet rebellions shape this story as much as the undeniable power of patriarchy and the restricted roles of women.

And if courts sometimes behaved unpredictably in personal matters, so too did petitioners. In 1727 Elizabeth Anderson of Maryland said that she had "received such intolerable abuse and usuage from her husband . . . as renders it impossible for her without the utmost danger to cohabit with him . . . he frequently beating her in amost cruel and barbarous manner." Unless the court saved her "from the hands of her most cruel and barbarous husband," Anderson concluded, "she must inevitably sink under the miseries she now labours [with]." Despite this fervent petition, the Andersons reconciled before their court appearance, and so ended the case.[168]

Or did it? The Andersons may genuinely have reconciled, or Elizabeth Anderson may have feared her husband's brutishness too much to continue her suit. The case itself may have been a turning point in their marriage, forcing some resolution of their problems, or it may have been one of many crises, one scene in a fitfully continuing drama. We cannot know. It is precisely this kind of ambiguity in the evidence, uncertainty in the possible interpretations as well as apparent inconsistency in behavior, that makes it so difficult to render uniform judgments about the meaning of court decisions and the effects of community intervention in marriages. The Anderson case offers a cautionary tale, not only to the colonial authorities who would have had them conform to particular norms of behavior, but also to historians who would now have them conform to particular interpretations of their behavior.

The colonial community supported marriage as an institution and protected vulnerable individuals in a number of ways. But it gave its support most emphatically, indeed almost exclusively, to the social functions of marriage. For the sake of order, morality, and its own economic interests, the community demanded stability in marriage. It encouraged love as a source of stability but showed little respect for or understanding of a couple's psychological needs. And though marriage serves many practical purposes in all societies, the colonial community exerted so strong an influence that, to an unusual degree, the private, emotional side of marriage was subordinated to its public uses.

There were exceptions. In some instances the community permitted private obligations to supersede public duties. In New Haven, for example, Henry Peck was excused from attending the General Court in 1648 because his wife was sick, and in 1697 Richard Haynie explained that his absence from the Virginia House of Burgesses was "occationed by my Wife's Sickness, who is far more likely to Dye then recover, (and I cannot in Conscience leave her)."[169] Courts made allowances for a special loyalty between spouses; when the wife of Francis Perry was arrested in 1654 for striking a man several times, the Essex County Court "decided it to be in defence of her husband, and she was admonished" rather than punished.[170] And courts granted some couples autonomy in deciding their own lives. John and Elizabeth Coggeshall of Rhode Island separated in 1655 "by mutuall and voluntarie consent," and in Virginia Edward Moore freed his wife from their marriage "for severall causes and reasons best known to myselfe."[171] Unfortunately, independence could cut two ways; when Jacob Hap appeared in a New York court for having "scandalously beaten and wounded his wife and thrown fire brands at her," the authorities decided that he was "not punishable for as it happened between man and wife."[172] Such cases remained exceptional in the early colonial period as autonomy and even affection in marriages found little support in ideology and less in custom. But they do suggest some haziness in the demarcation of marriages. Over the course of the colonial period, that ambiguity became less bearable as tensions between the public and private purposes of marriage became more evident and more difficult to accommodate within existing arrangements.

The strain of community expectations surfaced most clearly in the lengths to which authorities went in fitting couples to their own mold, in an apparent belief that coercion could heal troubled marriages and in blatant indifference to private pain. Indeed, many cases suggest not that authorities blithely ignored statements of personal unhappiness but rather that they simply did not know how to respond to them or how to weigh them against community prerogatives. Beatrice Berry of Salem complained in 1676 that her husband's "base, brutish and Inhumane carriage" made it "Impossible for any poore woman specially a woman of my Age to live with such a person." She submitted "to the mercy of the court, for what ever I suffer I am not able to live with such a Tyrant." The court ordered her to go home. The following year she complained again that she was "continually abused by my husband, with most vile, threatening and opprobrious speeches." Neighbors amply supported her claims, yet the court stopped at fining Edmund Berry for "being distempered with drink and for abusive carriages and speeches to his wife."[173] In New York in 1681 Anneke Schaets said her husband was "not a man with whom she can live and that she would prefer to be dead or imprisoned for life rather than live with him." She was forcibly returned to her husband before agreeing to a reconciliation supervised by two officials.[174] The Kingston, New York, court found no "legal reasons for a separation" when Jeronimus Douwersen declared "that his wife cannot serve him as a wife and will not serve him as a servant, and further says that she has never loved him."[175] And in 1656 in western Massachusetts Joanne Miller was ordered whipped for calling her husband "foole and vermine; and that shee said shee did not love him but hated him: yea shee here said shee did never love him and shee should never love him."[176]

Schaets and Douwersen and Miller found their aspirations for affection and love within marriage thwarted not only by the shortcomings of their spouses but by their community's, and their own, expectations and definition of married life. Some participants in these cases spoke of love and happiness; others spoke of duty and peaceableness. The difference between the language of affection and the language of social obligation points eloquently to the distinct and ultimately contradictory values placed on colonial marriages. It was difficult, perhaps impossible, to reconcile the differences in a culture that, to use Douwersen's revealing words, expected women to serve as servants when they would not serve as wives, and in which the distinction did not much matter .

One New Amsterdam case shows how formulaic prescriptions for marital behavior trapped community authorities and consequently couples. In 1658 the New Amsterdam court asked Merritje Joris "how it happens that she behaves so that her husband complains of her, and that she goes drinking in all the groggeries and holes, and being drunk he cannot keep house with her and does no good." She answered that she paid for her liquor out of her own money but also that "he himself goes drinking, rollicking and full, and she has not slept with him a long time, but were she a young woman he would have more affection for her, and he complains of me etc." The court passed over the melancholy of her reply and told her "to live in peace with her husband, so that no more complaints should be heard of her." Joris said she would leave her husband since he often beat her and shut her out of the house, "and she is not disposed to live so." Her request for separation was denied. Five years later the couple again appeared in court. The husband, Nicholas Boot, demanded a separation "because of her ill behavior; communicating the same in writing and detailing it at length." But the court found "no sufficient reasons to separate parties from each other, but order them to live together in peace."[177]

Occasionally authorities conceded something to the vagaries of human relationships. In 1673 the New Amsterdam court told a petitioner whose wife had left him "to conduct himself in the future and henceforward so civilly, peaceably and friendly towards his wife, that by his good behavior his wife may be induced to dwell with him again, as she ought."[178] But more often authorities acted in such cases as though marital harmony could be restored by fiat. Some went even further. When Massachusetts officials learned in 1669 that Christopher Lawson and his wife had lived irregularly and unhappily for years, they ordered the couple "to live quietly and peaceably together as man and wife, which, if either party refuse or neglect to doe . . . the said party shall be committed to the house of correction, or forthwith to depart this jurisdiction."[179]

Judged as inducements to connubial bliss, such official injunctions seem not only futile but absurd. They make more sense when considered in light of the community's concerns. The community was less interested in the happiness of couples than in ensuring that couples discharged their responsibilities as if their marriages were intact. In many cases a couple's social obligations remained compatible with their wishes and needs but, when they clashed, the community promoted its own interests and sacrificed those of the couple. Divorced for four years, Ann Gray in 1672 sought a Virginia court's help in getting support from her husband; instead the court ordered Miles Gray "to consider his said wife and maintaine her and live as man and wife together."[180] The New Amsterdam authorities spent months throughout 1665 trying to reconcile Arent Lantsman and his wife. They deputed mediators to restore the couple to "love and friendship" even as they warned that if either rejected the mediators' efforts "then proceedings may be expected according to the style and custom of law as an example to other evil housekeepers."[181]

But officials willingly abandoned hopes for reconciliation if separation promised more order for the community. A Rhode Island court found no grounds for divorcing Henry and Elizabeth Stevens in 1669 "but notwithstanding, takeing notice of his turbulencye of speritte, which may prove destructive," ordered the magistrates "to take course, soe to order them apart as his Majestyes peace be not broken."[182] New Amsterdam authorities made a clear choice between public order and marital unity. In 1659 Hendrik Sluyter and his wife were charged with fighting, and the wife was sentenced to imprisonment for "having, in presence of a respectable company, who were with their wives, hoisted her petticoats up to her back, and shewed them her arse; being an offence not to be tolerated in a well ordered province." The court excused her from prison only when Sluyter promised "to send his wife away to Holland" and paid a fine.[183]

Community influence in marriage also bred personal frictions and resentments, and it was on this informal level that individuals proved most ready to challenge interference. When William White cautioned Daniel Ela in 1682 about mistreating his wife, Ela became "very angry and told White that he was a meddling knave and bade him go home and order his own wife, for said Ela 'I knu how to order mine before you knu mee.'"[184] In 1743 Ann Bowell of Maryland regretted that she had "Rashly (by the advice and Insinuations of sum ill minded Persons) made a Severe Complaint" against her husband.[185] And sometimes the neighbors rued their actions. In 1672 George Parker of Virginia sheltered and advised a woman abused by her husband only to see her suddenly leave his house to return to her husband; another neighbor told him "that should be a warning for him for meddling betwixt a Man and his wife again."[186] Even courts sometimes protected couples from unwanted personal interference. New Amsterdam authorities called the in-laws "the chief and principal cause of the trouble" between Arent Lantsman and his wife in 1665 and told them to stop meddling, and a Maine court warned a woman in 1660 that if her son-in-law brought further complaints against her for "Occasioning future differences betweene him and his wife," she would be removed from their house or sent to prison.[187]

Individuals found it far more difficult to resist official intervention, although some did. When a New Hampshire court refused to allow Richard Andrews to marry Jane Avery in 1682 because he could not prove that he was divorced from his first wife, he "broke forth very peremptorily, saying that she was his wife, and desiring the people all to take notice that he took her for his wife; presently saluting her, saying, Come, wife, with other peremptory words, and contemptous carriage."[188] One Maine settler charged with beating his wife in 1666 asked, "What hath any man to do with it, have not I power to Correct my owne wife?"; the following year another swore he would continue to beat his wife, "for it was below him to Complayn to Authority against his wife"; and in New York in 1672 Edward Whitaker, when asked "why he treated his wife so badly . . . answered that he could do with his wife as he pleases, that nobody was to prescribe to him how to treat his wife."[189]

The evident pathology of these challenges negated any legitimacy they might have had; it was hard to respect a wife beater's demand for privacy. But even cogent statements of autonomy failed. Massachusetts Bay refused to divorce Mary Drury from her husband in the 1670s even though he was impotent and unwilling to live with her. She argued in vain that "because our first Law or Fundamentall Liberty Is that noe persons goods or estate shall Bee Taken away or aney wayes endamadged but By virtue or equeaty of Some expresse Law of the Cuntrey warranteing the same etc" and that she had not broken any law by leaving a man who was "Not Truley hir husband."[190] In the seventeenth century such statements remained exceptional and ineffective, easily overwhelmed by the weight of colonial authorities and the assumptions people commonly made in running their lives. Only later, by the mid-eighteenth century, as tensions persisted and objections gained greater ideological force, did it become easier to challenge not only the effectiveness of community involvement but its very legitimacy.

CHAPTER 4

The Ambiguities of Family:
Childrearing

Childrearing in colonial America reveals more clearly than any other activity the community context of family life. The community helped define parental responsibilities, upheld parental authority, reinforced and often provided parental care. Childrearing responsibilities were dispersed to relatives, neighbors, masters, even strangers. Many parents and children benefited from a myriad of family-community ties. But the extent and variety of communal influence also reflected and in some ways deepened the ambiguities of parent-child relations, which were marked by an often confusing mix of indifference and affection, economics and love. Colonial assumptions and practices in childrearing contrasted sharply with those that emerged in the mid- and late eighteenth century, which rested on a more limited, explicitly demarcated role for the community in family life and a more private, affective tie between parents and children. The practice of "putting out" children, rather than being exceptional or abnormal, reveals starkly the assumptions—and limits—of colonial childrearing.

In the early colonial period, the influence of friends and neighbors in childrearing ranged from casual advice to outright adoption. The need for outside intervention pressed most urgently in the case of parental death, and this in turn loomed as a problem far more often in the Chesapeake than in other regions. Orphanhood was rare in New England, whereas most children in seventeenth-century Maryland could expect to lose at least one parent before coming of age.[1] But community influence was not simply a response to extreme crisis; it seeped into everyday patterns of childrearing and cushioned the effects of many difficulties short of parental death. Although brute demographic facts subjected families in different regions at different times to critically different stresses, all of colonial America accepted community influence in childrearing at many levels. And in all regions established forms for child care and education built on an unstable compound of filial affection and economic need.

Orphans were naturally dispatched to the closest or most convenient relatives. Their disposition ranged through all immediate family ties.[2] For children in the southern colonies, however, family ties remained only a fragile buffer against parental death through the seventeenth century. The same conditions that took their parents often left orphans without close relatives as well, and often relatives proved hard to find. Daniel Howard of South Carolina, for example, provided in 1684 for his two sons to be sent to England to live with his brother after his death.[3] Southern children were not only more likely to become orphans but also—in the seventeenth century—more likely to need help outside the family.

Even when one parent survived, relatives commonly shared or assumed a parental role. The position of a widow was more ambiguous than that of a widower, so much so that sometimes courts felt obliged to formalize her authority.[4] In addition, widows often found themselves bound by testamentary instructions. These ranged from the exhortatory—in New York Esther Hunting was told "to take a parental care" and Teunis Day asked his wife to act "as a pious mother, for God's sake, is bound to do"—to the concrete.[5] Relatives often guided, sometimes reinforced, and sometimes superseded widows in the care of their children. In 1676 the Plymouth court gave John Fuller's widow the use of his estate for raising his children and asked her father and father-in-law to "be healpful to her."[6] A Connecticut court let Abraham Finch's widow choose between keeping her child or committing him to her father-in-law, "who tenders to educate it at his owne Coste."[7] But in New Hampshire Edward Clarke's widow had no choice and saw her stepdaughter bound out to her aunt.[8] This decision was unusual, however, and no doubt owed much to the fact that the widow was a stepparent.

Relatives influenced the care even of children they were not raising themselves. The children of James Bick were not orphans, but they were destitute. Coming to Providence in 1698, they seemed "likely to perish" if "not speedely provided for with clothing and other nessessaryes." They "Repared unto their unkle Jonathan Sprague desireing of him Relief," which he gave with the town's aid.[9] Sarah Longhorn of Massachusetts, "who was left yong and of Tender agge," was raised by her father's executor and chose Daniel Wickam as her guardian when she reached the age of fourteen. Her grandmother, Constance Crosbie, disapproved of Wickam and petitioned the court to wait until Sarah's uncle consented, for, Crosbie conceded grudgingly, "he takes more Care of the children than I expected he would have don."[10] Similarly, in 1677 Elizabeth King complained that through her son-in-law's negligence her grandchildren "suffered very much for want of food and raiment and [their inherited] land for care"; the court named her and two other relatives among the children's guardians.[11]

Often born of necessity, the intervention of relatives in many cases drew upon genuine affection. Basil Waring of Maryland, "Stand[ing] the nearest in Blood to the Said Children and having a tender Concern for their Welfair," became guardian to his brother's orphans in 1750.[12] In the settlement of William Gillson's estate in 1649, a Plymouth neighbor testified that Gillson raised two of his sister's children "which hee looked upon as his owne," and in Massachusetts Bay Mary Washburne "tooke uppon her the trouble" of administering her son-in-law's estate because of her "maternall affection towards her parentlesse Children to whom she is a Granmother."[13] The material and emotional benefits of such family ties are obvious. Certainly they required no elaboration for children who tasted some of the bitter alternatives. Bound to a master who did not "decently maintain" her, Mary Love of Baltimore was released in 1710 to "her Kinsman," who promised to take better care of her.[14] In the same year George Hack of Virginia complained that his sister's master "hath very much misused her and now disposed of her to some other person to her great damage and utter ruine"; he offered "to take her and educate her as it becomes a Christian," and his sister "humbly" prayed that he be allowed to do so.[15]

But kinship did not guarantee refuge. In 1742 Henry Eggerton of Georgia reclaimed his son from his father-in-law when he learned that the boy was "used very ill by his Grandfather."[16] John Selby complained to a Maryland court in 1741 that his brother "contrary to the Laws of Humanity doth vilely abuse your petitioner making no respect betwixt his negroes and [him] in any manner Except being more favorable to them in usage."[17] Physical abuse by relatives was perhaps unusual, but conflict among kin over the disposition of children was not at all uncommon. Who should raise the child, decide how to educate him, control his estate, bear the costs of his upbringing: these decisions frequently revived half-buried family grievances or gave birth to new ones. Childrearing arrangements, even when ratified by law, remained subject to review—and sometimes to unraveling—by attentive relatives. Physical custody itself could be an issue. In 1641 William Bucknam of Charlestown, Massachusetts, petitioned for the return of his son, whom his mother-in-law kept from him "against the good will of this peticioner," an action, he added mildly, "which is like to be a breach of peace between us."[18]

The continued interest of kin proved a blessing in some cases. In Georgia in 1739, for example, the Gilberts opposed in vain their son-in-law's decision to place his children with a Moravian family while he went to England. One child died. Some time after, Mrs. Gilbert learned that the surviving child was ill. At first refused permission to visit her grandchild, she returned with a neighbor and gained entry to the Moravians' house. There they found the child "in a most miserable Condition, with cruel Usage, and uncommon Severity." She had been "scourged in a most terrible Manner, most piteous to look at, and her Flesh torn, after the Manner of what a Criminal used to have, at the Hands of a common Executioner."[19] In this case, the disagreement was clear-cut and amply justified. In many other cases, though, family conflicts were amorphous, befogged by bickering, jealousy, and greed. After tracking the complicated disposition of the Thompson orphans in 1667, the New Haven court advised "all relations concerned on both sides to endeavor the promoteing of love, peace, and unity with another, as becomes the rules of their relations."[20] But the rules of relations were often observed in the breach.

True to the cliché, family disagreements often centered on a stepparent. People *expected* stepparents to cause problems, and their anxieties must have been at least in part self-fulfilling. Fathers tried to protect their children and their estates by including in their wills alternative provisions if "they're Stepfather doth abuse them" or if he "prove unlovinge to the Child or Children or wastefull" or if "my sayde wife should marry and That my Children should suffer in their Estates or good Edicature."[21] Stepfathers posed special dangers if not hedged in by testamentary provisions and vigilant executors because they controlled the estate and presumably dominated their wives. By contrast, when Lewis Morris of Morrisania, New York, anticipated problems between his wife and her stepchildren, he urged conciliation on the children. Noting that "differences arising in families are always attended with the worst consequences," he asked that "all my children use their best endeavours to cultivate a good understanding with each other, and be dutiful to their mother, who, although she is a mother-in-law to some of them, has done them equal justice."[22]

Complaints about stepparents frequently reached beyond the family circle to the courts, especially if the case involved an estate. In Maryland in 1668 the executors of Roger Gross's estate charged that his orphan was "abused and not lookt to by the deft. [defendant] theire father in law, and that the Estate is imbezill'd and made away withall," and friends of Henry Coggen told the Plymouth court in 1659 that they believed his children "suffer wrong in sundry respects" at the hands of their stepfather.[23] In 1716 Evan Lewis of South Carolina sued his wife's stepfather for mistreatment of her and her siblings; in particular, Lewis complained, "there was very little difference or distinction made between the said Children . . . and the Negroes."[24] Sometimes the orphans themselves complained. Mary Woodley and Sarah Wallis asked a Maryland court for a new guardian in 1665 because their stepfather "did severall all times abuse your Petitioners . . . and hath all this time turned them out of his house."[25] Aaron Prother in 1726 asked permission to choose his own guardian, noting that "he has had the mishap sometime since to fall under the lash of an unfortunate father in law."[26]

Relatives sometimes took matters into their own hands if the court did not redress their grievances against stepparents. A case in Maryland shows how much death, remarriage, and jealousy could complicate colonial family life, especially in the Chesapeake. Captain Edward Brock's daughter married Matthew Magbee, had children by him, and died. Magbee remarried and then he too died, leaving his second wife with the children of his first marriage (as well as some of their own). In 1709 Brock sought custody of his grandchildren; the court left them with their stepmother, since she needed their help and was of "a Gennerall good Caracter." The following year the children went to Brock without their stepmother's knowledge, enticed, according to her complaint, by Brock's "fair and insinuating promises." Brock's gambit failed, however; the court ordered him to return the children "which he by soe Clandestine and unjust manner Detaine[d]."[27]

Some relatives sought minor victories. Cornelia De Peyster of New York claimed to love her grandchildren "as her own" and if their stepfather, David Provoost, were not obliged to maintain them, "she would give them board for nothing, but it would be giving it to a stranger, not to make David Provoost pay for it."[28] But not everyone could stomach this familial guerrilla warfare. Andrew Norland of Maryland felt cheated by his stepfather, but he was "loth to goe to law with his owne Mother"; he hoped "to avoyd further Trouble" by having the court assign his mother's share of the estate so that he could claim his own without conflict.[29]

Colonial authorities joined relatives in mistrusting stepparents. Special orphans' courts or orphanmasters along with regular courts protected children from abuse and their estates from mismanagement or embezzlement; these special courts proved particularly important in the Chesapeake.[30] In addition to wills, legal protections for orphans appeared in estate settlements, apprenticeship and service indentures, and marriage contracts. In Albany, for example, Jan Tyssen married a widow with four children. When she died he settled "in all love and Friendship" with the children's guardians arrangements for their inheritance and upbringing, promising to treat them "not as a step-father but as one's own father could and should do."[31] Nicholas Velthuysen seemed less willing to accommodate the children of his deceased wife's first marriage. In 1659 one of the children complained to a family friend that Velthuysen "got drunk daily and squandered the property." The friend informed the Orphanmasters, who demanded an inventory of the property "for preventing harm to the children." Velthuysen resisted with "strange and improper answers," but eventually agreed when threatened with imprisonment. All Velthuysen's delays and creative accounting could not conceal a "great difference" between his inventory and the one prepared by his wife's executors; specifically, "there was not so much wampum as stated." The Orphanmasters put Velthuysen and his doctored books under house arrest until he agreed to repay the defalcated sum.[32]

Authorities levied other penalties as well, and they acted in all regions throughout the colonial period. Boston's First Church excommunicated Robert Parker in 1636 for "scandalous oppression of his wives children in selling away theire inheritence from them, and other hard usage both of her and them."[33] In Baltimore Thomas and Christopher Durbin were taken from their stepfather in 1716; in Massachusetts Joseph Langton's stepson went to live with his grandfather after Langton was presented for "evil usage" of him in 1652; and in 1669 Henry Davys of Virginia was allowed to live alone to escape his stepfather's "hard usadge."[34] Actual abuse was not the only reason for removing a child. In Massachusetts in 1677 Edmund Berry's stepchildren left because "he would not bring them up as their mother by their father's will was to do."[35] In short, stepparents often discharged their responsibilities while burdened by the suspicions of folk wisdom, the resentments of relatives, and the surveillance of officials. Even colonial authorities sometimes sympathized with stepparents in their unenviable lot. One Virginia court cautioned that "the office of the overseers" of an estate was not to harass the stepparents but "onely to see that the said orphants are not abused or missused and their estates imbessled."[36]

Guardians often fared better than stepparents, at least in part because they were chosen—either by the courts, by deceased parents' wills, or by the children themselves if they were of age. Guardians tended to be relatives or persons close to the family in some other respect.[37] If an orphan had no relatives or family friends, the court made do; in appointing Samuel Seabury guardian to "a poor orphan left att Plymouth" in 1681, the court noted that "his frinds many of them [were] deceased."[38] In other cases, guardianship formalized arrangements of long standing or altered the terms of apprenticeship or educational agreements.[39] Rearrangements of this sort may have changed little in the daily lives of the children, but they were more than dry formalities; they gave the guardian parental authority and control over any estate the child inherited. Indeed, control of the estate figured as the major concern in most of these proceedings.

In practice, the cares of guardianship varied considerably. Many guardians confined themselves to financial arrangements, but even this task extended beyond the probate of the estate to securing the child's inheritance, supervising and "improving" the estate, and accounting to authorities for their actions. Building on their explicit authority, guardians often became general advisers and protectors for the orphan or the family and in many cases assumed direct care of the children.[40] Some guardians took on more than their share of family burdens: in New Hampshire Joseph Daniell administered Thomas Chesley's estate, raised one of Chesley's children, and eventually married Chesley's widow.[41]

But not all guardians and wards were so well matched. Some guardians refused outright to accept the job, which suggests that they were not consulted beforehand and in other cases the widow or even the children objected to the designated guardian, both before and after appointment.[42] Most complaints against guardians attacked their administration of the estate. In 1670 John Edloe of Virginia charged that his guardian had ruined his estate, while in Maryland Matthew Rolinson claimed that his guardian withheld from him the profits of his own property.[43] Other difficulties arose over the quality of care. Roger

Moore of Maryland, for example, complained in 1661 that his guardian did not clothe him adequately.[44] More heatedly, Joseph Bridger petitioned Governor Nicholson of Virginia in 1691 to replace his godson's guardian, who was "a Professed Papist and contemner and slighter of the Publick worship of God," among those unfit "to have the Education of their owne children, much less" anyone else's; in Maryland too, in 1734, Isaac Wood rescued his godson from "the Care of a Certain John Crow who is a profest roman Catholick."[45] For the most part, though, guardianship worked smoothly. Many guardians acted not only out of a sense of duty to a friend or the community but also in the knowledge that the care they gave their wards might well become necessary for their own children; in both ways, guardianship fit into a sense of community responsibility and reciprocal obligation.[46]

In matters of childrearing, the influence of neighbors was more diffuse and less weighty than the explicit authority of relatives or guardians, but it was still significant. Neighborhood interest in the disposition of children and neighborly actions for their care broadened the sources of support for the family and wove community concerns into family life. Indeed, a "community" itself appeared in many forms to aid families and children. In about the year 1639 Thomas Blanchard took passage to America on the *Jonathan* of London with his family, but his wife died on board. Blanchard's fellow passengers, as many who came to reside in Newbury, Massachusetts, later testified, so sympathized with him that they "made a gathering [collection] for him in the shippe to helpe to put his child to nurse."[47] The influence of neighbors is easiest to document in the extreme cases, and this is not simply an accident of the surviving evidence. Although it is impossible to prove a negative, it seems almost certain that in normal circumstances neighbors did not do much to shape the day-to-day care of other people's children, that in fact their direct intervention was usually confined to emergencies.

Even so, neighborhood action in crisis drew on a steady watchfulness and willingness to intervene, an alertness that testified to the daily permeation of community influence into family matters. In Maryland in 1659, Anne Barbery was tried on suspicion of murdering her bastard child. Thomas Cobham testified that one night, as he was taking a walk and smoking his pipe, he heard a child cry. Attributing the noise to Indians in the tobacco house, he "went to Bed thinking nothing." The next morning, however, "the Cry running still in his mind," he returned to the tobacco house and found an infant, still alive. He brought the child to Anne Barbery who admitted, under his questioning, that the child was hers and she named the father. He "willed her to have a Care of it," and he and Thomas Nobs went on to another neighbor's house to help with a house frame. "Discourseing about the busines" with these neighbors, Cobham and Nobs "thought best not to leave the woman alone," but by the time they returned the child was dead.[48]

Other neighbors showed better timing, and often their help was invaluable. The neglected children of John Blano of Massachusetts were among the beneficiaries. According to neighbors' testimony in 1677, the children "suffered both for food and raiment": indeed, "they suffered very much and had it not been for their friends through pity taking some of them from him and relieving them, they might have perished."[49] Such kindly interference was not confined to close-knit New England villages. In Maryland, for example, in 1676 Richard Leake, "being a neer neighbour" to Thomas Ward, asked the court to act when Ward and his wife died, leaving four young children with only a small and encumbered estate; and in 1673, when "some of the Neighbourhood" complained that Thomas Vaughan "had inhumanely beaten and abused" his stepdaughter, the court removed her to a neighbor's care.[50]

Parents and authorities sharply checked some forms of neighborly interference. When a neighbor's child climbed a tree, apparently at some hazard to himself, Dorothy Clarke pulled him out of it. Partly because she acted too roughly and, it seems, partly because she was in some disfavor anyway, the Plymouth church summoned her in 1689 to explain herself. The elders charged that "she was in a passion, when she pulled the lad out of the tree with her hand, and then threw him over the fence; that she ought first to have told the mother of the childs fault in getting up to the tree and not have toucht him herselfe; that there was violence appeared in her carriage to the child."[51] Though Dorothy Clarke does seem to have used more force than was necessary, it is suggestive that the church believed she should have notified the mother instead of acting herself—even though the child may have been in danger. New York authorities put the point more clearly. In 1680 Juriaen Teunise appeared in court for spanking a neighbor's child who had beaten his own son. The court found no case for assault against Teunise; "nevertheless," they continued, "they consider that the defendant acted very badly in interfering with someone else's children," and ordered him to pay the court costs.[52] Such cases denote a strikingly clear limit to neighborly influence, a boundary of privacy that was conspicuous by its absence in many other areas of colonial life. This implicit restriction on the direct authority of neighbors over other people's children may well have stemmed from a strong sense of children as the dependents and inferiors—in fact, the property—of their parents. If so, it seems that neighborly restraint arose less from an acknowledgment of family privacy than from respect for the hierarchical order of social relations.

Within such limits, however, parents not only acknowledged the breadth of community interest in their children but often relied on it. John Warner of Providence was bound for England in 1652. Since "care and conscience bindeth mee to take care for the well ordering of my child in my absence," he "Intreate[d] and also betrust[ed] my loving friendes the Towne of Providence with the care thereof." He went on to say that "because the season of the yeare is very difficult with (respect of business) to gett the Towne together, to acquaint them with my desire, I doe more particulary Intreat my faithful and worthy friendes [naming five men] to be as [trustees] in behalf of mee and the Towne of Providence."[53] Warner held the town collectively responsible for his daughter, would not have hesitated to lay the matter before an open town meeting, and rendered the appointed trustees accountable to the town as well as to himself. His confidence rested on high expectations and long experience of community involvement in family life.

In some cases, such dependence on community goodwill outlasted the society that created it. In colonial America childbirth was virtually a public event, almost a ritual, attended by many female friends and neighbors. But even as childbirth became more private and midwifery more formal, something of the former sense of community bonds, of neighborly helpfulness, persisted. In regulating midwives, for example, New York City in 1731 required them to swear that they would help poor as well as rich women, and that "in time of Nessessity You shall not forsake or leave the Poor Woman to go to the Rich."[54] Towns were larger, neighbors were less intimate, and midwifery was a business— but the community still owed something to women in childbed.

Loyalty and affection form one thread in the involvement of kin and neighbors in childrearing arrangements; economic considerations form another. Concerns for and conflicts over money emerged most explicitly for children who inherited some estate. Family members often disagreed over the division of property, or they suspected profligacy and bad management. Even charges of deliberate embezzlement were far from rare.[55] Many formal arrangements and informal negotiations sought to alleviate such fears and smooth the way to family peace. Problems nevertheless persisted, in part because of human nature but also because difficulties inhered in the financial relationship of children to their relatives. One New Yorker clearly recognized his conflict of interest. In 1656 Joost van Beeck asked to be excused as guardian to his nephew; he doubted that his brother's marriage had been legal and "therefore he would not know, how to govern himself in this case," and also "because he is a party in interest, as he has some claims on the estate of his deceased brother."[56]

More subtle difficulties arose over the value of children's labor. In general, children contributed to the family economy in diverse ways, and courts as well as parents recognized this. In assigning the Widow Magbee custody of her stepchildren in 1709, the Maryland court noted that the youngest children required support "and that those bigger Children might be a great help" to their stepmother in providing it.[57] Parents and guardians sought—and usually received—recompense if a child's worth proved less than expected. When Walter Lord of Virginia relinquished the guardianship of Emma Edwards in 1669, he was allowed to keep her cattle for three more years, he "haveing had great losses in her cattle, and alsoe putt to some trouble with her in her minority"; and in Maryland in 1712 Thomas Stonestreete had his taxes abated because his seventeen-year-old stepson was "a Naturall foole and will doe nothing for your Petitioner but puts him to charge in maintaineing [him]."[58]

In assigning custody of children to relatives or guardians, authorities often formalized it as an *economic* arrangement, usually an apprenticeship between male relatives.[59] William King of Massachusetts took an unorthodox route in 1651 when he left his brother's care to "be apprenticed to his mother."[60] It is hard to say just what King's apprenticeship to his mother meant. Surely she did not teach him a trade, and probably the term "apprenticeship" was used loosely to denote King's authority over her son. But Joseph Crooker's formal articles of agreement held no such ambiguity. In Oyster Bay, New York, in 1686 Crooker bound himself to his stepfather, John Rogers, "with him to dwell after the manner of a servant" during the lifetime of his mother. Crooker promised that he "well and faithfully shall serve [his stepfather] and his Lawfull and Humble Comands alwaies shall do." In the standard form of service indentures, Rogers in turn promised to provide "sufficient meat drink and Apparell both Linen and woollen and Lodging and all other things necessary for him the said servant."[61]

Such agreements went beyond recognizing a child's contribution to the family's welfare. They explicitly tied a child's care to economic value and implicitly rested on financial return rather than family affection. These agreements typically stipulated protections for the child: requirements for a certain standard of treatment, education, freedom dues, and so on. But the basis of these arrangements—the expectation of profit and the weakness of affective family ties—opened the way to abuses as well. The case of John Chiffers Jr. may suggest the potential dangers in a child's usefulness to his relatives. John Chiffers of Maryland planned a trip in 1710, but "he Could not tell what to do with his Child," seven-year-old John Jr. The boy's uncle, John Gaterall, told him to "take no Care for the Child I will take care of him untill you returne," and Chiffers agreed. When Chiffers returned he asked his stepson, Thomas Whitehead, to take custody of John Jr. (his half-brother). Chiffers then left again, this time for good. Whitehead asked his uncle for his brother. Gaterall refused. Whitehead, "in Consideration of Our relation to the said Gaterall and his then indigency" and seeing that the boy "was a very Great help to his Uncle both within Doors and without," yielded. The boy could stay until matters improved for the uncle "or at least" on the condition that Gaterall teach him some trade. But in 1719 Gaterall, "by Cuning insinuation and frightfull Threatning," sought to have the boy bound to him. Thomas Whitehead, along with his three brothers, objected that "Our Uncle not Valuing affinity nor regarding Honor or Honesty has basely and Sinisterly Misrepresented the Matter . . . to get a Servant a Slave and a Drudg." If his brother remained with his uncle, Whitehead foresaw, he would end up no "better than a Negro." The Whiteheads won their suit, but even then John Chiffers' refuge lay not in fraternity but in a formal apprenticeship. Thomas and William Whitehead agreed to train him in carpentry, to teach him to read and write, "and at the Experation of his time of Servitude to Give him an Intire Suite of Clothes."[62] This coupling of a child's upbringing and his labor, troublesome enough among relations, proved even more problematic in the system of "putting out".

Putting or placing or binding out were terms applied interchangeably to a variety of childrearing arrangements, and definitions blur in explaining this widespread practice. Generally, though, the terms referred to placing a child in another family on the understanding that the family would receive recompense while the child received adequate care and some sort of training; the child normally stayed until he or she reached maturity. Apprenticeship and service were, in effect, the most formal and most clearly defined versions of putting out. Some other practices may be distinguished from putting out, however, even though they share some of its features.

Some parents hired out their sons (and daughters, though less commonly) to neighbors for specific tasks or for brief periods.[63] This practice was quite rare in the southern colonies but apparently common elsewhere. In New England, Ray Potter worked for a farmer "through the season" when he was ten and was intermittently "engaged to" families as a day laborer until the age of seventeen; Richard Lee was "put at work at five years old as steady as a man."[64] Samuel Buckman of Massachusetts had been apprenticed to John Atkinson to learn felt and castor making; but in 1682 a neighbor testified that Atkinson "several times let out Samuel Buckman to husbandry work and employed him a great deal in that work himself."[65] Farming absorbed most of this child labor, and often enough to establish a going rate of pay; in Albany in 1679, for example, Teunis Carstenz, aged fourteen, agreed "to dwell with . . . Claes Teunisz and help him during the whole harvest of this present year, he paying therefor the ordinary wages given by others."[66]

Children were often "nursed" as well as employed by neighbors; the task began with wet nursing but extended to foster parenthood. Puritan mothers in particular were enjoined to nurse their own children on moral and hygienic grounds, but sickness and death often intervened. Mary Sturgiss of Connecticut died in 1729, "leaving a young child in her father's house, which has been nursed and supported by his estate."[67] In 1675 Bethiah Lothrop of Massachusetts testified that her cousin had died, leaving an unweaned child. "The next day," she said, "there came a friend to our house a woman which gave suck and she understanding how the poor babe was left being Intreated was willing to take it to nurse, and forthwith it was brought to her."[68] And in Maryland in 1661 Eleanor Empson, who was widowed, offered two heifers "with thear Increas" in order to "put out her Child to nurse for too years."[69]

Children were sent out for other kinds of nursing as well. In Virginia Richard and Sarah Brooker agreed in 1728 to take William Apperson, "a poor Lad with a sore Legg," until the next levy "and Endeavour to Cure his Legg."[70] Henry Green brought his daughter to Ann Edmonds of Lynn, Massachusetts, to be cured of a sore leg in 1660; Edmonds agreed to accept a cow as payment for the girl's board since Green had no money and she told him "to leave the child a fortnight or three weeks and she would see what she could do."[71] Neighborly care extended to some very unusual cases. When the children of John Goodwin were thought to be bewitched, Cotton Mather "took the Eldest of them home to my House" to observe and cure her. "The young woman," he reported, "continued well at our house for diverse days."[72]

Other arrangements lasted as long as putting out, but without the financial underpinnings. These cases most closely resembled adoptions, and some participants explicitly understood them in that context. Sometime before 1673, for example, John and Anna Allin of Plymouth "tooke Josias Leichfeild as theire adopted child, with purpose to bring him up, and to do for him as theire child"; in Maryland in 1638, Captain Robert Winter cleared William Naufin of any service obligation, explaining "that he brought him not over as a servant but to keepe him company, and to breed him up at schoole."[73]

The bonds of affection revealed in some of these cases distinguish them from putting out far more dramatically than simply the absence of financial exchange. Before he died in King Philip's War, Thomas Lothrop of Massachusetts adopted his cousin's orphaned daughter. Even though he died intestate, the court allowed his widow to provide for the girl as Lothrop had planned to do. Another relative, eager to share in the estate himself, objected, arguing that the girl had no more claim on the estate than an ordinary servant. But the widow replied that the girl "was not counted a stranger by himself [Lothrop] neither did he put his name upon her for complements sake but as he owned her for his adopt child. She was dearer in his affections than I can express. If my dear husband did have the power to adopt a child then I humbly apprehend that he did as really and truly accept of that child for his adopted daughter as he accepted me for his wife." Lothrop had fully intended to leave the child "something to live upon" after his death, Bethiah Lothrop persuaded the court. "And while it was an infant my dear husband was a tender nursing father to it and many times when himselfe hath had her in his arms and when he hath sate by and I have held the child he hath solemnly taken notice of the providence of God in disposing of the child from one place to another till it must be brought into his house that he might be a father to it."[74] The quality of this relationship was quite different from most instances of putting out.

Even with distinctions such as these, however, putting out remains an umbrella term for a spectrum of arrangements and conditions for raising children. At the most formal and clearly defined end of this spectrum lay apprenticeship. Children were bound by themselves or their parents for a limited period, usually from adolescence to the age of twenty-one. Girls as well as boys became apprentices, usually in housewifery.[75] Apprenticeship indentures followed a standard form that specified, often down to the smallest detail, the mutual obligations of master and apprentice.[76] Masters were held closely to their duties; in 1647 John Legate of Massachusetts successfully sued William Fuller on behalf of Samuel Fogg "for not teaching him the trade of a locksmith."[77]

Despite its apparent precision, the definition of apprenticeship blurred at the edges. The terms servant and apprentice were often used interchangeably, occasionally even in the same indenture, and sometimes the duties of one belonged more strictly to the province of the other.[78] In addition, there were two kinds of apprenticeship. Industrial appr nticeship required vocational training, but in poor-law apprenticeship children were bound out primarily to be maintained at minimal expense to the town or parish. For all practical purposes, poor-law apprenticeship was indistinguishable from other cases of putting out. And though specific vocational training was the distinctive feature of industrial apprenticeship, it was not its only, sometimes not even its most important, function. Apprenticeship, in fact, shared with putting out a number of broader social purposes.

As an alternative to parental care, putting out was most significant in times of family crisis. It was the common response to a host of family disruptions, the major means of community support for families in difficulty. Indentures frequently linked putting out to the death of a parent.[79] Although parental death accounted for many cases of putting out in all regions, it was certainly most likely to be a factor in the Chesapeake. Chesapeake indentures were also more likely to refer to the absence of other relatives to take the place of deceased parents. James Kempe, for example, asked a Virginia court in 1719 to bind to him an orphan named Mackenzie Boggs, "there being none of his kindred to take care of him."[80] Parents incapacitated in other ways were forced to put out their children as well. William Coke of Maryland put out his three children in 1705, after his wife "Eloped from him whereby he is disabled to keep house and maintaine his children at home."[81] In 1725 Elizabeth Jones of Virginia and in 1731 Mrs. Arden of New York bound out their children because their husbands had gone insane; in Providence in 1687, Anne Waters put out her son when her husband, a convicted felon, was transported; and in Connecticut Goodwife Johnson's child "was born in the prison" and apprenticed in his infancy in 1651.[82] Some parents continued to hope that such steps would be unnecessary. Samuel Fuller of Plymouth, whose wife was ill, arranged for his daughter to live with Goodwife Wallen and his other children to go to his brother after his death. But he stipulated in his will that "if it shall please God to recover my wife out of her weake state of sickness then my children to be with her or disposed by her."[83]

Illegitimacy commonly led to putting out. Josiah Clarke of Massachusetts, charged as the father of Sarah Warr's child in 1672, asked for "liberty to put it out to some honest man until it be twenty-one years of age," and in Maryland in 1699 Abigail Clifford's "base borne Child" was bound out at the age of five months.[84] Children born to servants out of wedlock were particularly troublesome, since servants were commonly prohibited from marrying by the terms of their indentures. The typical solution in the Chesapeake, where this ban was more likely to be enforced, was to compensate the master "for the disgrace and trouble of his house" with an additional year's service, and then to bind the child to the same master. In other regions the master or authorities were more likely to encourage a marriage to legitimize the child, although this often proved impossible because the father had fled or was unidentifiable. Chesapeake masters almost always acquired another servant instead, in the person of the newborn child.[85]

And some parents simply abandoned their children. The children of Thomas Trowbridge were put out in 1644 when Trowbridge left New Haven, his children, and many debts behind, and in Virginia John Hayes became an apprentice in 1711 when his father "departed this County and took no care for him."[86] In Maryland Mary Webb was bound out in 1706 at the age of five, "her father and mother both being Runn away," and Samuel Mansell was apprenticed in 1720, "the father being runaway and the mother dead."[87] In many cases the courts merely formalized existing arrangements; typically in such cases a family had agreed to care for a child temporarily only to find that the parents could not or would not return. Abandoned by both parents in Warwick, Rhode Island, Sarah Rysbie lived with Job Almy for two years before becoming his apprentice in housewifery in 1666; and in 1726 George Wilson asked a Maryland court to bind to him "a poor young child now at his house whose continuance has been for seven weeks" since the child "was left there by his mother who is since dead and the Father is runaway to Virginia."[88] Authorities faced more ambiguous situations as well. In a case that suggests some vagueness both in child-care arrangements and in the official sense of geography, New York authorities allowed Isaac Bedlow to be apprenticed by his grandfather in 1730; the court considered Bedlow's parents to be as good as dead, "the father being somewhere beyond sea and the Boy's Mother in the Province of New Jersey."[89]

Most commonly, though, putting out was associated with poverty. Sometimes as a cause in itself, often by compounding other family problems, financial strain influenced most cases of putting out. Solomon Mack, the maternal grandfather of the Mormon prophet Joseph Smith Jr. and born in Lyme, Connecticut, in 1735, lamented that through "the more complicated evils attendant on the depravity of the sons of man, my parents became poor, and when I was four years old the family, then consisting of five children, were obliged to disperse and throw themselves upon the mercy of an unfeeling and evil world. I was bound out to a farmer in the neighborhood."[90] Some parents even put out their children as a way of meeting their debts. Susanna Rogers of Massachusetts, a widow with four children, observed in 1664 that her husband had left her only a small piece of land on Plum Island which her "poore Children was put out prentis to pay for"; and pressed by creditors for years, Francis Johnson "affirmed that he was poor and that they could have his two or three children, as he had nothing else."[91]

But such offers were quite rare: parents almost always put out their children simply because they could not afford to keep them. In 1647 Samuel and Elizabeth Edeth gave over the care of their son Zachary to John Browne because they had "many children, and by reason of many wants lying upon them, so as they are not able to bring them up as they desire."[92] When Andrew Edmunds deserted his family in Providence in 1693, his wife found herself "unable to maintaine his family but must be forced to put forth theire children"; in Virginia in 1729 Elizabeth Glidewell, "a poor Widow and Not able to Take Care of her Children," apprenticed her son; and in Pennsylvania the orphans of John Boyd were put out in 1748 after "being left destitute without any effects to support them."[93] Such families often turned to putting out only as a last resort. In 1683 John Collyer asked the Baltimore court for control of his younger brother's and sister's land; he hoped that "some pains and Industry bestowed upon their fathers Land" would yield an income that would spare them "the shame of seing themselves Reduced to the Indigent necessity of submitting themselves to the Service and Command of others."[94] But not every inheritance assured freedom. Rowalls Rodger of Virginia was forced to apprentice out Sarah Taylor, an orphan under his care, because "he Could not afforde to maintaine her out of the profitts of her Estate it being so very small."[95]

Poverty or fear of poverty was most likely to stir official interest as well. Partly for the welfare of the children, primarily to thin the relief rolls, authorities assisted or coerced the apprenticeship of poor children.[96] Officials presented their financial interest in these apprenticeships quite straightforwardly. New York City church wardens apprenticed Richard Blanck to a watchmaker in 1714 because at the age of ten he was "fatherless and Motherless and destitute of Other friends or Relations and . . . likely to be Chargeable to this City," and in 1725 Providence voted to apprentice Mary Owen "as a poore Child that is fallen to the Tow[n]s Care for Releiff."[97] Authorities typically took less care to bind out children for whom they could disclaim responsibility; when, for example, Richard Gillum of Virginia took an apparent orphan into his home in 1698, his parish ordered the church wardens "forthwith to take Care that the Said Child be returned from whence it Came or to Caus the Said Gillum to give Good Securitie to Save the parish harmles."[98]

In some cases, almost exclusively in New England, authorities used putting out to reform character. In 1691 Michael Towsley appeared with his wife and daughter before a magistrate in western Massachusetts. All were charged with "diverse misdemeanors." Neighbors testified that the Towsley children were "Theevish pilfering lying etc.," that the father was a troublemaker or worse, and that the family was a continual source of grief to their community. On this day the judge convicted the Towsleys of "greivous mischiefes." To turn the daughter from these "Sinfull and dangerous and to be abhorred practices," the court ordered that she be "wel whipt on the naked body with eight Lashes" and that the Suffield selectmen "take effectual care to have said Mary put out to Some meet Person or Persons to Service with whom she may be wel educated." The court drew confidence in this case (although New England courts were rarely diffident) from "the child herself Saying, that she can do [no] better or reforme whyle She continues with her Parents or father."[99] In an even more punitive spirit, a Connecticut court ordered in 1651 that Sarah Gibbs "bee put to service" or else sent to the house of correction "if Shee doth not give good

Satisfaction to the said Courte, that Shee hath seene and reformed her evill wayes."[100]

More broadly, New Englanders viewed putting out as a remedy for improper upbringing. New England legislators frequently rebuked parents who neglected their children's education and decried the fruits of such conduct. Connecticut ordered town officials in 1650 to "have a vigilant eye over theire brethren and neighbours, to see first, that none of them shall suffer so much Barbarisme" as not to teach their children the rudiments of learning; Plymouth authorities also complained of the neglect of education, "whereby Children or Servants may be in danger to grow Barbarous, Rude or Stubborn, and so prove Pests instead of Blessings to the Country."[101] Fears of disorder coursed unmistakably through these warnings. Massachusetts officials suggested in 1669 that the neglect of family education, "as by sad experience from court to court abundantly appears, doth occasion much sin and prophanes to increase among us, to the dishonor of God." In particular, they worried about those "who do live from under family government, viz. doe not serve their parents or masters, as children, apprentices, hired servants or journeymen ought to do, and usually did in our native country being subject to there commands and discipline."[102]

To stem these evils, local officials were empowered to bind out children whose education did not meet their standards; and though no evidence appears to support Edmund Morgan's contention that Puritan parents put out their children in order to avoid spoiling them, the record does show parents who had that step forced upon them.[103] William Scant was bound over to the Suffolk County Court in 1675 "to answer for his not ordering and disposeing of his Children as may bee for theire good education," and for defying the advice of the Braintree selectmen in the matter. After considering "the State of his Family," the court upheld the selectmen's decision and directed them to find places for Scant's children.[104] The Dorchester selectmen summoned Robert Stiles in 1679 "to answer or give an account how he did improve his time for himself and Children" and told him "that he should look out for a place for one of his Children at least, or elce the Select men would provide a place."[105] When the same selectmen advised Francis Bale to put out two of his children in 1680 and he answered "that his wife was not willing," they "perswaded him to perswade his wife to it."[106]

But even New Englanders tended to identify poor education, disorder, negligence, and lack of discipline with poverty. William Williams, for example, pointed to "Parents who from the Numerousness of their Children, or low outward Circumstances, are uncapable to do what is proper and necessary towards their good Education." His recommended solution: "They should otherwise provide for it by disposing of them into good and virtuous Families, where they may be well educated and fitted to serve God and their Generation; and not live in Rudeness and Ignorance, and in Idleness and Sloth, as many do, which is the occasion of abundance of Sin and Wickedness."[107]

Poverty in itself did not alarm Puritans, or colonial Americans generally, nor were the poor deemed inherently vicious or immoral. On the contrary: poverty was accepted as natural, even inevitable, as part of the divine plan; a hierarchical society, after all, required its lower orders, those who would remain "mean and in subjection." But *idle* poverty—as opposed to honest and industrious poverty—clearly signaled an unfit parent. The town of Andover accused Samuel Hutchinson in 1675 of being "an idle, slothful person who will not work nor provide for his family." Neighbors testified that his "manner of living made him an imprudent person," and "although much had been said to him . . . to reclaim him, but it had done no good and he was likely to come to extreme poverty." They ended with a plea to bind out the children in order to "deliver them from much suffering."[108] In 1651 the New Haven court ordered William Bunill's son put out despite the objections of his father, "for it was said that the boy is not only a charge, but he will be spoyled for want of government."[109] This conflation of poverty and unfitness meant that in practice New Englanders imposed apprenticeship for better education only upon poor children.

In fact, in all the colonies, authorities bound out compulsorily only the children of the poor. After finding Joseph Coats incapable of supporting and bringing up his children, in 1735 a Virginia court ordered his church wardens to bind out his children, and in New York in 1746, "whereas there are parents of children at Marbletowne which are very like to become a charge to the said towne," the court answered the complaint of the town poormasters by directing that if these parents "do not put out such Children as aforesaid within two months time that then the poormasters shall put them out untill they are of age."[110] Gradually the laws themselves were framed in ways that made clear their limited application. As early as 1641, Plymouth decreed that, for families that received public relief and had unemployed children, towns could "order that those children shalbe put to worke in fitting imployment according to their strength and abilities or placed out by the Townes," and after 1692 all colonial legislatures adopted apprenticeship laws exclusively for poor children.[111]

Economic considerations not only prompted many cases of putting out; they formed the basis of the system and determined its workings at every level. Masters and families who took in children expected a financial return, usually from the child's labor. In complaining that her son-in-law put out her grandchildren, a Georgia woman noted in 1739 that "to make Payment for the breeding up of these two Children, of the Age of about seven or eight Years, their Father contracts for their Servitude in all Kinds of Work implicitly, till their attaining the Age of Twenty-four, and so leaves them."[112] In some cases masters did receive other kinds of compensation. Apprentices often paid a fee when they began their training, and local officials regularly paid persons who cared for destitute children.[113] Officials sometimes responded to special demands in such cases: in 1726 a Virginia vestry increased the allowance for keeping Lucy Gilles because she "Was More then Ordinary troublesome."[114]

Some fortunate orphans could offer the profits of their estate in exchange for maintenance.[115] But most children who were put out earned their keep, and parents and authorities who paid masters usually did so only for children too young to work. Maryland judges compensated the masters of Hannah Thickpenny "in Consideration of her being Soe young," Hannah Burke, "being of Such Tender age," and Elizabeth Litchell, "in consideration of the Child's Infancy."[116] More often children compensated for their unproductive early years with service throughout adolescence; masters commonly justified their request for legal indentures by the costs of early child care.[117] Many masters feared that they would lose their right to a child's labor just as he was reaching an age when he was likely to be useful. Asked by George Whitefield to free an orphan for outside work in 1740, a Georgia master replied that "he thought it would be a great Hardship to have that Boy taken from him, now he is grown capable of doing him some Service, after living so long with him when he could do him none."[118]

An indenture, then, was one means of protecting their investment, and masters sought other protections as well. In 1651 William Nicolls asked the Essex County Court in Massachusetts to rule on the disposal of a child bound to him if he, Nicolls, died, "in order that he might not lose the expense he had incurred in caring for the child." Presumably he was comforted by the court's decision that the boy would be placed in the custody of his heirs.[119] Any number of things might threaten a master's financial return: his own death, the child's death, an ambiguous contract, a parent who changed his mind—even shady dealings. Peter Carr of Maryland asked to have Elizabeth Lylly bound to him in 1672 because he had raised her from her birth without payment, and now that she was twelve years old he was "fearefull that Shee may be enticed by Some or other from him."[120] Such fears were not entirely far-fetched. William Roe told the Baltimore court in 1741 that he had supported William Jones "ever since his Infancy and now he is by the perswations of other Persons left him." Not only was Jones his stepson, but Roe had "in all parts don his Duty for him, and as he had left your Petitioner Now and he's Just Able to gett his bread it is a Considerable Disadvantage to him." The court agreed and ordered Jones to return.[121]

Guarantees for the master on one side, protections for the child on the other, and the quest for financial advantage on all sides complicated the process of placing out a child. Indeed, the negotiations to place a child were filled with actuarial calculation and bargaining that sometimes seemed more stubborn than shrewd. Life expectancy was just one of the variables these agreements tried to fix in some way. Since most masters who took very young children received some cash at the same time, authorities usually prorated their compensation if the child died.[122] Agreements provided for the death of the master as well. Hannah Buckmaster of New York was to be freed if her mistress, Jane Latham, died; the rationale obviously was that Joseph Latham could not assume his wife's responsibility for teaching Hannah "to make Mantos, Pettycoats, Sew and marke plain worke."[123] Hannah Buckmaster's case is unusual because she was a girl, but the principle applied generally: the more specific the training, the more formal the apprenticeship, the more likely the child was to be freed if the intended teacher died. Conversely, in agreements that did not emphasize training in a particular craft or skill, the child was likely to continue in the household or at least at the disposal of the master's heirs. Thus when Joanna Crawley of Maine placed her grandson with Alexander Maxwell in 1671, she expected him to learn to read and write during the term of his "service"; and she agreed that if Maxwell died during the boy's term that he would "serve the remainder of his tyme with his Dame Annas Max[w]ell."[124]

A more immediate consideration in placing a child was the amount of money or other valuables to be placed with him. Although it would certainly vary by time and place, there seems to have been some sense of a "going rate" for placing a child. A reported exchange between Henry Gold and Sarah Warr in Massachusetts suggests as much; in 1677 neighbors testified that "they heard Gold tell Sarah that if she lived in some houses they would make her pay 10 li. per year for keeping her child."[125] And in New Haven authorities blamed Goodwife Wheeler for failing to place a boy: "She was told her demands are too high, elc it is like she might have put him forth before now."[126] But many factors could drive the rate up or down. It was always most expensive to place a child upon favorable terms with a skilled craftsman, and difficult to place a child incapacitated for work. There was room too for simple disagreement on a fair price. In providing for the two Horton boys in 1641, the magistrate William Pynchon of Springfield deferred a decision until a set sum was "indifferently judged fitt for their bynding out."[127] Even as they chastised Goodwife Wheeler for unreasonable expectations in placing her child with a tailor, New Haven authorities asked Thomas Kimberly "to speak with others of that trade and let the Court understand what they thinke may be a just consideration for him."[128] In these circumstances there was a general temptation to test what the market would bear, and town governments as well as parents and masters succumbed. Watertown, Massachusetts, echoed many colonial communities when it ordered its selectmen to put out the children of the widowed Mary Boyington "as Cheap as they can."[129]

So many issues and parties to the transaction often meant that it took a while to match a child to a home. In New Haven, in September 1663, the widow of Robert Hill decided to put out her stepson. The town authorities approved her decision. (Even when they were not placing the child themselves, local officials, particularly in New England, oversaw the procedure, offering advice and assistance.) The following month she reported to the town that she had met "with some discouragements from some persons about keeping the child," but she remained hopeful, having heard that "one Topping a hatter at Milford had a desire to have it." This promising lead came to nothing. In March 1664 Mrs. Hill, her stepson still in tow, appeared again before the town to express her desire that the boy "might be well placed." Asked if she had any prospects in mind, she replied "that her thoughts was of Mr. Tuttle, and it would be satisfying to her." At this point the town took a more active part. Tuttle, whose wife apparently was related to the Hills, was "asked about the business and he declared that his wife had spoken to him about it." He had thought it over and, at least in part because of his own children, "he had some inclination to take it"—to take it, that is, "if he liked of the tearmes." Fortunately the parties agreed, and the boy and sixteen pounds went to the Tuttles.[130]

As this case suggests, one frequent effect of official involvement in putting out was to hasten the result. Their interest in orderly households and minimal relief responsibilities strengthened the authorities' desire to expedite the business. They did this by assisting at a critical moment, as in the Hill case, or by ordering parents to act quickly. The Providence town council, for instance, told Zachary Field's widow in 1695 to put out three of her children "and to doe it betweene this day and the next day of our Councill meeting and at our next Councill meeting to appeare and give them information where and who the persons are."[131] When they had full authority to dispose of a child, officials deliberately—and avowedly—wasted no time. In settling the fate of James Hall's orphans in 1685, a Pennsylvania orphans court determined to act "with what expedition may be," and when a female infant was abandoned in New York in 1728, the church wardens were ordered to provide for her nursing until she could be put out "and that they take Care to put out the same as soon as possible."[132]

But this did not always mean that local authorities callously unloaded children wherever they could. Several cases show authorities weighing the fitness of prospective masters. Some even upheld special standards: in 1740 Georgia officials refused to commit an apprentice to a Mr. Duchee "who was known to be a professed Deist, and a Ridiculer of Christianity." George Whitefield, for one, objected that "he could not, in Conscience, agree to it."[133] Still other cases demonstrate genuine concern for the children and a careful consideration of their welfare. Consider the case of John and Elinor Vinton, two orphans who fell to the care of New Haven officials in 1664:

The Court having had some thoughts of giving liberty for the disposing of the Children as orphans according to order. But understanding that the Children had received a Letter from Mr. Purchase Clarke of the iron-workes at [Lynn], which was presented and read (and is alsoe kept upon file) wherin he shewes much affection to the Children and Earnest desire of their comming thither where their parents had formerly lived, and they bred and Borne, and most of their friends and some remote relations being there, he alsoe promised to take the Care of them and too see them disposed off for their good.

After receiving assurances that Purchase was "an able man and of good repute for Godliness" and finding that the children had "an earnest desire to goe thither," the court committed the orphans to his disposition. They later learned, from a former servant of Purchase who came to New Haven, that "the Children were loveingly received by Mr. Purchase . . . and very well disposed of as might be for their good."[134]

In other instances too, courts (and parents, when they were available) consulted the wishes of the children. When a New Amsterdam man asked that William Samuel continue in service with him in 1662, the orphanmasters told him "first to speak with Willem and then to come with him to the next session of the Board"; before placing two Carter orphans with their elder brother in 1689, the Orphans' Court of Bucks County, Pennsylvania, dispatched two officials to "speake with the said orphans of theire willng[nes]s to be placed with their brother."[135] Some children were given leeway on particular points. William Legg of New York, for instance, directed in 1730 that his son was to be placed "to learn a trade as he best likes," and when a Maryland court placed John Prindowell in 1726 they ordered that, if the master died during his indentured time, it would "be in the lad's Election either to be bound out anew or remain" with his master's executor.[136]

But for the most part children found their choices extremely limited. For one thing, they remained in every sense at the disposal of either their parents or the local authorities. New Haven, for example, ruled in 1659—to his advantage—that Edward House's indenture was invalid as "being the boyes act, without consent of either his parents or authority." Since he was only twelve or thirteen at the time, "he was not capeable of making an indenture"; finally the court suspected that he had been coerced into signing.[137] New Haven considered Edward House too young at twelve or thirteen to make his own decisions; yet he was fairly old to be put out. Very few children were bound out after the age of fourteen except in very formal services or apprenticeships in which little was left to the discretion of the child. At the same time, children in all the colonies were frequently put out at very young ages— certainly too young to have had anything to say about it. Thomas Seddon of Virginia in 1691, Elizabeth Brown's daughter in New York in 1725, and James Reyner of Maryland in 1730: all were put out before

they could walk.[138] In fact, officials sometimes considered children simply too young to be put out at all. In 1686 the Essex County Court
called Sarah Saverie's illegitimate child "too young to be taken from its
mother"; Georgia officials considered the case of German immigrants
in 1745 and decided that several children ranging in age from six to
nine "were too young to be separated from their Parents."[139]

But exigency even more than age circumscribed children's options in
putting out. Most children simply went where they would be welcomed
or were bound where they happened to end up. And these children
were often the lucky ones. Some children fell—disastrously—through
the cracks of family care and formal authority. In a 1678 petition,
James Kiely of Maryland asked the court to appoint an estate administrator. His father, he explained, had died about five years before. His
mother became the executrix of the estate but then died intestate a year
later, leaving three children and a maidservant in the house. No one
took charge of the estate or of them. "Wee lived in my fathers house
soe long as wee had Victualls and haveing noe Creditt for more Every
one shifted for themselves." The two brothers bound themselves by
court order, "and my Sister lived with a neighbor and the maide servant
went about the Countrey to Worke for Victualls." They waited in vain
for an administrator and took no steps to improve or rent the plantation "for feare" that "the Administrator when he came would take itt
away." After living like this for four or five years, Kiely sought a resolution. The judge agreed to appoint an administrator, although "he did
not conceave he was Enabled by any Law to meddle with the Lands of
the deceased."[140] Nothing quite like this could have happened in New
England; even by Chesapeake standards it was an extreme case. Still it
suggests something of the fluidity of colonial child-care arrangements
and of the buffer putting out could provide against so much uncertainty.

The actual conditions of service in putting out—provisions for treatment, education, freedom dues, and so on—fell within a fairly narrow
range of practice and were easily standardized in the formulaic terms
of indentures. The essential features of apprenticeship or putting out
were so predictable, in fact, that indentures often forsook specifics for
such phrases as treatment "according to the custom of the country" or
"as it is usual for such masters to do by orphans" or "as is appointed
for servants by indenture or custom."[141] Georgia officials wrote into

law their standing arrangement with one master, resolving in 1733 that "every Parish Boy or Girl" bound to Roger Lacy would receive twenty acres of land as part of their freedom dues "accordingly with the usual Limitations and Conditions."[142]

Many indentures spelled out provisions a little more fully, especially those concerning education. Virtually all indentures required the master to teach the child to read (at least in the Bible), and many also required writing and "cyphering." Some even elaborated a careful educational program. One Albany indenture required Meyndert Fredericksen in 1680 to teach his apprentice "the smith's trade as he shall be able and to send him to the evening school for three winters, namely, two months each winter, and to pay the school tuition"; in 1701 a New York City indenture gave Jonah Thomasson "Liberty to goe Six winters in the Night School that is to Say three Months in Every winter upon the Charge of his Master."[143] By contrast, with an offhandedness not uncommon in southern indentures, John Middleton of Maryland promised in 1704 to give Giles Bowers, an orphan, "2 years Schooling, when opportunity presents before his age is Expired."[144] In New Haven in 1653 John Jones was not even required to teach Henry Yeats his apprenticed trade of husbandry after he took over his indenture because "the boy hath (as himselfe saith) no desire to learne."[145]

Some additional provisions were not standard but were nevertheless very common. Southern indentures very often prohibited masters from using their female apprentices in agricultural work. In most colonies the parties to a formal apprenticeship expected implicitly that an apprentice would not be employed to the exclusion or detriment of his specific craft training. In the South the proscription for female apprentices was rock-ribbed because the degradation associated with slaves' work was apparent. Hence female apprentices were not to "work in the ground for the making of either Indian Corne or Tobacco," nor to "give her assistance towards the making of Tobacco or Corn etc.," "no ways to be put in the Ground to work but to be brought up wholly to houseworke"; the master was "not to suffer her to work in the Ground" or "not to turn her to worke either at the howe or mortar or any such labor."[146] The ban on farm labor was less common and less than absolute for boys in the South; William Nicholls, for example, was apprenticed as a carpenter in 1709 and was "wholely to be Employed therein Except three weeks yearly in Tending Corne."[147] Indentures in general left it to the master to determine what was appropriate work for an apprentice. Thomas Disrowah of Maryland was to serve

his master "in such imployment and service as [the master] shall lawfully require," and in New York Alexander de Bonrepos was apprenticed to "Serve in all Such Service or Imployment as his Said Master
Shall have for him to doe or Shall Sett him about from tyme to
tyme."[148]

Another clause common in southern indentures forbade masters to
move with their apprentices out of their original jurisdiction.[149] These
provisions aimed at keeping the apprentice within the range of official
protection. Such provisions carried far less importance in New England. There a master who moved was likely to find the authorities in
his new home every bit as inquisitive and forceful as the ones he had
left behind. In fact, after keeping Jeremiah Chichester and his mother
for a couple of months in 1658, Edward Taylor decided to leave Salem;
then the selectmen of Salem and Marblehead bound Jeremiah as an
apprentice to Taylor precisely so he would *not* leave the boy behind to
become a charge on the town.[150]

A child ordinarily served in the apprenticed household until reaching
the age of majority—twenty-one for boys, eighteen or marriage for
girls—but a master's plan to move was only one of the circumstances
that could overturn that expectation. The death of the master was
probably a more common problem. In that case the child sometimes
returned to the parents.[151] Sometimes too the child was simply transferred to another master, but most often the apprentice remained at the
disposal of the master's heirs or family. The unexpired time of apprentices commonly appears in estate inventories and testamentary lega-
cies.[152] Indentures also specified that an apprentice remain in the deceased master's family or at least provided for some compensation if
he or she left. When a Connecticut court bound John Gennings to Jeremiah Adams in 1661, it determined that Gennings would finish his
term with Adams' widow if he died, with another relative if they both
died, and if it became necessary to "otherwise dispose of Gennings the
benefit is to return to Jer[emiah Adams] or his assignes."[153]

Dissatisfaction or incapacity as well as death led to relocating a
child. Phoebe Seales of Boston left John Coggeshall for another master
in 1637 after she "proved overburdensome to him," and Daniel Sutton
of West New Jersey surrendered his apprentice in 1696 after complaining against him "for running away and stealing and Cheating."[154] In
1664 Cornelius van Schelluyne's apprenticeship to an Albany shoemaker was to be voided "in case of disability on either side"; in Pennsylvania Joseph Walley's apprenticeship ended in 1734 after he "had

become disordered in his mind"; and in 1761 Adam Bedinger found a new master to learn a new trade because "he was not capable to learn the Art or Mystery of a Taylor."[155] Peter Atterbur's experience was virtually a catalogue of reasons for transferring apprentices. Orphaned in Maryland at the age of two, he was placed with his godfather, who died not long afterwards. His godfather's executor, Henry Barn, took over the estate and Atterbur "as part thereof." Barn later passed on Atterbur to his son-in-law, James Sims, who in turn, "for a valuable consideration," transferred him to Joseph Chew, under whose authority he reached his majority.[156] Benjamin Skarlet's experience was at the other extreme of stability. At the age of fifty-four, he testified in 1678 that "at his Cominge into this Country," Massachusetts Bay in 1635, he was bound by his mother as an apprentice to Governor Endicott, "and from that time until now//2 years excepted// . . . lived either with him or upon a peice of his land adjoy[n]ing to his farme (which he gave unto me)."[157]

The impermanence of many putting-out arrangements was of course inconvenient to the officials who had to find new homes for children thus displaced. Salem selectmen spent a fair amount of time settling—and then resettling—Sarah Lambert. They provided for her in April 1662 and again in December and then again two years later, in November 1664. By 1673 the selectmen found their charge doubled: Sarah Lambert bore an illegitimate child whom she could not support. Between January 1673 and November 1679, they placed Lambert and her child (sometimes separately) at least fourteen times. The selectmen of Salem must have spoken ruefully when they cleared another town of responsibility for Lambert in 1679, admitting that they did "looke att her as a burden belonging unto our towne."[158]

Such impermanence was much more than an inconvenience, however. It reduced putting out to only a stop-gap solution to family instability. Even worse, it produced instability anew. It certainly disrupted the education of the children and probably undermined the fragile emotional attachments that putting out permitted. Although it is impossible to measure accurately the duration of children's stays in one family, it seems likely that most children outside the South in the seventeenth century enjoyed fairly stable and long-term arrangements; it was after all in the master's interest to prolong the term of service. But for children who were moved—children who had already left their own families—the experience must have been wounding. The very circumstances of relocation were likely to be grievous. Mary Thacker—"a poor Child," as she termed herself—petitioned the Frederick County, Maryland, court in 1749. After both her parents died, she, "haveing noe friends . . . was bound at Anarundel County Court to a certain William Hayward of this County." She reported, in a phrase that proved itself, that Hayward "never gave me noe Scooling." She moved with Hayward twice before he—in debt to Joseph Hill—sold her as "a Servent to the said Hill for three Years to pay the Debte." She asked the court for liberty from service and a guardian; instead she was bound to Hill until the age of sixteen. Mary Thacker was not yet fourteen when she appeared in court.[159]

Putting out bred several other kinds of problems and disagreements. Many complaints stemmed from flawed or misunderstood indentures, others from fraud or coercion.[160] Two particular issues generated most of the substantive complaints about putting out: nonperformance and cruelty. Charges of nonperformance—which came most often from parents but sometimes from authorities—ranged from the failure to teach a trade to the failure to provide proper freedom dues.[161] Many orphans complained that they were too busy doing manual labor to learn anything, and some masters failed to give their charges any education at all. The Orphans' Court of Kent County, Maryland, charged Thomas Hicks in 1696 with keeping two orphans who were "brought up to nothing but the Hoe," and in 1702 Elizabeth Padgett of Prince George's County complained that though her son's master had promised to provide three years schooling he had "utterly neglect[ed] to give him any."[162] The problem spanned time and region. In 1746 George Whitefield lamented the condition of Georgia orphans, many of whom "were at hard Services, and likely to have no Education at all"; his complaint came a century after Dorothy Flute informed John Winthrop that her son's master had promised "faithfully to bringe my Child upp att schoole" but "ever since imployed [him] to keepe hoggs and goates, and by this meanes he is like not only to bee deprived of his means but also of educacon or any Calling by which hee may hereafter subsist."[163]

Inadequate care was another common complaint. John Bryan of Virginia in 1678 and Humphrey Edwards of Maryland in 1694 both charged that their masters gave them inadequate clothing; Henry Colie of New York City made the same complaint in 1716 on behalf of his son; and Stephen Longman of Maryland testified in 1699 that his master worked him and the rest of the servants "very hard and cloth them very thin and indifferent."[164] In 1663 Adriaan Jansen of New Amsterdam explained that he wanted to leave his master because, among other things, "he gives him nothing to eat," and in Hempstead, New York, Joseph Dodge was freed from his apprenticeship in 1739 after charging that his master did not give him "Sufficient Meat."[165] Masters were charged with spiritual as well as corporal neglect; the Charles County Court in Maryland presented Honor Boughton in 1664 for raising an orphan "in the Roman Catholick Religion Contrary to the Religion of his dead parents."[166] Finally, masters were brought to court for failing to pay freedom dues and for denying their servants freedom altogether. Richard Middleton of Pennsylvania sued for his freedom dues in 1732, and John Winbery of Virginia and Susannah Preston of Maryland sued on behalf of their indentured children.[167] In 1673 Christopher Batson of Maryland charged that though he had served his time his master "yet will not set him free," and in Pennsylvania when Joseph Helon's master refused to free him in 1742 he "absented himself."[168]

Some masters were clearly guilty of extreme neglect and deliberate cruelty. In 1643 a Virginia court considered the charge that John Wilkins "hath most unhumanely beate and abused" his apprentice; Daniel Rumble of Massachusetts appeared in court in 1644 for "beating his boy 50 blowes"; and in 1701 two Maryland orphans complained that their guardians "mightily abused them."[169] In rare cases an indentured child died as a result of mistreatment. A Plymouth jury indicted Robert Latham in 1655 "for fellonious crewelty done unto John Walker, his servant, aged about 14 yeares, by unreasonable correction, by withholding nessessary food and clothing, and by exposing his said servant to extremities of seasons, wherof the said John Walker languished and immeadiately died." Latham was subsequently convicted of manslaughter, and his wife was found "in a great measure guilty, with her said husband, in exercising cruelty towards their late servant."[170]

Children luckier than John Walker were protected from extreme abuse by local authorities. No one questioned the right of masters to punish physically their servants, but officials distinguished between appropriate correction and cruelty. Charges against masters often specified that they had erred in the degree of force or in giving punishment disproportionate to the offense. In 1716 John Southworth of Pennsylvania complained that his master "beat him unlawfully More than Common Correction for Servants."[171] Authorities often freed children from abusive masters, although not from abusive parents.[172] But the line between "common" correction and cruelty was not always easy to draw, and it could be moved or erased by a master's whim. Even when they punished masters, authorities' reactions to cruelty seem oddly mild. Their lack of surprise—not to say outrage—speaks eloquently to colonial standards of corporal punishment, and also to their expectations of treatment for the class of indentured children. In a triumph of understatement, a Massachusetts court presented Philip Fowler for abusing his servant boy in 1682, "and although [the] court justified any person in giving meet correction to his servant, which the boy deserved, yet they did not approve of the manner of punishment given in hanging him up by the heels as butchers do beasts for the slaughter, and cautioned said Fowler against such kind of punishment."[173]

A child's other major protection against abuse lay in the vigilance—and intervention—of relatives or neighbors. Samuel Magee of New York complained that his son's master beat him; in Maryland Margaret Brown petitioned for her child's release in 1753 because it was "very Barbarsly used and . . . they whip it almost to Death . . . and it Can be proven by Severall persons that they use said Child after an Unhuman Manner in all Shapes and Wickedness"; and according to testimony given in 1639, a neighbor in Salem, Massachusetts, told Marmaduke Pierce's wife "to give [their servant] some victialls and to spare any further correction for that time for that he thought the boy had sufficient correction."[174] To their regret, Benjamin Jones and his wife ignored the advice of their neighbors in Gloucester, Massachusetts. Warned to stop beating their servant, Goodwife Jones answered that "the more people talked about it the worse it would be for the child." In this case the neighbors prevailed, and in 1682 the boy was removed from the Jones household.[175] But many children were less fortunate.[176]

Corporal punishment and other forms of strict discipline for children and servants were widely sanctioned in colonial America—so widely sanctioned that one study has found that even when punishment by parents or other caretakers resulted in the death of a child, it elicited relatively mild punishment.[177] Even in less extreme cases, the standards for such discipline—what contemporaries would have deemed inappropriate or cruel—differ from the standards of most twentieth-century Americans. It may even be that by colonial standards only a minority of indentured children were "abused." But it should also be emphasized that the system of putting out itself—and not simply individual depravity or sadism—virtually guaranteed that some children would be abused. Putting out was inherently exploitative in that it extracted labor from children who were necessarily weaker than their masters. Children who were put out because they were orphaned or abandoned or impoverished—which is to say, most children who were put out at all—were vulnerable to abuse for the same reasons. Henry and Jane Stacy of Marblehead, Massachusetts, bound out their daughter Martha as a servant to Joseph Crocker of Newbury. Hearing in 1680 that she was mistreated, they visited her and found her "beaten black and blue, with many marks on her body, so that some doctors despaired of her life." The Stacys had no money to file a suit against Crocker, but at their request the court sent William Beale to investigate and take evidence. Beale learned that neighbors had urged the Crockers to return Martha Stacy to her parents "rather than abuse her," to which the Crockers "replied that her parents were poor and kept by the town and cared not what became of her."[178] In this instance the Crockers underestimated the affection and wherewithal of the Stacys, but they identified clearly enough their exposed position. All indentured children were vulnerable; cruelty to indentured children followed the lines of greatest vulnerability; and those lines were drawn and reinforced by the workings of the system itself.

The problem of cruelty stemmed in part from the contradictory nature of putting out. Putting out was an economic arrangement clothed in familial terms. It performed the custodial and educational duties of family life while economic pressures molded its every feature. Of course the colonial family itself was, in large part, an economic arrangement so that its functions were at first easily transferred to putting out. But by the late colonial period, as people placed higher personal and emotional demands on family life, as they came to expect the family to be unique and distinct from other social units, the disjunction between family life and putting out grew too great to ignore. The particular purposes of putting out—welfare, education, labor—were formalized and increasingly removed from a familial context. At the same time, the special character and prerogatives of family life were clarified and elaborated.

The clearest sign of stress between putting out and an emerging sense of affective family life came in conflicts over authority between parents and masters. Indentures and putting-out agreements rested implicitly on the assumption that during the term of service the master assumed the role of a parent; he exercised parental authority and was to behave as a parent to the child. This expectation was often made explicit. In

Maryland in 1655, Joseph Weeks promised to give Hance Hanson "his freindly or otherwayes fatherly Care Charge and Education"; in 1668 John Jushup of Southampton, Long Island, agreed to take Caleb Dayton "and to doe for him duering the time as for his owne"; and in Albany Richard Pretty and his wife promised in 1674 to raise Johanna Hans "as if she were their own child," and her mother specified "that said employers shall be to her as a father and a mother."[179]

But it is not always easy to say exactly what behaving "like a parent" meant. Certainly in some cases the injunction meant only that the master should behave humanely, guided by the obligations of all social superiors to their inferiors and dependents. When John Reeves was bound to Jonathan Covell in 1720, Covell agreed to "behave himselfe in all respects well towards the said John Reeves So as is Decent and becoming a Master towards his Servant or a Guardian towards his Ward."[180] Though his testimony was self-serving (he was contesting a bequest to an adopted child), Ezekial Cheever of Massachusetts suggested that such terms might intend to protect the master more than the child. He argued in 1675 that Thomas Lothrop had taken Sarah Gott "not upon loose terms, as he did [another servant], but as his own: so that her father might not have power to take her away from him, when she might grow up to be serviceable, as is oft done in such cases." Cheever went on to note the looseness of familial terms: "As for her calling them father and mother, it is no more but what is ordinarily done to nurses servants, and what another, whom he [Lothrop] had brought up before, was used to do."[181]

Despite the broadness of familial terms, it seems to be true—and significant—that parental care was the standard by which a master's care was measured. To care for a child as a parent was better than caring for him or her simply as a master. In 1656 Jan Hendrick defended himself from the charge of mistreating his servant by maintaining that he "treated him only as his own child"; in Massachusetts Richard and Mary Littlehale testified in 1657 that they had seen "at Thomas Davis' the kind and tender usage of the boy [Davis' servant], like parents"; and in Maryland when Thomas Cornwallis took Hester Nicholls as a servant in 1658, he promised to "take as much care for her as his owne Child."[182] One of the arbitrators in a Massachusetts case involving a neglected apprentice concluded in 1670 that "if it was my child I should look upon him as undon."[183] The hope that masters would match parents in ideal affective terms was probably doomed by the system's workings as well as its economic underpinnings; and the affective quality of the parent-child relationship itself is ambiguous for most of the colonial period. But people understood apprenticeship and service in paternalistic and familial terms; masters did provide the kinds of basic care that parents owed their children; and in all practical ways children *were* masters' children for their terms.

Where did this leave the natural parents? Their position vis-à-vis their own children, as well as their children's masters, was ambiguous and ridden with conflict. Some children who were placed out seem not only to have sensed the anomalous position of their parents but even to have exploited it. In Massachusetts, for instance, an unnamed adolescent, probably a boy, self-consciously described his progress in a letter that subverted Puritan pieties even as it espoused them. In 1659 or so he wrote to his mother that "through my master's diligence wt mee and God's blessing I have greatly Benefitted myself for my time but I hope hereafter to show better fruits of my learning." He went on to reveal in a very striking way his sense of independence from—and indeed advantage over—his mother. He asked for ten shillings, a fee for his extra schooling in algebra, and added with a reproachful undertone and a hint of blackmail: "I pray bee not [bac]kward for my preferment for I hope to bee a comfort to you in your old age Allso I would desire you—Apparell me like an Apprentice for you know how . . . I pray Mother that which [I ask] doe lett itt bee done Chearefully."[184] This boy must have been unusual among placed-out children in many respects: in his maturity, in the advantageous terms of his apprenticeship, and in his shrewdness. But his letter does suggest the elements of calculation and pragmatism that characterized so much of filial relations in the colonial period. It suggests too how the extension of childrearing responsibilities in practices such as putting out might subtly shift the balance of power in family relations.

The balance of power between parents and masters was even more precarious and more openly problematic. Many indentures sought to prevent conflicts by demarcating and reducing parental influence. In the 1650s William Baker of Warwick, Rhode Island, put out his son to Thomas Bradley "to bringe up as his owne child, for which end I passe over my fatherly Authority unto him," and in 1706 Elizabeth Hogg of Providence gave her daughter to Mr. Thomas Field and his wife "for them to bring up. Tutor and instruct, and to dispose of as their Owne."[185] In Huntington, New York, Sarah Davis' indentures included the stipulation that her father "doth comand his said daughter to obey al her said dames lawfull comands all her fore mentioned time."[186] One measure of a master's authority was his right to dispose further of the child. Mary Hobson of Rhode Island, Rachel Lead of Virginia, and Edward Garnum of New York, for example, were all apprenticed by consent of their current masters.[187]

Certainly no vagueness clouded two agreements from Virginia in 1644. Elizabeth Cooper allowed Anthony Hodgkins "to have possess keep and mayneteyne [her daughter] as his owne natural Child and Respectively to Governe Nurture and dispose of the said Child as becometh a naturell parent," while she "henceforth disclayme all interest and acknowledgement in the said Child or in anything belonging unto her. And doe further bynde myself that from henceforth I shall not doe nor procure to bee done unto the said Anthony Hodgkins any trouble incumbrance or molestation whatsoever For or by any reason of the said Child or anything belonging or appertayneing to it."[188] Richard and Mary Hudson also promised, when they "freely and absolutely" gave their daughter to John Judson, "never to trouble nor desire to have her again" as long as the Judsons lived.[189]

Most parents, however, were not so neatly excised from their children's lives. In general, parents could retrieve their children by compensating the master for room and board. In Huntington, New York, John Smith took John Wood in 1662, agreeing that if his parents wished to remove him within a year and a day "that they have their liberty to do so, Provided that they Defray and Discharge" his expenses; and in binding Mary Tudor to James Simmons in 1694, the court of Norfolk County, Virginia, ordered that "in case her said father [who had left several years before] shall come and require her aways, she still to continue with the said James Simmons, unless he Sattisfie him for his Care, Charge and keeping, for the time she hath been with him."[190] Such provisions recognized the potential fluidity of colonial family life: parents forced or inclined to put out children one year might find it possible or desirable to reclaim them the next. In addition, many children were expected to return to their parents if their apprenticeships were cut short; Robert Doughaley of Maryland and John Eddy of Plymouth, for example, were to return to their parents if their masters died.[191]

Much of parents' influence over children raised in other households necessarily remains intangible, but there are some clear suggestions of parents and children who sustained their relationships. Apprenticed to a weaver in Rowley, Massachusetts, in 1664, Samuel Hadley had "liberty once in a year during his apprenticeship to go to see his friends," and in Kingston, New York, Jacomyna Cornelis' daughter left her service to return home when Jacomyna fell sick.[192] Most children probably continued to live fairly near their parents. Certainly authorities tended to place children within the bounds of the town or parish. Georgia's trustees ordered in the case of German immigrants in 1745 that "the Children Who are placed out from their Parents . . . serve in the same District in Which their Parents are placed out, if it conveniently can be."[193] John Pulcipher of Massachusetts lived close enough to convey regularly to his parents stolen goods; in 1679 he confessed to filling his pockets and walking home with about half a bushel of wheat, several large pieces of pork, and ten pounds of sugar.[194] John Pulcipher's master was not alone in regretting the proximity of parents. Thomas Tiddeman of New Amsterdam sued the Hendrick Obes, senior and junior, in 1668. The younger Obe, who was Tiddeman's servant, had "Run away out of his Service to his father's house, who gives him Entertaynement Contrary to Lawe." A neighbor testified that some time before he had mentioned Obe's son to Tiddeman, who replied with irritation "that the Boy Would do better by him in Case his father's howse Was not soo nye to his."[195]

In some cases parents and masters worked out something like joint custody. James Davy of New York City was apprenticed in carpentry in 1718 on the usual terms, except that his father agreed to provide his clothing during his apprenticeship.[196] Francis Wynne's arrangement was more elaborate. Apprenticed to an Albany shoemaker in 1674, Wynne's master agreed "to furnish said boy with proper food and clothing, after the manner of burghers," while his father agreed to pay the cost of making the clothes if the master paid for the materials; the father also promised to pay for the washing and mending of the clothes, and the master allowed the boy to "help his father three weeks every year in the harvest."[197]

And from time to time masters received reminders of what they owed to parents while they benefited from the labor of their children. In 1655 Mary Clarke of New Haven got into trouble for misbehavior with John Knight. Knight was in serious trouble himself. Considered by the court "a lewd, prophane, filthy, corrupting, incorridgable person, a notorious lyar," he was condemned to hang for attempted sodomy with a teenaged boy. As "for Mary Clarke, the court lookes upon her as wofully corrupted by John Knight." The precise character of her undoing must be inferred, since the published records omit about three pages of the original manuscript "as containing matters of a nature deemed unfit for publication." But whatever the misconduct the court did not blame Mary Clarke alone. They censured her employers, Goodman Judson and his wife, for not watching her more strictly. By their failure, the court said, "they have neglected their trust and duty towards Mary Clarke and her parrents." The Judsons were fined as "a warning to governors of families to be more carefull and watchfull over the charge and trust they take upon them."[198]

The number of complaints that parents lodged against masters further suggests their continued interest in their children. The complaints themselves reveal the prickliness of the relationship between parents and masters. Arien van Laer of New Amsterdam complained that Grietje Provoost "beat her little boy, ill-treated him and shewed him bad example"; when Jan van Hoesem of New York sued Joachim Wesselson for kicking his daughter, rendering her unable to work, Wesselson answered that van Hoesem's daughter "was admonished by his wife to mend her ways as she was a young maiden, whereupon, she making some retort, the woman was moved to chastize her."[199] In Massachusetts Abraham Whitehaire sued Robert Gray for leaving his son in Virginia; Dermot Matthew complained that George Strange had sold his son to another master to his "great grief of heart"; and William Piggott lamented that his son had fallen "into the hands of an unreasonable man, who hath indeavered Contrary to the Custom of the Country, and hath Dealt Deceitfully towards the Lad and us his parents . . . hee hath by his Indiscreet and passionat usage Dishartned the boy, that it made him weary of his life."[200]

More telling than complaints about mistreatment were the fights between parents and masters for the custody of a child—or, at any rate, the right to the child's service. These cases suggest how much putting out blurred the boundaries of family life. In Massachusetts Thomas Chandler sued Job Tyler in 1662 for "taking away his apprentice Hope Tyler, and detaining him out of his service," and in New York Barent Mynderse sued William Hoffman in 1677 for the same reason. In both cases the child was returned to his master.[201] Most of these cases involved a master suing for the return of an indentured child, and the master's hand was usually stronger than the parent's; masters after all held an indenture. Although he lost his case, John Jypson voiced a common presumption in 1716 when he exclaimed that it was "a thing never heard of before that any power or authority can take a man's apprentice from him the master not haveing violated or broken any part of his Indenture."[202] Plymouth Colony sternly backed the claim of John Cook to his servant, Joseph Billington. Billington, who was five years old, "did ofte dep[ar]te his said masters service" to return to his parents' home. The court immediately returned Joseph to his master and ordered him to remain there. The court further ordered that if his parents "do receive him, if he shall again [depart] from his said master without his lycence, that the said Francis, and Christian, his wyfe, shalbe sett in the stocks every lecture day during the tyme thereof, as often as he or shee shall so receive him."[203]

Some parents had more luck. Rebecca Mobberly of Maryland sued successfully in 1730 when Robert Wall refused "to let her have her child again" after his term.[204] But sometimes parents themselves displayed mixed motives and feelings. One of the most revealing of these custody cases was William Buckley's suit in 1661 against Thamar Quilter "for harboring and witholding his apprentice," Joseph Quilter. Thamar Quilter, a widow, apprenticed her only son to William Buckley in Ipswich, Massachusetts. When the boy fell sick, Goodwife Quilter nursed him at Buckley's house for about three weeks until she herself became ill. She returned home, but not before observing "his master to be soe harsh to him (tho the boy as is well known was in great extremytye)." Buckley then brought the boy home to his mother "and there left him, not Inquireing of me whether I would receive him, and Indeed upon some considerations I was unwilling." But since her sick child had already been left, and she did feel "a mother bowell yerneing toward my child," she "did not turne him backe; feareing he might perish." Nevertheless, she complained that in ten additional weeks of nursing the boy, Buckley never "brought or sent any thing to releeve him."[205]

This case sums up the wavering lines of responsibility and affection that linked parents, masters, and children. Thamar Quilter worried enough about her son to move to his master's house for three weeks, but she did not want to care for him without compensation. Buckley left a sick boy, for whom he was legally responsible, with his widowed mother for over two months, yet sued—successfully—for the boy's return as soon as he recovered. Such conflicts point up the confusion both in the definition of family life and in expectations of putting out. These anomalous situations reveal the contradiction between an emerging sense of the family as a private, affective unit and a labor system that approximated the trappings of family life. This anomaly, this deepening contradiction, forced a more precise definition of community child-care arrangements, especially in the use of child labor, and a narrower scope for community influence; it also promoted a special, but more separate, place for the family within the community.

Afterword: Transformations

More than any other force, the demands of community determined the conduct of private life in colonial America. The specific character and intensity of these demands were not constant or uniform: the evidence reveals any number of variations by region and religious group and class, and perhaps even more variations that attest to the inescapable effects of idiosyncrasy or whim in any record of human behavior. But through all the variations by region or group or simple quirkiness, the interrelationship of family and community emerges from the record as an abiding fact of colonial life. And from the very beginning of colonial society, the influence of the community on personal relationships generated conflicts. In particular, three kinds of problems emerged.

First, relationships in the community at large strained under the weight of social assumptions and expectations. The interpenetration of public and private concerns, the pressures of communitarianism, and the daily effects of close neighborhood bonds sowed contentiousness. Attempts at arbitration revealed not only the extent of conflict but the difficulties of restoring harmony. Slander suits, so widespread and so emotionally charged, reflected the importance and vulnerability of good name and public esteem. Colonial Americans accepted the right of their neighbors to examine and judge their lives, and the realities of community life gave them every opportunity to do so. But inevitably the obsessive concern with reputation, with the power of gossip, and with the threat of public shame generated resentment, conflict, and a search for resolution.

Second, contradictory expectations of family life and the community's role surfaced. This problem appeared most clearly in the demands placed on colonial marriages. Colonial society supported the concept of companionate marriage but only within closely circumscribed limits. Whereas authorities hoped for affection and happiness in marriage, they demanded stability. They were unwilling to take the risks true companionate marriage presented or to grant the independence and privacy it required. Motivated by fear of scandal, disorder, immorality, and greater poor-relief responsibilities, authorities used every means, from counseling to coercion, to keep couples together. Individuals and couples accepted community involvement—in effect, community partnership—in their marriages. But in supporting the interests of stability and patriarchy, community goals and pressures played havoc with people's lives. Colonial marriages were expected to fulfill private needs as well as social obligations, and they suffered from their cross-purposes.

Third, the lines between family and community and often the very definition of family were blurred. The experience of parents and children illustrates this point most clearly. The delegation of childrearing responsibilities, above all through the system of putting out, hampered the development of parent-child bonds in simple practical terms. Even more significant, the dispersion of responsibility for childrearing raised questions about the meaning of such bonds. If a master performed all the functions of a parent, if indeed a master's authority could not be distinguished from a parent's—then what did it mean to *be* a parent and how was the relationship to a child defined? Throughout the colonial period this distinction remained unclear. Its ambiguity led to conflicts and custody fights between parents and masters, conflicts that expressed eloquently the fluidity of family definition and relationships in this period.

Just as these problems appeared from the beginning of the colonial period, so too did complaints about them and objections to community demands. These objections failed to carry much weight for several reasons. They were usually quite limited and personal: a person would challenge the court's disposition of a particular case or a specific action rather than its assumptions and purposes. Persons rarely challenged the *right* of the community to intervene in private life or to attempt to bring behavior into line with its broader goals. Further, these isolated challenges were often deviant in some way, a wife beater complaining of interference or a criminal protesting neighborly nosiness. The self-interest and occasional pathology of such objections robbed them of credibility. Indeed, they may have reinforced the prevailing colonial wisdom that only a person up to no good wanted privacy and autonomy.

But in the end even reasonable objections foundered, overwhelmed by the power of community influence and expected behavior. Such challenges remained anomalous in the most fundamental sense. They failed because they ran contrary to deeply entrenched expectations of community and individual behavior, because they challenged customs of local life, patterns of authority, and social ideals that were endorsed by religion, by the state, and by generations of use. Such challenges would not succeed until they could ground themselves in different patterns of community life and different expectations of families and of society.

That is precisely what happened in the mid- and late eighteenth century. The colonial community based its influence on shared assumptions, on the accessibility of neighbors, and on the interconnectedness of their lives. But in the second half of the eighteenth century, a number of developments eroded the practical bases of traditional community life. The shattering of religious consensus, the increasing complexity of economic relationships and the influence of the market, population growth, migration: all pushed private life and individual decisions beyond the reach of the community. At the same time, the cultural paradigm of family and community—all the assumptions, expectations, ideals, and limits built into colonial life—faced profound and, ultimately, irresistible challenges. Early American society accepted and tried to conform to traditional European ideas about family and community, as well as European ideas about most other things; indeed, throughout the colonial period, Americans deeply regretted that they did not conform *more* closely to traditional ideas and social patterns.[1] Inevitably, in applying traditional notions to some of the peculiar conditions of American society, European settlers produced hybrid, distinctive societies, ranging from that of the religious radicals of Rhode Island to that of the adventurers and indentured servants of Virginia. In fact, at the same time, traditional European society was itself undergoing all kinds of important changes, and many European ideas about society were more unstable and more fluid than the image of traditional society usually allows.[2] Both the dynamism of seventeenth-century European society and social thought and the special conditions of colonial settlement meant that American ideas and expectations of society, including family and community, were born in flux.

But though the traditional model of family and community life may have been losing its resemblance to reality even in Europe, though it might never have applied fully to American society—though in these ways the "traditional" paradigm of family and community life may have been unstable, it was still very powerful. It dominated and defined American family and community life until the middle of the eighteenth century, when it began to yield to new forms. By then a set of new ideas about the individual and the family had emerged, ideas that increasingly emphasized the affective family and individualism in both social and political terms. These ideas grew from many sources, but to some extent they were elaborated in response to the changing realities of family and community life, including the kinds of tensions that resulted from the close involvement of family and community in the American setting. These strains formed part of the social experience in which these intellectual and cultural changes were rooted; and, in their turn, such fundamental intellectual and cultural shifts reinforced and propelled further changes in society.

Any discussion of such fundamental changes in colonial society and comparisons with nineteenth-century society raises many conceptual and methodological problems. At least three of them require specific attention here. First, it is important to avoid teleological arguments. It would be misleading to suggest that colonial society was an inchoate or incomplete or flawed form of social organization, which then matured or evolved into a better, more coherent, and more rational form. In their definition and conduct of family and community life, colonial America and nineteenth-century America represent different cultural systems, with different configurations of values and behavior, and with different problems and conflicts. A comparison of the two should help clarify the distinctiveness of the two cultures, but it should not privilege one and deride the other; nor should it suggest that early American social development followed a course marked out as right or natural or inevitable.

A second problem is more narrowly evidentiary. As community influence in family life declined, many of the issues that appeared so clearly in seventeenth-century records, especially court, town, and other local records, simply disappeared from the eighteenth-century records. By the middle of the eighteenth century, community life was not leaving the same tracks. This is itself a suggestive development, in its own way as revealing as the dog that did not bark in the night. It becomes necessary, then, to shift to records other than traditional local ones and also to recognize that local records after the mid-eighteenth century are not comparable in most respects to those of the earlier period. This presents problems of comparability and symmetry not only in the evidence for the eighteenth century but in the arguments that can be built on it. On balance, though, the difficulties of different evidence seem preferable to those of no evidence.

A final problem inheres in any attempt to link results to causes, to explain the developments we may be able to describe. Historical explanations often rely on leaps of faith, and explaining the shifts in family and community life in colonial America promises to be no exception. It is impossible to argue for a uniform cause for the reorientation of family and community in eighteenth-century America or to argue that the reorientation occurred in the same way to the same extent at the same time throughout the country. It is possible to suggest, however, broad sets of conditions that contributed to this change and to suggest some basic ways in which family and community life by the late eighteenth century differed from that of the colonial period.

The broadest changes in eighteenth-century life have received so much attention in so many ways from so many historians that they now seem to constitute the usual suspects in any causal analysis. Yet it is worth reviewing these changes, if only briefly, in order to emphasize their multiplicity and the ways in which they affected the relationship between family and community. Lawrence Stone's term, "affective individualism," comprehends many of these new ideas and expectations. Affective individualism marked a break from an older pattern of family and personal relations characterized by "distance, deference and patriarchy," a shift Stone calls "perhaps the most important change in *mentalité* to have occurred in the Early Modern period, indeed possibly in the last thousand years of Western history." Families cast in the mold of affective individualism gave greater scope for expressions of the self, emphasized affection and autonomy, and sought privacy for both individuals and families. In England this pattern of family values had established itself among the middle and upper classes by 1750, spreading more slowly and more tenuously among the lower classes.[3]

The growth of affective individualism converged with and was reinforced by another significant eighteenth-century development, the widening influence of Lockean psychology. John Locke's *Essay Concerning Human Understanding* (1690) and *Some Thoughts Concerning Education* (1693) forced a thorough reconsideration of childrearing ideas and practices. His view of the mind as a tabula rasa and sensationalist epistemology implicitly rejected the doctrine of original sin; gave nurture rather than nature primary importance in forming a child's mind and character; and suggested that love and reason instructed a child more effectively than external restraint and coercion. Children were not inherently depraved beings whose sinful natures had to be curbed and their obstinate wills broken. Instead their minds were blank, impressionable slates and their characters were to be molded by responsible, loving parents. Not only was Locke's own work often reprinted, but by the 1740s his ideas were popularized in a growing body of didactic literature.[4] In addition, as Jay Fliegelman has discussed, a striking number of English and American novels in the later eighteenth century preached the "Lockean gospel," dramatizing the problems of parental tyranny and filial disobedience.[5]

Lockean principles of childrearing did not translate into practice immediately, uniformly, or universally. Philip Greven's work on childrearing and religion suggests the persistence of an "evangelical" approach to childrearing, that is, an approach that was authoritarian, often brutally harsh, and emphasized the arduous struggle against wickedness necessary to avoid damnation. Evangelical childrearing practice was reinvigorated by the Great Awakening of the 1740s and continues into the twentieth century. Yet along with this pattern, other styles of childrearing, the "moderate" and "genteel," were consistent with Lockean ideas and were becoming familiar currency in the mid- and late eighteenth century.[6] These ideas conformed to a model of family life very different from the one prevailing in colonial America. Lockean ideas promoted a special place for children and childrearing within the family and gave the relationship between parents and children unique importance. Parents—not kin, not masters, not neighbors— held the greatest responsibility for and exerted the greatest influence over children. And as the relationship between parents and children tightened, the relationship between family and community loosened. As Philippe Ariès writes, when the eighteenth-century family organized itself around the child, it "raised the wall of private life between the family and society."[7]

One effect of Lockean ideas on parent-child relations was to undermine patriarchal authority within the family. Other factors contributed to this erosion, including economic changes. One of the props of patriarchal authority, in New England at least, was control over a limited supply of land. Greven has presented the starkest picture of the ways in which fathers influenced their sons' choices and limited their independence by controlling their inheritance.[8] But in many areas of New England by the 1730s and in many more by the 1760s, the steady subdivision of lands and their declining productivity meant that fathers had less and less to offer their sons in return for obedience. Sons typically faced the choice of buying land for themselves or migrating in search of better opportunities; either way, they chose a life of greater independence from their fathers. Both the original strength of patriarchal control and the steepness of its decline in colonial America have probably been exaggerated: the evidence on the strength of patriarchy in other regions is more mixed; patriarchal relations in the South actually may have strengthened in the eighteenth century; and evidence even from New England often reveals remarkable tenacity in eighteenth-century patriarchs.[9] But on balance it seems clear that patriarchal control faced increasingly stiff challenges in the eighteenth century, from practical as well as ideological sources.

In fact, the challenges to paternal authority belonged to a much broader reconsideration of the nature of authority in the mid- and late eighteenth century. Patriarchalism as a political ideology had weakened under attacks from the mid-seventeenth century on and declined rapidly in influence after 1690.[10] The Great Awakening further exploded traditional ideas of authority and social order in the colonies. The ideas of the Great Awakening emphasized the essential division of regenerate and unregenerate rather than social distinctions; undermined the establishment of churches; and questioned the foundations of social and political authority as well. Its solvent effects on traditional forms of authority appeared on many levels, from conflicts within families to open attacks on social and political elites.[11]

One area in which changing conceptions of authority clearly had an effect was in the use of a familial paradigm for political authority. For most political thinkers of the seventeenth century, authority within the state mirrored patriarchal authority within the family; even the critics of Sir Robert Filmer, the foremost theorist of political patriarchalism, accepted his assumptions on this point to at least some degree.[12] Colonial Americans accepted the familial paradigm as it applied to politics within the colonies and also as a description of their relationship to England. As one historian has argued, "the parent-child analogy was no mere decorative metaphor, but rather the paradigmatic basis for . . . an understanding of the imperial union."[13] But by the middle of the eighteenth century, the familial ideal itself was changing radically, with equally radical implications for politics. Fliegelman has demonstrated persuasively the thematic connections between the fundamental reconsideration of family relations and values in the eighteenth century and the changing bases of political authority. A host of eighteenth-century popular novels, influential on both sides of the Atlantic—*Robinson Crusoe* and *Clarissa* foremost among them—justified filial disobedience in response to parental tyranny. The political echoes were unmistakeable: John Adams himself said, "The people are Clarissa."[14] As Fliegelman argues, "The problems of family government addressed in the fiction and pedagogy of the period—of balancing authority with liberty, of maintaining a social order while encouraging individual growth—were the larger political problems of the day translated into the terms of daily life."[15] By the late eighteenth century, the traditional familial model no longer fitted with political views that stressed the voluntary, contractual nature of political relations. By the late eighteenth century, in fact, the traditional model no longer described family life.[16]

The strain on the familial model is only one of many indications of a changing conception of authority both within the family and beyond it. Other evidence also suggests the emergence—halting, incomplete—of a new understanding of family and community life, with different assumptions and expectations. The second half of the eighteenth century, and particularly the period after the Revolution, introduced a new emphasis on personal happiness in marriage as well as the autonomy of the partners. In June 1775 after leaving England and his own unhappy marriage behind, Thomas Paine published "Reflections on Unhappy Marriages." Here Paine upholds the importance of affection in marriage and endorses these words of "an American savage": "if any should be found so wretched among us as to hate where the only commerce ought to be love, we instantly dissolve the bond: God made us all in pairs: each has his mate somewhere or other; and tis our duty to find each other out since no creature was ever intended to be miserable."[17]

New expectations manifested themselves at both the beginning and the end of marriages. By the late eighteenth century, parental direction and economic considerations increasingly yielded to personal preference and affection in choosing a spouse. Most colonies continued to require parental consent for children's first marriages, but children began to wield their own weapons in intergenerational battle. In New England, it has been suggested, young couples wrung consent to marry from their parents by deliberately conceiving a child. In Hingham, Massachusetts, for example, the rate of premarital pregnancy rose from 10 percent of all conceptions in 1700 to 30 percent in 1750, and in Bristol, Rhode Island, half the women married between 1740 and 1760 gave birth within eight months.[18] This phenomenon suggests both declining parental control and rising expectations within marriages.

And when these expectations were frustrated, they increasingly led to demands for divorce. In a study of eighteenth-century Massachusetts divorce petitions, Nancy Cott found a steep increase in petitions after the middle of the century; of petitions and decrees recorded between 1692 and 1786, more than half came after 1764, and more than a third after 1774.[19] Cott attributes the increase to a new spirit of self-assertion and generally "modernizing" attitudes toward marriage.[20] The numbers of divorce petitions rose before any changes in the law itself; in fact, after considering a 1787 case from Pennsylvania in which arbitrators provided for a separation where the law did not, Marylynn Salmon concludes that, "As such a case of community initiative demonstrates, popular attitudes favored easier divorce laws long before lawmakers acted to create them."[21] It is by no means clear that these changes in attitudes and the accessibility of divorce significantly improved women's legal position,[22] but they do indicate different expectations of marriage and the duties it imposed. This shift, not only in marriage but in family life as a whole, appears in other regions as well. Writing of the Chesapeake, Daniel Blake Smith notes that "what is most striking in the post-1750 period is the development of a more openly affectionate, intimate family environment in which emotional attachments were deeply valued, indeed cherished."[23]

In the larger community too, relationships changed as firmer boundaries between private life and public influence began to be recognized. Colonial neighbors had assumed not only the right but the duty to supervise one another's lives. In the second half of the eighteenth century that assumption breaks down; it is replaced by a new caution about interfering in personal matters and a new regard for privacy. In 1747 John Barnard warned that some matters are better left untouched. Writing of "other People's Quarrels" he advised: "Be likewise warily silent in all concerns as are in matter of dispute between others: for he that blows the coals in quarrels he hath nothing to do with, has no right to complain if the sparks fly in his face; it being extremely difficult to interfere so happily, as not to give offence to either one party or the other."[24] A Pennsylvania man put the matter succinctly fifty years later. When John Owens, curious about his neighbor's nighttime visitor, "proposed going to see who it was," his brother refused, "saying that offence might be given in a matter which was none of his concern."[25] Owens went anyway, which suggests the persistence of old habits as well as the power of nosiness, but his brother's objection strikes a new note in the conduct of personal relationships and signals a shift in attitudes.

Another measure of changing relations in the community, and in the relationship of the individual to the community, lay in the attenuating power of slander. By the late eighteenth century, slander had lost much of the emotional freight it had carried throughout the colonial period. The frequency of slander suits declined, and their focus was increasingly restricted to economic concerns or the importance of a good business reputation.[26] Individuals who were slandered rarely faced the same public scrutiny, condemnation, or lamentable consequences that earlier victims had feared. Like many plaintiffs before him, Solomon Inglee of Plymouth claimed, in suing Jacob Albertson for slander in 1795, that "his good name had been greatly injured, he had been rendered liable to criminal prosecution, and he had 'undergone a great deal of fatigue and bodily labour to falsify the said rumours.'" But unlike most plaintiffs throughout the colonial period, Inglee agreed to a private arbitration and settlement. Inglee revealed none of the interest in public vindication so remarkable in earlier cases.[27] This suggests the greater insulation of the individual from criticism in the community and a considerably less urgent need for public approval. Andrew Jackson's mother spoke for a more privatized, more individualistic society, as well as a rougher kind of justice, when she taught young Andrew not to sue for such things as slander: "Always *settle them cases yourself!*"[28]

Furthermore, by the end of the century the community found it increasingly difficult to impose its views, even if it could justify them. The size of towns, the ease of movement, ethnic diversity, the weakening of religious sanctions—all tended to diminish the community's ability to enforce its demands. Population growth alone presented a formidable challenge to the cohesiveness of community life. The white population of British North America not only grew substantially through the eighteenth century but, outside New England, grew more diverse. The population of New England, the region best documented, grew very rapidly in the seventeenth century and then, after about 1670, grew at a steady—but still quite high—rate of about 2.4 percent; this meant that the population of New England nearly doubled every twenty-five years. After 1670 the Chesapeake posted a slightly higher annual growth rate of 2.7 percent, and its population was far more diverse than New England's: more than 30 percent of the white population was non-English, primarily Scots and German. The Middle Atlantic colonies grew at a spectacular rate, about 3.4 percent a year from the 1690s to the end of the colonial period. High rates of immigration to the Middle Colonies continued through the eighteenth century, with the result that by 1790 non-English Europeans and their descendants made up more than half the population. The lower South, despite almost certainly the highest mortality rates in the colonies, grew after the 1690s at a rate of roughly 4.4 percent a year; its white population showed the same kind of ethnic diversity as the Middle Colonies.[29]

And this growing population was mobile. As early as the 1720s, New Englanders had begun to escape population pressures and declining land productivity by migration to western Massachusetts and New York. The cessation of hostilities between the British and the French and the Treaty of Paris in 1763 opened the trans-Appalachian frontier for settlement—settlement that proceeded despite the ineffective effort by the British to prevent it in the Proclamation of 1763. The northern frontier too grew remarkably quickly through large-scale migration. In 1770, for instance, Maine and Vermont had populations of less than 10,000; by 1776 they had more than doubled, reaching 20,000.[30] At the same time, immigration to the colonies continued to transform American society. Bernard Bailyn has painted an illuminating portrait of the impact of European immigration and settlement in the era of the Revolution. From Nova Scotia to the Floridas, from the eastern coast to the Ohio Valley, this was a society of extraordinary dynamism and diversity.[31]

The rapid growth of the colonial population, its fluidity, and its diversity (outside New England) all worked against the values and enforcement of community life which had rested, to at least some degree, on stasis, homogeneity, and consensus. Authorities bemoaned the loss of their former influence but could not restore it. In 1764 exasperated Maryland church officials could only record their dismay that, after frequent warnings to stop illegal cohabitation, a couple did "not in the least [mind] or [pay] any regard to our severall Admonitions [but] still continue in and follow their illegall Practices."[32] Informal pressures proved no more effective. The force of community opinion dissipated as towns grew and individuals experienced for the first time not only privacy but relative anonymity. Even William Bentley, who made it his business to keep track of his neighbors in Salem, complained in 1791 that "the parties married this evening were not in the most respectable condition, but were entire strangers to me."[33]

Salem of course was a fairly large and active commercial town. But even New England villages, the strongholds of community life, felt these changes by the end of the century. The pastor of Rockingham, Vermont, offered a virtual catalogue of social changes in late-eighteenth century America. "The unhappy disputes in Politics which at several times have run so high among us, have evidently been unfavourable to the flourishing of Religion," he wrote in 1798. The splintering of churches that followed the Great Awakening had taken its toll. The "disputes and divisions in Respect to Religious principles which have had a great run among us. tho' they may not have lessened the Quantity of Religion, have been unfavourable to the Communion and Numbers of the Church." Turning to broader problems, he observed that the "increase of Wealth in this Town and the Introduction of Luxuries, the Changes in Civil Government, the endeavours and attempts which have been made for Obtaining some Publick funds for providing a decent house and supporting Public Worship therein, and the disappointements which attended these attempts, and the common Disputes which have arisen in Civil matters"—all vitiated "the flourishing state of outward Religion among us."[34] Community life in America had indeed undergone a sea change if villages such as Rockingham could feel its effects so completely.

By the late eighteenth century, then, many of the daily realities of family and community life, many of the assumptions and conditions on which that life had rested throughout the colonial period, had changed or weakened. By the end of the century, the ideology and conduct of private life as colonial Americans had conceived it yielded to a new definition of the family and its relation to the community, along with new expectations for the individual and society, which received full-blown expression in the first part of the nineteenth century. In practice, this paradigm was far more circumscribed by class, by region, and by religion than the colonial paradigm was. In its details, these new standards of family life described primarily the lives of northern, middle-class, relatively urban, mainstream Protestant families. On the central question of the relation of the family to the community or to the state, however, this paradigm did apply broadly, and it sharply distinguished private life in colonial society from private life in nineteenth-century America. But even as this new pattern responded to changes in eighteenth-century American society, and even as it resolved some tensions in colonial society, it rested on still other tensions, on other unresolved questions. These tensions would prove especially acute in the definition of authority and power in the new republic, in gender relations, and in the proper degree of individual responsibility to society.

At the heart of the redefinition of private life lay a new conception of the family. By the turn of the century, the ideal family was understood to be affectionate, voluntaristic, and private; this has in fact been characterized as the "republican" family.[35] "It is a duty to exclude everything permanently disagreeable from the family," Catherine Sedgwick wrote, "for home should resemble heaven in happiness as well as love."[36] Marriage was to be a voluntary contract based on mutual affection. As one American magazine put it in 1784, "Wherein does the happiness of the married state consist? In a mutual affection, a similarity of tempers, a reciprocal endeavour to please, and an invariable aim to each other's comfort"; according to another in 1790, "Where there is a necessary union of persons, of cares and of interests, there a union of hearts and affections is indispensable."[37]

Changes in the law in this, "the formative era of American domestic-relations law," reflected and ratified this new conception of marriage.[38] As Michael Grossberg has shown, in the late eighteenth and early nineteenth centuries, the law increasingly emphasized the contractual, consensual nature of marriage. In addition, in a departure from colonial practice, the law emphasized that while marriages had social consequences they were private compacts rather than public institutions. As Grossberg put it, "Though the law continued to portray marriage as a civil contract, in a vital transition the accent shifted from the first word to the second."[39] Divorce reform came slowly in the postrevolutionary era, an incomplete concession to the greater autonomy of the partners. In 1785 Pennsylvania enacted the most liberal divorce statute in the new states, providing absolute divorces for adultery, willful desertion for four years, bigamy, and knowledge of sexual incapacity before marriage; Connecticut and Massachusetts continued to allow absolute divorce for adultery, desertion, and uncontrollable cruelty; New York passed its first divorce statute in 1778, under which the Court of Chancery could grant a divorce for adultery and separations for cruelty and desertion; the Virginia and Maryland assemblies began to enact private bills for divorce, a prerogative they surrendered to the courts only in the 1840s. As so often in American history, South Carolina proved a conspicuous exception: South Carolina law made no provision for absolute divorce in any circumstances. Although divorces remained fairly rare and difficult to obtain, the numbers of both divorce suits and separations increased in the postrevolutionary period.[40] Lawmakers and judges remained persuaded that strong marital and family ties were crucial to the well-being of the state, as the resistance to broader divorce reform demonstrates. But by the nineteenth century, the law reflected a different understanding of how the state might best define and support stable families; at the same time, it reduced drastically the scope for state intervention in married life.[41]

As in the case of marriage, ideas about childrearing and the relationship between parents and children also changed in this period. The late eighteenth century saw a distinctively new emphasis on the role of the mother in childrearing.[42] Colonial writers had often blurred the distinction between father and mother in delineating childrearing responsibilities, usually addressing their advice to the generic "parent." In fact, insofar as one parent enjoyed special prominence, it had been the father. Cotton Mather, in glossing the proverb "A wise son maketh a glad father, but a foolish son is the heaviness of his mother," observed that "the Father ordinarily has most Share in procuring, and most Sense in perceiving, the Wisdom of his Children. When Children are come to such Maturity, that their Wisdom does become Observable, ordinarily the Mother has more dismissed them from her Conversation than the Father has from his."[43]

But in the late eighteenth century, the mother moves to the foreground. The responsibilities and special purposes of motherhood receive careful elaboration; before this period, only one advice book published in the colonies addressed itself specifically to mothers, but now "advice to mothers" proliferates.[44] Mothers are portrayed as uniquely fitted to care for children. In part, this was a simple matter of practicality. From the late eighteenth century on, as the separation of work from the household became more usual, mothers remained home to care for children while their husbands left for work.[45] As a New Hampshire clergyman put it, "Business, and many cares, call the father abroad, but home is the mother's province—here she reigns sole mistress the greatest part of her life."[46] Supposed female attributes deepened this division of labor; increasingly, maternal affection was contrasted with paternal harshness. A 1797 tract, for instance, asked:

Where are the tender feelings, the cries, the powerful emotions of nature?
Where is the sentiment, at once sublime and pathetic, that carries every feeling
to excess? Is it to be found in the frosty indifference and the rigid severity of so
many fathers? No; it is in the warm impassioned bosom of the mother . . .
These great expressions of nature, these heartrending emotions, which fill us
at once with wonder, compassion and terror, always have belonged, and always will belong to women. They possess . . . an inexpressible something,
which carrie[s] them beyond themselves. They seem to discover to us new
souls, above the standard of humanity.[47]

The exaltation of motherhood received a final boost from the requirements of a republican society: as the reponsibility for cultivating
a republican citizenry came to rest first with mothers, their influence
widened in significance. Mothers were to inculcate civic virtue in their
sons, prepare them for membership in republican society. Mothers, the
minister William Lyman announced in 1802, "hold the reins of government and sway the ensigns of national prosperity and glory. Yea, they
give direction to the moral sentiments of our rising hopes and contrib-
ute to form their moral state."[48] The most influential proponent of this
view, Benjamin Rush, argued in his *Thoughts Upon Female Education*
(1787) that in order to fulfill this trust, women themselves had to be
better educated. And in fact, between 1780 and 1830, women's literacy
and opportunities for education improved significantly—but always
circumscribed by the definition of women's education as a means to
promote the republican experiment. In explaining the goals of wom-
en's education, one graduate of a female academy clearly marked its
limits: "A woman who is skilled in every useful art, who practices every
domestic virtue . . . may, by her precept and example, inspire her brothers, her husband, or her sons, with such a love of virtue, such just ideas
of the true value of civil liberty . . . that future heroes and statesmen,
when arrived at the summit of military or political fame, shall exalt-
ingly declare, it is to my mother I owe this elevation."[49]

Motherhood and mothers gained stature in tandem with childrearing and children. The nineteenth-century middle-class family, steeped
in both Lockean psychology and liberal Protestantism, placed the child
at its center. The law also gave increasing prominence to the rights of
children, rejecting the view that children were the property of their parents. In an 1838 custody decision, a Maine federal district judge observed that "as soon as a child is born, he becomes a member of the
human family, and is invested with all the rights of humanity."[50] A

father's right, according to an 1852 law treatise, was "not an absolute one, and is usually made to yield when the good of the child, which, especially according to the modern American decision, is the chief matter to be regarded, requires that it should."[51] The emergence of the "best interests of the child" doctrine joined with the spreading view of women as uniquely fit for childrearing to chip away at the primacy of fathers' rights over children. The presumption of paternal rights and paternal custody remained powerful, but in the early nineteenth century it was no longer absolute.[52]

Apprenticeship law in the early nineteenth century reflected some of this reorientation of children's status—and in fact changes in apprenticeship itself demonstrated much of the larger reorientation of family and community in this period. In undermining the presumption of paternal control and in stressing the state's interest in the welfare of the child, early nineteenth-century legal decisions seemed to open the way to emphasizing the familial nature of apprenticeship and strengthening a master's parental role. But in reality something very different happened in the late eighteenth and early nineteenth centuries. The character of apprenticeship—and the judicial disposition of children— diverged very sharply according to class lines, with profound implications for the class basis of later family law. In its legal forms and appearance, voluntary apprenticeship survived well past the Revolution—but several factors diminished its importance and use. The expanding commercial and early industrial economy drew much more heavily on free labor than on older forms of dependent labor; a gap between employers and employees widened in this period, a gap that did not encourage familial bonds; the decline of craft labor reduced the demand for training apprentices; and, finally, the greater emphasis on maternal nurture and the importance of childrearing and the home increased the desire of middle-class parents to keep their children in the bosom of the family.[53]

But if voluntary apprenticeship declined in practice, involuntary apprenticeship flourished, primarily as a form of poor relief. Authorities had always encouraged involuntary apprenticeship or putting out largely for poor children; now they did so exclusively and explicitly for poor children. Georgia authorities articulated this policy as early as 1743: children who were destitute, liabilities to the parish, were put out; "but if any Person will maintain them, so that they are not chargeable to the Parish, then the Parish doth not meddle with them."[54] In theory, the laws of apprenticeship protected children whether their ap prenticeship was voluntary or involuntary. But the differences between voluntary and involuntary apprenticeship proved enormous, and the "equal" protections of the law evoke Anatole France's observation that, in its "majestic equality," the law forbids rich and poor alike to sleep under bridges at night. In reality, what protections the law offered were inconsistently enforced. Poor children were commonly, and not surprisingly, bound out on terms inferior to those of voluntary apprentices; freed black children fared especially badly.[55]

Ironically, the "best interests of the child" doctrine increased the courts' willingness to apprentice poor children for their own good, especially since in the minds of many judges poverty itself sufficed to make an environment unfit for a child. As the Indiana Supreme Court ruled in 1841, "Overseers of the poor have no right to meddle with the children of living parents, unless they be found unable to maintain them."[56] They were not called overseers of the poor for nothing. And, as Michael Grossberg notes, "Judges, like most propertied Americans of the nineteenth century, assumed that dependent poverty was but one component of an unsalubrious nexus: ignorance, moral license, idleness."[57] The appearance of immorality or irregularity or deviance of some sort often prompted authorities to act. In 1812, for instance, a Maryland court removed John Matzon from his home because he was "likely to be brought up in a very improper manner, the mother of him the said John living with a negro man."[58]

Courts soon extended this logic to justify the commitment of poor children to asylums. In Ex Parte Crouse, the Pennsylvania Supreme Court ruled, in defiance of her father's wishes, that Mary Ann Crouse should remain in the Pennsylvania House of Refuge. The girl, according to the judges, had "been snatched from a course which would have ended in confirmed depravity; and, not only is the restraint of her person lawful, but it would be an act of extreme cruelty to release her."[59] Families like the Crouses were vulnerable to state intervention because they failed to meet middle-class standards of family life. By their dependency, courts assumed, they forfeited the full rights of membership in a republican society; moreover, their dependence threatened that society. The law, then, as Grossberg observes, "placed the poor and deviants in a dependent legal position that matched their economic, material, and cultural ones. As with race, family law treated them with special, and generally repressive, treatment."[60] In the colonial period, all families contended with the review of their neighbors and authorities. By the early nineteenth century, only poor families had to submit to continued moral supervision and legal coercion. The middle-class family, except in extraordinary circumstances, regulated itself.

Ideally, even the middle-class child regulated itself. Early nineteenth-century childrearing stressed the value of self-restraint, self-discipline, and self-censure. Catherine Sedgwick's extremely popular novel *Home,* first published in 1835, illustrated just such an approach to childrearing. In a chapter entitled "A Glimpse at Family Government," the Barclay family is gathered in full force around the hearth: father reading the newspaper, mother and daughters pursuing a domestic task, the youngest child Haddie playing with the kitten. The plot thickens. Haddie gives the kitten a kite belonging to her brother Wallace, and a treasured possession. The kitten, following some relentless and inscrutable feline instinct, shreds the kite. Wallace, aged eight or so, enters the room to find the tattered remnants of his kite and, in an access of fury, seizes the unfortunate kitten and plunges it into a pot of scalding water. After several moments of horrified silence, Haddie generously observes that Wallace must feel great remorse for having done such a terrible thing. Wallace, however, feels no such thing. His father sends him to his room, saying "You have forfeited your right to a place among us. Creatures who are the slaves of their passions are, like the beasts of prey, fit only for solitude."

For several days Wallace is quarantined from his family, leaving his room only to attend school. Finally Wallace presents himself to his father, says that he understands the value of this lesson and that he has learned to curb his temper. The proof of his reform lay in the fact that on that very day, though much provoked by the school bully, Wallace bit back angry words and stayed his hand. Only after passing through this trial did Wallace feel worthy to rejoin the company of his family. Although only the most dull-witted of readers could have missed the point here, Sedgwick spells it out. "Mr. Barclay held whipping, and all such summary modes of punishment, on a par with such nostrums in medicine as peppermint and lavendar, which suspend the manifestation of the disease, without conducing to its cure. He believed the only effectual and lasting government—the only one that touches the springs of action, and in all circumstances controls them, is self-government."[61]

Evangelical Protestants provided a counterpoint to this tendency among middle-class liberal Protestants, persisting in their efforts to break the will of children and often relying on harsh means to do so. In 1831, Francis Wayland, a Baptist minister and president of Brown University, published an account of his struggle to break the will of his fifteen-month-old son. After a show of bad temper, Wayland isolated the baby for over a day until he became "mild and obedient."[62] But, increasingly, mainstream middle-class Protestants, like the Barclays, emphasized reason and self-restraint.

Thus by the early nineteenth century the family had come to define its special character, its unique role within society. At the same time the family, notably the middle-class family, increasingly distinguished itself and separated itself from society. Colonial writers had always considered the family a microcosm, a "lively representation" of society as a whole; and, throughout the colonial period, the lines between family and community were so faint and so often crossed as to be almost meaningless. But by the early nineteenth century the family is celebrated for its *difference* from the rest of society. The family becomes a refuge from the outside world, from an impersonal, mercenary, competitive world. It preserves moral values under siege elsewhere and buffers the individual from the wilderness. In a typical passage, one writer in 1830 coupled a paean to the family with an indictment of society:

We go forth into the world, amidst the scenes of business and of pleasure; we mix with the gay and the thoughtless, we join the busy crowd, and the *heart* is sensible to a desolation of feeling: we behold every principle of justice and of honor, and even the dictates of common honesty disregarded, and the delicacy of our moral sense is wounded; we see the general good, sacrificed to the advancement of personal interest; and we turn from such scenes, with a painful sensation, almost believing that virtue has deserted the abodes of men; again, we look to the *sanctuary* of *home;* there sympathy, honor, virtue are assembled; there the eye may kindle with intelligence, and receive an answering glance; there disinterested love is ready to sacrifice everything at the altar of affection.[63]

Colonial Americans had not felt, and would not have recognized, so sharp a break between the experience of the family and that of the larger world; for them, as John Demos has written, "family and community, public and private, formed part of the same moral equation."[64] But the changing character of the family, especially its increased emotional importance and the separation of work from the household, upset that equation.

The separation of family and society received its fullest elaboration in the nineteenth-century cult of domesticity, or the doctrine of "separate spheres." Whereas men took on the cares of business and politics, women devoted themselves to the life of the home. "To render *home* happy, is women's peculiar province; home is *her* world."[65] Advice books poured forth to explain the importance of women's distinct role and to instruct them in the science of domesticity. And just as the idea of home changed, so too did actual homes. Beginning in the 1840s, a steady stream of tracts, guides, and "pattern books" described model homes and the domestic settings that best promoted ideal family life. The romantic revival in architecture expressed and reified changing conceptions of domestic life. While Federalist architects had sought to portray such values as balance and moderation in public buildings— above all in Washington, D.C.—romantic reformers emphasized private behavior and expressed the kind of discipline and self-control that was central to middle-class domesticity. Romantic architecture created more specialization within the home, reflecting more specialized roles, and addressed itself especially to the needs of women. This style of architecture also placed much more emphasis on privacy within the home and gave scope to the individual, private development of family members. Indeed, as one historian has noted, "Middle class Americans valued privacy in the nineteenth century as never before."[66]

If architecture expressed a new sense of boundaries between family and society and even within the family, the law was central in defining and protecting those boundaries. American law itself was transformed in the generations before and after the Revolution.[67] The period before the Revolution witnessed increasing demands for a better educated bar and a more efficient, more professional legal system. Lawyers continued to battle deep popular prejudices against them, and they continued to be identified with social strife, disorder, and moral decay. In Virginia, for example, after 1755 the *Virginia Almanac* vented antilawyer sentiments increasingly often, printing morality tales about lawyers alongside cautionary tales about other social vices such as drinking and gambling.[68] One such story, in 1762, summed up common attitudes toward lawyers (as well as the Court-Country split in ideology) in its concluding line: "I know not . . . what distinction there may be in *London;* but I am sure, by sad experience, *we in the country know no difference between* a lawyer *and a liar.*"[69]

Nevertheless, the American bar expanded steadily in the generation before the Revolution and received better training; lawyers even began to enjoy "creeping respectability," in the words of John Murrin.[70] Ironically, in some colonies, notably Massachusetts, improvements in the training and status of lawyers resulted from their emulation of the British legal system, in effect, from an Anglicization of American law on the eve of the Revolution.[71] The state and federal constitutions lent greater coherence to the legal system and significantly expanded the powers of the judiciary. In fact, the powers of judges in such areas as domestic relations law grew so much that Michael Grossberg has referred to the creation of a judicial patriarchy in this period.[72] Views of the law and its role in society changed as well. An instrumentalist view of the law gained more and more prominence in this period; law was seen less as a set of fixed, fundamental principles and more as a flexible, creative instrument of social policy and social change. Morton Horwitz has traced the profound effects of this shift on nineteenth-century economic and social development.[73] Significantly, too, the law concerned itself less and less with traditional offenses against the community. As A. G. Roeber finds in the case of Virginia, the law was increasingly seen less as the enforcer of a homogeneous community's moral standards and more as an "instrument of a complex and diversified social order."[74]

The character of arbitration by the end of the colonial period demonstrated the growing reliance on the law and a growing demand for the precision, clarity, and formality that law brought to personal dealings. Arbitration was originally praised for its flexibility, its informality, its calculated vagueness, its commonsense fairness, its spirit of compromise—and always it was praised for saving people from the clutches of the law. But by the late eighteenth century the angle of vision had shifted dramatically, and these same attributes were seen as disadvantages. Implicit faith in the judgment and even the honesty of arbitrators fell away. In 1788 a Maryland petitioner complained of "prejudices and prepossessions" of arbitrators, and in 1770 Landon Carter refused an arbitration and chose to go to court instead "because from Long experience I had discovered Arbitrators not generally sworn acted partially upon one side or the other."[75] Even more telling, arbitration was criticized for differing from the law. A Maryland litigant complained in 1768 that in his case "exact care was not taken in the Stating and Settling" of the award, and in Pennsylvania a defendant objected to an award in 1795 because it was "not Sufficiently certain," not drawn "with Sufficient precision."[76] Another Pennsylvania litigant put the complaint most clearly in 1788. "The Referees have found for the Defendants," he objected, "when by Law they ought to have found for the Plaintiffs."[77]

Attitudes toward the law and arbitration had so flipflopped by 1767 that a Boston pamphleteer could ask whether an arbitration decision robbed a litigant "of his freedom, the natural and inherent right of a freeborn citizen, the darling privilege of every British subject? Is it not the privilege of every Englishman to be tried by a jury of twelve honest men."[78] This particular writer's vehemence undoubtedly stemmed from prevailing fears of British encroachment on liberties and legal rights, including fears of the overreaching power of vice-admiralty courts in the colonies. But it reflected the general tendency of the eighteenth century to formalize arbitration, to make it resemble the law, until finally it was replaced by the law altogether.[79] Even Quakers, who continued to rely on arbitration, explained their preference less by their consensual goals than by their desire to defeat the law. In 1787 the residents of Germantown, Pennsylvania, resolved to use arbitration because "we know not a more exalted act of charity and benevolence than that of presenting a shield against the rapacity of the law, which in the increase of costs, and delay of justice in our courts has become such an enormous and oppressive evil, that it is the duty of every real friend to the community to prevent the people from wasting their property by the chicane of laws, or corruption of our courts."[80] But they knew, as their defensive tone suggests, that they were fighting a losing battle against the preeminence of the law in the new republic.

Redefining the boundaries of the community and the purposes of the family constituted a revolution in private life in eighteenth-century America. In a broader sense, these developments demonstrated the emergence of private and public spheres in society, a separation that appeared in other areas as well, in politics, in religion, in education, in economics.[81] But its effects were nowhere more important or more pervasive than in the reorientation of family and community ties. The realignment of these relationships was a fundamental shift in our history. The character of that shift reveals much about the quality of social change in early America. It was critically important that the ties between family and community developed naturally, from the bottom up, and that they were widely accepted rather than imposed. By contrast, early modern German community life was supported more forcefully from above, by *Heimatrecht,* which ensured the preeminence and protected the insularity of the home towns. But, as Mack Walker argues, when the political and economic conditions that supported *Heima-*

trecht were destroyed in the creation of the Second Empire, the major features of home-town life were also destroyed. The experience was shattering in many ways for individual Germans, and its destruction of the social fabric had terrible consequences for Germany as a nation.[82]

Nothing like that happened in America. Even though American community life was also supported by legal forms and political institutions, the community rested on a more solid bedrock of family and neighborhood ties, of informal networks and local customs. These ties, which themselves changed gradually, made the community more flexible and adaptable, in a way more dynamic than the German home town. Though they could not prevent dislocations and the human costs of social change, they could cushion the impact. The challenges to community life in America came not from drastic political change but from inner tensions and gradual economic and social change. The effects of change on community life were ragged and uneven, and the adjustments to them gradual.[83]

The adjustments were in some ways incomplete and troublesome as well. Traditional conceptions of authority in a patriarchal, hierarchical society gave way to republicanism, individualism, and contractualism. Yet, from its very beginning, republican society in America rested on exclusion, the exclusion of blacks, native Americans, women, and the lower classes from power. The potential conflict between virtue and commerce also plagued America from the outset. The contradictions of republicanism revealed themselves most glaringly in the issue of slavery, but there were other signs of strain, other early challenges as well. Cathy Davidson's stimulating book *Revolution and the Word* suggests the subversive power of the novel in early America and its defiance of established authority. The sentimental novel subtly criticized the limitations placed on women, and the picaresque novel gave a voice to the classes of men excluded from political power and even from accepted political discourse. In fact, Davidson argues, many of the apparent contradictions and unsatisfying, forced resolutions of early American novels reflect the irreconcilable—and often unrecognized—conflicts and tensions of American society in the early nineteenth century.[84]

Changes in family life brought their own problems. Greater emphasis on affectionate private life raised the expectations of family members and greatly raised the possibility of disappointment. To ask, as Catherine Sedgwick did, that home resemble heaven in happiness, was to ask for trouble. When divorces became easier to obtain, the rising divorce rate testified eloquently to the higher and perhaps unrealistic expectations of marriage and family life.[85] The problem was especially acute for women, who were specially charged with family happiness. "The task of perfecting the home," as Kirk Jeffrey notes, "was ultimately an impossible one," and it made women's role inevitably a frustrating one.[86] The cult of domesticity, even as it glorified women's position, proved an effective trap. The doctrine of separate spheres undercut and delayed recognition of equality of women, and women's identification with family life and family responsibilities erected a formidable stumbling block to full equality. The putative benefits of the doctrine, such as the extension of women's influence into such areas as reformism, must be understood within the strict confines of political and social inequality. Even the ideal of companionate marriage, which promised women a kind of domestic parity, must be seen alongside the crippling legal and economic disabilities of women, disabilities that made the idea of companionate marriage something of an oxymoron. As Suzanne Lebsock has wryly observed, companionate marriage "was rather like the companionship between a seven-year-old and a ten-year-old: They may have the best of times together, but everyone knows who is in charge."[87]

Finally, in many ways the relationship between family and society remained ambiguous and troubled. The scope of legal intervention in family life narrowed as domestic-relations law accorded privacy and autonomy to middle-class families. Still the poor, the dependent, and the deviant remained subject to the direction and coercion of the law and of public authorities. The law retained its influence in many areas of private life, including divorce, contraception, abortion, child welfare, homosexuality, and sexual equality. Domestic-relations law rests on the premise that society has some stake in how individuals and families conduct their private life. But the boundaries of society's interest in private life have shifted, and continue to shift, and how far the law may direct or constrain family and individual behavior remains open to debate.[88]

Just as the extent of society's responsibility for individuals and families remains a troublesome question, so does the extent of the individual's responsibility to society. In the eighteenth century, the shift in focus inward—to the self, to the family—diminished engagement with the larger society and discouraged commitment to public life. Jan Lewis has perceptively traced the gradual abdication of public responsibility by the Virginia gentry in the postrevolutionary period, as civic virtue and civic responsibility gave way to an emphasis on private happiness and domestic affection.[89] Jay Fliegelman observes that "as the loss of the family had been the price of choosing the world . . . so the price of choosing the family is the loss of the world, a sense of anxious separateness from it."[90]

That price seems disturbingly high to many who call for greater responsibility and accountability for society. The question of how the individual defines his or her responsibility to society not only continues in our own time but seems to have gained new urgency. *Habits of the Heart,* a recent work from a group led by Robert Bellah, explores just this tension between individualism on the one hand and community and commitment on the other.[91] Other works, notably Richard Sennett's *The Fall of Public Man* and Christopher Lasch's *The Culture of Narcissism,* take a harsher line, offering acute and troubling critiques of a society that has lost its sense of public responsibility.[92] Such works are often deeply flawed. Their criticisms of modern society carry more than a hint of nostalgia, a yearning for harmonious, cooperative communities that are hard to locate in the historical record; colonial America certainly offers no such model. Moreover, they often construe public and political life in narrow and stultifying terms, ignoring what feminists and others have argued persuasively, that the personal *is* political. But, whatever their flaws, such works address a fundamentally important question, a question that lay at the heart of the relationship between family and community in colonial America, and a question that remains open today: To what extent is private life a right or a luxury?

Primary Sources

Manuscript Sources

MARYLAND. Hall of Records, Annapolis

COURT RECORDS

Chancery Court Proceedings, vols. II–XXI, 1671–1791.
Testamentary Proceedings.

Allegany County
Orphans' Court Proceedings, liber A, 1791–1820.

Anne Arundel County
Court Judgments and Proceedings, 11 vols., 1703–1723.
Guardians for Infants, 1791–1805.
Indentures, 1795–1820. 2 boxes.

Baltimore County
Baltimore County Court Proceedings, 1682–1686, 1691–1696, 1708–1725,
   1728–1734, 1736–1747, 1750–1751, 1754–1756. 26 vols.
Orphans' Court Proceedings, vols. I–IV, 1777–1803.

Caroline County
Caroline County [Criminal] Judgments, 1774–1792. 3 vols.

Cecil County
Cecil County Judgments, 1683–1701. 5 vols.
Indentures.

No. 1, Proceedings of the Orphans' Court: Minutes, 1798–1817.
No. 2, Proceedings of the Orphans' Court: Records of the Proceedings, 1817–1821.

Charles County
Court and Land Records, vols. V–XIX, 1674–1700.
Orphans' Court Proceedings, 1777–1803. 7 vols.

Frederick County
Frederick County Court Judgments, 1749–1770. 11 vols. (including Judgment Records, liber M (1763–1766), on microfilm, reel CR 11669).

Kent County
Kent County Court Proceeedings, 1676–1698, 1701–1705. 3 vols.
Orphans' Court Proceedings, 1803–1822. 2 vols.

Prince George's County
Circuit Court Records, 1699–1820. 49 vols.
Orphans' Court Proceedings, 1790–1805. 6 vols.

Queen Anne's County
Court Papers, 1733–1786. 1 box.
Orphans' Court Minutes, vols. I–III, 1778–1801.

St. Mary's County
Orphans' Court Proceedings, 1801–1809.
Orphans' Court Proceedings, 1807, 1810–1826.
Orphans' Court Minutes: no. 1 (1777–1786); no. 2 (1787–1789); no. 3 (1796–1801).

Talbot County
Proceedings of the Justices of the County Court in the Settlement of Orphans' Estates, 1751–1775. 2 vols.
Orphans' Court Proceedings, 1787–1825. 7 vols.
Orphans' Court Minutes, 1787–1804. 4 vols.

Somerset County
Orphans' Court Proceedings, liber E.B. no. O, 1778–1792.
Guardian Bonds, liber E.B. no. 2, 1778–1790.

Washington County
Washington County Judgments, 1782–1800. 5 vols.
Orphans' Court Minutes, 1786–1801.

Worcester County
Orphans' Court Proceedings, 1777–1800. 6 vols.

EPISCOPAL CHURCH RECORDS

Anne Arundel County
All Hallow's Parish. Vestry Minutes and Accounts, 1761–1845 (reel M221).
St. Anne's Church. Vestry Minutes, 1713–1767 (reel M1156); Vestry Papers, 1764–1788 (D15 [8–14]); Vestry Minutes and Accounts, 1767–1818 (reel M1156–1157).
St. James Parish (Lothian). Vestry Minutes, 1695–1820 (12320–21).

Baltimore City
St. Paul's Church. Vestry Minutes, June, 1777 (reel M994).
Trinity Church. Vestry Minutes, 1817 (reel M248).

Baltimore and Harford Counties
St. John's Church. Vestry Minutes, 1792–1822 (reel M679).

Calvert County
All Saints' Church, Sunderland. Vestry Minutes, 1703–1717, 1720–1753 (reel M269).
Christ Church, Port Republic. Vestry Minutes, 1781–1825 (reel M270).

Caroline, Queen Anne's and Talbot Counties
St. John's Church, Hillsboro. Vestry Records, 1752–1770 (G114).

Cecil County
St. Stephen's Church, Earleville. Vestry Minutes, 1693–1820 (reel M333).

Charles County
Old Durham Church, Ironsides. Vestry Minutes, 1774–1824 (reel M226).
Trinity Church, Newport. Vestry Minutes, liber A, 1750–1795 (reel M227, M228); liber B, 1802–1841 (reel M229, M260).

Dorchester County
Christ Church, Cambridge. Vestry Minutes, 1758–1886 (reel M680).

Harford County
St. George's Church, Penyman. Vestry Minutes: book A, 1718–1771 (reel M1157–1158); book B, 1772–1850 (reel M1158).

Kent County

St. Paul's Church, Fairlee. Vestry Minutes: vol. II, 1693–1726 (reel M302); vol. III, 1725–1799 (reel M303); vol. V, 1800–1862 (reel M303).

Shrewsbury Church, Kennedyville. Vestry Minutes: vol. II, 1701–1730 (reel M339); vol. III, 1745–1794 (reel M339); vol. IV, 1799–1822 (reel M339).

Queen Anne's County

St. Paul's Church, Centreville. Vestry Minutes, 1694–1762 (D376[1]); 1762–1819 (D376[2], reel M940).

St. Mary's County

All Faith Church, Huntersville. Vestry Minutes, libers A, B, C, 1692–1824 (reel M230, M250).

Christ Church, Choptico. Vestry Minutes, 1799–1825 (reel M231, M252).

Somerset County

St. Mark's Church, Kingston. Vestry Minutes, 1772–1821 (reel M347).

All Saints' Church, Monie. Vestry Minutes, 1766–1825 (reel M337).

Talbot County

Christ Church, Easton. Vestry Minutes, 1708–1710, 1717–1766 (reel M295, M296).

QUAKER MEETING RECORDS

Baltimore

Yearly and Half-Yearly Meetings in Maryland: Minutes, 1677–1821 (reel M547, M547a, M549).

Minutes of the Women's Meeting: Half Years, 1677–1683; Yearly Meeting, 1684–1790, 1759–1791, 1810, 1812 (reel M776).

Christian Advices, Yearly Meeting for Pennsylvania and New Jersey, 1681–1763 (reel M558).

Quarterly Meeting for the Western Shore

Minutes, 1680–1688, 1682–1702, 1736–1749, 1710–1822 (reel M571, M571a, M637).

Minutes of a Particular and 4th Monthly Meeting at Richard Harrison's, 1699–1716 (reel M571a).

Minutes of the Women Friends, 1775–1805 (reel M571, M571a).

Monthly Meeting at the Clifts
Minutes, 1677–1771 (reel M605, M637); 1698–1759 (reel M637); 1771–
1778 (reel M640); 1778–1782 (reel M639); 1772–1817 (reel M638).
Minutes of the Women's Meeting, 1776–1808 (reel M640).

Gunpowder Monthly Meeting
Minutes, 1739–1768 (reel M627, M627a); 1768–1784, 1785–1797 (reel
M627); 1797–1824 (reel M628).
Minutes of the Women Friends, 1739–1767 (reel M629); 1767–1776 (reel
M627); 1776–1819 (reel M629).

Virginia Yearly Meeting
Minutes, 1702–1825 (reel M810).
Minutes of the Women Friends, 1763–1825 (reel M811).

NEW YORK. Historical Documents Collection, Queens College, City University of New York

Minutes of the Court of General Quarter Sessions of the Peace, 1691–1776
(reel CMS1-CMS2).
Ulster County, Minutes of the Court of General Sessions of the Peace, 1731–
1750 (reel UC50).
Court of Oyer and Terminer, Kingston, Ulster County, June 1684 (reel UC
50).

PENNSYLVANIA. Pennsylvania State Archives, Harrisburg, Pennsylvania

Record Group 33: Records of the Supreme Court, Eastern District Minutes,
Dockets, Precepts, and Case Files of Oyer and Terminer, 1757–1761,
1763, 1765–1776, 1778–1827. 7 boxes; 2 vols.
Appearance and Continuance Dockets, vols. I–III, 1740–1764.
General Motions and Divorce Docket, 1750–1837 (GM); 1800–1805 (D).
Divorce Papers, 1786–1815. 3 cartons.
Miscellaneous Court Papers, carton 1, 1745–1806.
Rules of Reference and Reports of Referees, 1765–1837. 2 cartons.
Petitions, 1781–1813, carton 8.
Record Group 21: Miscellaneous Papers, Provincial Council, 1664–1775. 2
boxes.

Allegheny County
Orphans' Court Docket, vol. I, 1789–1820 (reel 866, 288).

Bedford County
Orphan Court Docket, vols. I–II, 1772–1814 (reel 5–23).

Bucks County
Orphans' Docket, 1683–1801 (reel 9–19–1–23).

Chester County
Orphans' Court Docket, vols. I–VII, 1716–1774 (reel 15–16).
Court of Quarter Sessions, Docket, 1714–1759; vols. A–E, 1759–1803 (reel 558,038 and 558,039).

Huntingdon County
Orphans' Docket, vol. A, 1788–1804 (reel 900–558).

Lancaster County
Miscellaneous Book; Orphans' Court Records, 1742–1767 (reel 36–19).

Philadelphia County
Orphans' Docket, books 1–6, 1719–1802 (reel 51–124–51–128).
Court of Quarter Sessions, vols. I–III, 1713–1784 (reel 46–111).

York County
Orphans' Court, vols. A–D, 1749–1781 (reel 67–11).

VIRGINIA. Virginia State Library, Richmond

Accomack County
Deeds, Wills [and Orders], 1663–1666 (reel 1).
Orders, 1666–1670 (reel 78).
Orders and Wills, 1671–1673, 1673–1676 (reel 2).
Orders, 1676–1678 (reel 79).
Wills, Deeds and Orders, 1678–1682 (reel 4).
Wills and Orders, 1682–1697 (reel 4).
Orders, 1690–1767 (reel 79–83).
Orphans' Accounts, 1741–1780 (reel 123).
Vestry Orders, 1723–1784 (reel 136).

Henrico County
Record Book, no. 2, Orders and Wills, 1678–1693. Transcript (reel 53).
Order Book, 1678–1693 (reel 53).

Lancaster County
Orders, 1655–1666 (reel 24).
Order Books, nos. 1–10, 1666–1756 (reel 24–28).

Middlesex County
Order Book, no. 1, 1673–1680 (reel 1).

Norfolk County
Order Book, 1675–1686, 1742–1755 (reel 53).
Deed Book 5, part 2, 1686–1695 (reel 2).
Deed Book A, 1637–1646 (reel 1).
Wills and Deeds B, 1646–1651 (reel 44).
Wills and Deeds D, 1656–1675 (reel 45).

Princess Anne County
Order Books 1–2, 1691–1717 (reel 38).
Minute Books 3–5, 1717–1744 (reel 39).

Surry County
Orders, 1671–1691 (reel 28).

Published Sources

"Abstract of the First Wills in the Probate Office, Plymouth." *New England Historic and Genealogical Register*, IV. Boston, 1850.
"Abstracts of Wills on File in the Surrogate's Office, City of New York, 1665–1800." *Collections of the New-York Historical Society*, XXV–XLI. New York, 1893–1909.
Acts and Resolves, Public and Private, of the Province of Massachusetts Bay, I. Boston, 1869.
Ambrose, Isaac. *The Well-Ordered Family*. Boston, 1762.
Ames, Susie, ed. *County Court Records of Accomack-Northampton, Virginia, 1632–1640*. Washington, D.C.: American Historical Association, 1954.
—— *County Court Records of Accomack-Northampton, Virginia, 1640–1645*. Charlottesville: University Press of Virginia, 1973.

Arnold, Samuel. *David serving his Generation.* Cambridge, Mass., 1674.

Balch, William. *Reconciliation with an Offended Brother, Explained and Inforced.* Boston, 1740.

Barnard, John. *A Present for an Apprentice.* Boston, 1747.

Bass, John. *A True Narrative of an Unhappy Contention in the Church at Ashford.* Boston, 1751.

Bates, Samuel A., ed. *Records of the Town of Braintree, 1640–1793.* Randolph, Mass.: Daniel H. Hoxford, 1886.

Belcher, Joseph. *Duty of Parents, and Early Seeking of Christ.* Boston, 1710.

Bellamy, Joseph. *The Law, Our School-Master.* New Haven, 1756.

Benson, John. *A Short Account of the Voyages, Travels and Adventures of John Benson.* N.p., n.d. American Antiquarian Society, Worcester, Mass.

Bentley, William. *The Diary of William Bentley.* 4 vols. Salem, Mass.: Essex Institute, 1905–1914; repr. 1962.

Blodgette, George, ed. "Early Church Records of Rowley, Massachusetts." Essex Institute, *Historical Collections,* XXXIV (1898), 77–116.

Bond, Carroll T., ed. *Proceedings of the Maryland Court of Appeals, 1695–1729.* Washington, D.C.: American Historical Association, 1933.

Boston Registry Department. *Boston Town Records.* 39 vols. Boston: Rockwell and Churchill, 1876–1909.

Bradford, William. *Of Plymouth Plantation.* Ed. by Samuel Eliot Morison. New York: Alfred A. Knopf, 1970.

Briggs, Lloyd Vernon, ed. *History and Records of the First Congregational Church, Hanover, Mass., 1727–1865.* Boston, 1895.

Brigham, Clarence, ed. *The Early Records of the Town of Portsmouth* [Rhode Island]. Providence: E. L. Freeman, 1901.

Brigham, William, ed. *The Compact, with the Charter and Laws of the Colony of New Plymouth.* Boston, 1836.

Brown, John. *The Examiner Examin'd. Or, an Answer to the Rev. Mr. Prescott's Examination of Certain Remarks on a Letter Relating to the Divisions of the First Church in Salem.* Boston, 1736.

Browne, William Hand et al., eds. *Archives of Maryland.* 72 vols. Baltimore: Maryland Historical Society, 1883–1972.

Calendar of Virginia State Papers, 1790–1792. 8 vols. Richmond, 1875–1890; repr. New York: Kraus Reprint, 1968. (Despite its title, this work contains material from 1652 to 1776.)

Calendar of Virginia State Papers and Other Manuscripts (1652–1839). 11 vols. Richmond, 1875–1893.

Cambridge, Mass. *The Records of the Town of Cambridge, 1630–1703.* 2 vols. Cambridge, 1901.

Cambridge Synod. *A Platform of Church Discipline* (1648). Cambridge, Mass., 1649.

Candler, Allen D., ed. *The Revolutionary Records of the State of Georgia.* 3 vols. Atlanta: Franklin-Turner Company, 1908.

Chamberlain, Mellen, ed. *A Documentary History of Chelsea [Mass.], 1624–1824.* 2 vols. Boston: Printed for the Massachusetts Historical Society, 1908.

Chamberlayne, C. G., ed. *The Vestry Book of Blisland (Blissland) Parish: New Kent and James City Counties, Virginia, 1721–1786.* Richmond: The Library Board, 1935.

—— *The Vestry Book of Kingston Parish, Mathews County, Virginia, 1679–1796.* Richmond: Old Dominion Press, 1929.

—— *The Vestry Book of Petsworth Parish, Gloucester County, Virginia, 1677–1793.* Richmond: The Library Board, 1933.

—— *The Vestry Book and Register of Bristol Parish, Virginia, 1720–1789.* Richmond, 1898.

—— *The Vestry Book and Register of St. Peter's Parish, New Kent and James City Counties, Virginia, 1684–1786.* Richmond: The Library Board, 1937.

—— *The Vestry Book of St. Paul's Parish, Hanover County, Virginia, 1706–1786.* Richmond, 1940.

—— *The Vestry Book of Stratton Major Parish, King and Queen County, Virginia, 1729–1783.* Richmond: The Library Board, 1931.

Chapin, Howard M., ed. *The Early Records of the Town of Warwick [Rhode Island].* Providence: E. A. Johnson, 1926.

Chauncy, Charles. *God's Mercy, Shewed to His People, in Giving Them a Faithfull Ministry and Schooles of Learning, for the Continual Supplyes Thereof.* Cambridge, Mass., 1655.

Cobbet, Thomas. *A Fruitful and Useful Discourse Touching the Honour due from Children to Parents, and the Duty of Parents toward their Children.* London, 1656.

Collections of the Rhode Island Historical Society, X. Providence: Printed for the Society, 1902.

Colman, Benjamin. *A Devout Contemplation of the Meaning of Divine Providence in the Early Death of Pious and Lovely Children.* Boston, 1714.

—— *The Duty and Honour of Aged Women.* Boston, 1711.

—— *The Honour and Happiness of the Vertuous Woman; More Especially Considered in the Two Relationships of Wife and Mother.* Boston, 1716.

Colonial Records of Pennsylvania: Minutes of the Provincial Council. 16 vols. Harrisburg and Philadelphia, 1838–1853.

The Colonial Records of the State of Georgia. 28 vols. Atlanta and Athens, 1904–1979.

Colonial Society of Pennsylvania. *Records of the Court of New Castle of Delaware, 1677–1681*. Lancaster: Wickersham Printing Company, 1904.

Cotton, John. *Spiritual Milk for Boston Babes in Either England.* Cambridge, Mass., 1656.

"Council Minutes [of New Netherland], 1638–1649." *New York Historical Manuscripts: Dutch*. IV, Baltimore: Genealogical Publishing Company, 1974.

Cox, John Jr., ed. *Oyster Bay Town Records, 1653–1763*. 6 vols. New York: Tobias Wright, 1916–1931.

Crozier, William Armstrong, ed. *Virginia County Records: Spotsylvania County, 1721–1800*. New York: Published for the Genealogical Association by Fox, Duffield, 1905.

Crumrine, Boyd, ed. "Minute Book of the Virginia Court Held at Fort Dunmore (Pittsburg) for the District of West Augusta, 1775–1776." *Annals of the Carnegie Museum*, I (1902), 525–569.

———— "Minute Book of the Virginia Court Held for Yohogania County, First at Augusta Town (Now Washington, Pa.), and Afterwards on the Andrew Heath Farm Near West Elizabeth, 1776–1780." *Annals of the Carnegie Museum*, II (1903), 71–140, 205–429.

Cummings, Archibald. *An Exhortation to the Clergy of Pennsylvania, at Philadelphia*. Annapolis, 1729.

Danforth, Samuel. *A Brief Recognition of New England's Errand into the Wilderness*. Cambridge, Mass., 1671.

Davenport, John. *A Discourse about Civil Government in a New Plantation whose Design is Religion*. Cambridge, Mass., 1663.

"Delaware Papers, 1664–1682." *New York Historical Manuscripts: Dutch*. XX-XXI, Baltimore: Genealogical Publishing Company, 1977.

Dexter, Franklin Bowditch, and Zara Jane Powers, eds. *New Haven Town Records, 1648–1684 and 1684–1769*. 3 vols. New Haven, 1917–1919, 1962.

Dod, John, and Robert Clever. *A Godly Forme of Household Government*. London, 1612.

Duvall, Lindsay O., ed. *Virginia Colonial Abstracts*. Series 2, 6 vols. Washington, D.C., and Wharton Grove, Virginia, 1952–1961.

The Earliest Volume of Staten Island Records, 1678–1813. New York: Historical Records Survey, WPA, 1942.

Ecclesiastical Records of the State of New York. 7 vols. Albany: J. B. Lyon, 1901–1905.

Edsall, Preston W., ed. *Journal of the Courts of Common Right and Chancery of East New Jersey, 1683–1702*. Philadelphia: American Legal History Society, 1937.

Eliot, John. *Communion of Churches*. Cambridge, Mass., 1665.

Evans, David. *Law and Gospel*. Philadelphia, 1748.

Farish, Hunter Dickinson, ed. *Journal and Letters of Philip Vickers Fithian, 1773–1774: A Plantation Tutor of the Old Dominion.* Williamsburg: Colonial Williamsburg, 1943.

Fernow, Berthold, ed. *The Minutes of the Orphan-masters of New Amsterdam, 1655–1663.* New York: Francis P. Harper, 1902.

———— *The Records of New Amsterdam, 1653–1674.* 7 vols. New York: Knickerbocker Press, 1897.

Fisk, Samuel. *A Just and Impartial Narrative of the Controversy between The Rev. Mr. Samuel Fisk the Pastor and a Number of the Brethren of the First Church of Christ in Salem.* Boston, 1735.

Fiske, John. *The Watering of the Olive Plant in Christ's Garden.* Cambridge, Mass., 1657.

Fleet, Beverly, ed. *Virginia Colonial Abstracts.* Series 1, 34 vols. Richmond, 1937–1949.

Folger, Peter. *A Looking Glass for the Times, or the Former Spirit of New England Revived in this Generation.* Boston, 1676.

Forbes, Harriette M., ed. *The Diary of the Rev. Ebenezer Parkman* (of Westborough, Mass.). Westborough Historical Society, 1899.

Fox, Dixon Ryan, ed. "The Minutes of the Court of Sessions (1657–1696), Westchester County, New York." *Publications of the Westchester County Historical Society,* II. White Plains, 1924.

Fox, George. *Gospel Family Order.* Philadelphia, 1701.

Frost, Josephine, ed. *Records of the Town of Jamaica, Long Island, New York, 1656–1751.* 3 vols. Brooklyn: Long Island Historical Society, 1914.

Gardiner versus Flagg. *A Short Vindication of the Conduct of the Referees in the Case of Gardiner vs Flagg, against the unjust Aspersions contained in two anonymous Pamphlets lately published and handed about.* Boston, 1767.

———— *Dr. Gardiner versus James Flagg, Merchant.* Boston, 1767.

———— *A Full Answer to the Pamphlet Intitled "A Short Vindication."* Boston, 1767.

———— *To Messieurs Edward Payne and Henderson Inches.* Boston, 1769.

———— *To the Public. A Small Pamphlet.* Boston, 1767 [?].

Gouge, William. *Of Domesticall Duties.* London, 1622.

Green, Samuel A., ed. *Early Church Records of Groton, Massachusetts, 1761–1830.* Groton, 1896.

Greene, Jack P., ed. *The Diary of Landon Carter.* 2 vols. Charlottesville: University Press of Virginia, 1965.

Gregorie, Anne King, and J. Nelson Frierson, eds. *Records of the Court of Chancery of South Carolina, 1671–1779.* Washington, D.C.: American Historical Association, 1950.

Hall, Clayton Colman, ed. *Narratives of Early Maryland, 1633–1684.* New York: Charles Scribner's Sons, 1910.

Hamlin, Paul and Charles Baker, eds. "Minutes of the Supreme Court of Judicature of the Province of New York, 1691–1704." *Collections of the New-York Historical Society*, LXXIX (1946). New York, 1952.

Hening, William Waller, ed. *The Statutes at Large: being A Collection of all the Laws of Virginia from the First Session of the Legislature, in the Year 1619*. 13 vols. Repr. Charlottesville: University Press of Virginia, 1969.

Hervey, James. *The Ministry of Reconciliation*. Philadelphia, 1760.

Higginson, John. *The Cause of God and His People in New-England*. Cambridge, Mass., 1663.

Hoadly, C.J., ed. *Records of the Colony and Plantation of New Haven, 1638–1649 and 1653–1664*. 2 vols. Hartford, 1857–1858.

Homes, William. *The Good Government of Christian Families Recommended*. Boston, 1747.

Hosmer, James K., ed. *Winthrop's Journal*. 2 vols. New York: Charles Scribner's Sons, 1908.

"Indentures of Apprentices, 1718–1727." *Collections of the New-York Historical Society*, XLIII (1909), 111–199.

"Indentures of Apprenticeship, 1694–1708." *Collections of the New-York Historical Society*, XVIII (1885), 565–622.

Jameson, J. Franklin, ed. *Narratives of New Netherland, 1609–1664*. New York: Charles Scribner's Sons, 1909.

Jarratt, Devereux. *The Life of the Rev. Devereux Jarratt*. Baltimore, 1806.

Keith, William. *The Experience of William Keith*. Utica, 1806.

Kingsbury, Susan, ed. *The Records of the Virginia Company of London*. 4 vols. Washington, D.C.: Government Printing Office, 1906, 1933, 1935.

"Kingston Court Records, 1661–1667." *New York Historical Manuscripts: Dutch*. XXV, part 1, Baltimore: Genealogical Publishing Company, 1976.

Konig, David, ed. *Plymouth Court Records*. 16 vols. Wilmington, Del.: Michael Glazier, 1978.

Lechford, Thomas. "Note-Book Kept by Thomas Lechford, Esq., Lawyer, in Boston, Massachusetts Bay, From June 27, 1638, to July 29, 1641." American Antiquarian Society, *Transactions and Collections*, VII (1885).

Lee, Richard. *A Short Narrative of the Life of Mr. Richard Lee*. Kennebunk, Me., 1804.

Lynn, Mass. *The Records of the Town Meeting of Lynn, 1691–1742*. 4 vols. Lynn Historical Society, 1949–1964.

Macfarlane, Alan, ed. *The Diary of Ralph Josselin, 1616–1683*. London: Oxford University Press, 1976.

Mack, Solomon. *Narrative of the Life of Solomon Mack*. Windsor, Conn., 1810 [?].

Mather, Cotton. *Cares About the Nurseries*. Boston, 1702.

—— *Corderius Americanus: An Essay Upon the Good Education of Children*. Boston, 1708.

———— *Early Religion, Urged in a Sermon, Upon the Duties Wherein, and the Reasons Wherefore, Young People Should Become Religious.* Boston, 1694.

———— *Family Religion Excited, and Assisted.* Boston, 1714.

———— *A Family Sacrifice.* Boston, 1703.

———— *A Family Well-Ordered.* Boston, 1699.

———— *A Good Master Well Served.* Boston, 1696.

———— *Help for Distressed Parents. Or, Counsels and Comforts for Godly Parents Afflicted with Ungodly Children.* Boston, 1695.

———— *Magnalia Christi Americana.* 2 vols. Hartford, 1820.

———— *Memorable Providences, Relating to Witchcrafts and Possessions.* Boston, 1689.

———— *Methods and Motives for Societies to Suppress Disorders.* Boston, 1703.

———— *Ornaments for the Daughters of Zion.* Boston, 1741.

———— *Orphanotrophium. Or, Orphans Well-Provided For.* Boston, 1711.

———— *Parental Wishes and Charges.* Boston, 1705.

———— *Parentalia.* Boston, 1715.

———— *Ratio Disciplinae Fratrum.* Boston, 1726.

———— *Repeated Warnings: Another Essay to Warn Young People.* Boston, 1712.

———— *The Will of a Father Submitted To.* Boston, 1713.

Mather, Eleazer. *A Serious Exhortation to the Present and Succeeding Gerneration in New England.* Cambridge, Mass., 1671.

Mather, Increase. *Pray for the Rising Generation, or a Sermon Wherein Godly Parents Are Encouraged to Pray and Believe for Their Children.* Boston, 1678.

Maxcy, Virgil, Rev. *The Laws of Maryland.* 3 vols. Baltimore: Philip Nicklin, 1811.

Minutes of the Common Council of the City of New York, 1675–1776. 8 vols. New York: Dodd, Mead, 1905.

Minutes of the Common Council of the City of New York, 1784–1831. 19 vols. New York, 1917.

Mitchell, Mary. *Short Account of the Early Part of the Life of Mary Mitchell.* New Bedford, Mass., 1812.

Moore, Caroline T., and Agatha Aimar Simmons, comps. and eds. *Abstracts of the Wills of the State of South Carolina, 1670–1740,* I. Columbia: R. L. Bryan, 1960.

Morgan, Joseph. *Love to Our Neighbours Recommended.* New London, 1727.

Morris, Richard B., ed. *Select Cases of the Mayor's Court of New York City, 1674–1784.* Washington, D.C.: American Historical Association, 1935.

Myers, Albert Cook, ed. *Narratives of Early Pennsylvania, West New Jersey and Delaware, 1630–1717.* New York: Charles Scribner's Sons, 1912.

"New Hampshire Province Records and Court Papers, 1680–1692." *Collections of the New Hampshire Historical Society,* VIII (1866).

New York. *The Laws and Acts of the General Assembly for their Majesties Province of New York* (1691). New York, 1694.

Norton, John. *The Heart of New-England Rent at the Blasphemies of the Present Generation.* Cambridge, Mass., 1659.

Nottingham, Stratton, comp. and ed. *Wills and Administrations of Accomack County, Virginia, 1663–1800.* First pub. 1931; repr. Cottonport, La.: Polyanthos, 1973.

O'Callaghan, E. B., ed. *The Documentary History of the State of New York.* 4 vols. Albany, 1819–1851.

——— *Documents Relative to the Colonial History of the State of New York.* 11 vols. Albany: Weed, Parsons, 1856–1861.

"Old Norfolk County Court Records, 1648–1681." *Essex Antiquarian,* I-XIII (1897–1909); Essex Institute, *Historical Collections,* LVI-LXVIII (1920–1932), LXX (1934).

Oliver, Fitch Edward, ed. *The Diary of William Pynchon* (of Salem). Boston: Houghton, Mifflin, 1890.

Paltsits, Victor Hugo, ed. *Minutes of the Executive Council of the Province of New York: Administration of Francis Lovelace, 1668–1673* (with "Collateral and Illustrative Documents"). 2 vols. Albany, 1910.

Parsons, Eben, ed. "First Book of Records of the First Church in Lynnfield." Essex Institute, *Historical Collections,* XXXIV (1898), 117–193.

Pennsylvania Archives. 122 volumes. Philadelphia and Harrisburg, 1852–1935.

Pierce, Richard D., ed. *The Records of the First Church in Salem, Massachusetts, 1629–1736.* Salem: Essex Institute, 1974.

"Plymouth Church Records, 1620–1859." Colonial Society of Massachusetts, *Collections,* XXII–XXIII. Boston, 1920, 1923.

Potter, Ray. *Memoirs of the Life and Religious Experiences.* Providence, 1829.

Prescott, Benjamin. *A Letter to a Friend, Relating to the Differences in the First Church at Salem.* Boston, 1735.

Probate Records of Essex County, Massachusetts. 3 vols. Salem: Essex Institute, 1916–1920.

"Probate Records of New Hampshire, 1635–1771." *New Hampshire State Papers,* XXXI–XXXIX. Concord, 1907–.

"Proceedings of the General Court of Assizes, New York City, 1680–1682, and Minutes of the Supreme Court of Judicature, 1693–1701." *Collections of the New-York Historical Society,* XLV (1912).

Providence, R.I. *Early Records of the Town of Providence.* 21 vols. Providence: Snow and Farnham, City Printers, 1892–1915.

Province and Court Records of Maine. 6 vols. Portland: Maine Historical Society, 1928–1975.

Records of the Church in Brattle Square, Boston, 1699–1872. Boston: The Benevolent Fraternity of Churches, 1902.

Records of the Colony of Rhode Island and Providence Plantations. 10 vols. Providence: J. R. Bartlett, 1856–1865; repr. New York: AMS Press, 1968.

Records of the Court of Assistants of the Colony of Massachusetts Bay, 1630–1692. 3 vols. Boston, 1901–1928.

Records and Files of the Quarterly Courts of Essex County, Massachusetts. 9 vols. Salem: Essex Institute, 1911–1975.

"Records of the First Church in Boston, 1630–1868." Colonial Society of Massachusetts, *Collections,* XXXIX–XLI. Boston, 1961.

Records of the First Church of Rockingham, Vermont, 1773–1839. Copied by Thomas Bellows Peck. Boston: David Clapp, 1902.

"Records of the Overseers of the Poor for the Old Town of Danvers, 1767–1768." Essex Institute, *Historical Collections,* II (1860), 85–92.

"Records of the Particular Court of Connecticut, 1639–1663." *Collections of the Connecticut Historical Society,* XXII. Hartford, 1928.

"Records of the Reformed Dutch Churches of Hackensack and Schraalenburgh, New Jersey." *Collections of the Holland Society of New York,* (1891).

"Records of the Reformed Dutch Churches of New Paltz, New York." *Collections of the Holland Society of New York,* III (1896).

"Records of the Suffolk County Court, 1671–1680." Colonial Society of Massachusetts, *Collections,* XXIX–XXX. Boston, 1933.

Records of the Town of Brookhaven. Port Jefferson, N.Y., 1888.

Records of the Town of East-Hampton. 5 vols. Sag Harbor, N.Y., 1887–1905.

Records of the Towns of North and South Hempstead, Long Island, New York. 8 vols. Jamaica, N.Y., 1896–1904.

Reed, H. Clay, and George J. Miller, eds. *The Burlington Court Book: A Record of Quaker Jurisprudence in West New Jersey, 1680–1709.* Washington, D.C.: American Historical Association, 1944.

Rice, Franklin P., ed. "Records of the Court of General Sessions of the Peace, Worcester County, Mass., 1731–1737." *Collections of the Worcester Society of Antiquity,* V. Worcester, 1883.

Robinson, John. *The Works of John Robinson.* 3 vols. London, 1851.

Salem, Mass. *A Copy of the Church-Covenants which have been used in the Church of Salem.* Boston, 1680.

Salem, Massachusetts, First Church. *A Faithful Narrative of the Proceedings of the Ecclesiastical Council Convened at Salem in 1734.* Boston, 1735.

"Salem Town Records, 1659–1680," Copied by Martha O. Homes. Essex Institute, *Historical Collections,* XL–XLIII (1904–1907), XLVIII–XLIX (1912–1913).

Salley, Alexander Jr., ed. *Narratives of Early Carolina, 1650–1708.* New York: Charles Scribner's Sons, 1911.

Saunders, William, ed. *The Colonial Records of North Carolina.* 10 vols. Raleigh, 1886–1890.

Sharples, Stephen, ed. *Records of the First Church of Christ at Cambridge in New England, 1632–1830.* Boston: Eben Putnam, 1906.

Shepard, Thomas. *Wine for Gospel Wantons: Or, Cautions Against Spiritual Drunkenness.* Cambridge, Mass., 1668.

Shewen, William. *A Brief Testimony Against Tale-Bearers, Whisperers, and Back-biters.* Philadelphia, 1701.

Shurtleff, Nathaniel B., ed. *Records of the Colony of New Plymouth.* 12 vols. Boston: William White, 1855.

—— *Records of the Governor and Company of Massachusetts Bay in New England.* 5 vols. in 6. Boston: William White, 1853.

Smith, Joseph H., ed. *Colonial Justice in Western Massachusetts, 1639–1702: The Pynchon Court Record.* Cambridge: Harvard University Press, 1961.

Smith, Joseph H. and Philip A. Crowl, eds. *Court Records of Prince George's County, Maryland, 1696–1699.* Washington, D.C.: American Historical Association, 1964.

Society of Friends. *Advice and Caution from our Monthly Meeting in Philadelphia Concerning Children and Servants.* Philadelphia, 1732.

Stoddard, Solomon. *The Necessity of Acknowledgement, of Offenses, in Order to Reconciliation.* Boston, 1701.

Stoughton, William. *New-England's True Interests.* Cambridge, Mass., 1670.

Street, Charles R., ed. *Huntington Town Records, 1653–1873.* 3 vols. Huntington, N.Y., 1887–1889.

Thomas, M. Halsey, ed. *The Diary of Samuel Sewall.* 2 vols. New York: Farrar, Straus and Giroux, 1973.

Tinling, Marion, ed. *The Correspondence of The Three William Byrds of Westover, Virginia, 1684–1776.* 2 vols. Charlottesville: University Press of Virginia, 1977.

Town of Bedford, Westchester County, New York. *Historical Records.* 8 vols. Bedford Hills, N.Y., 1966–1977.

Town Records of Newcastle, Mass., 1756–1778. N.p., n.d. Accession US11402.36. Widener Library, Harvard University, Cambridge.

Town of Weston, Mass., containing "Church Records, 1709–1825." Boston, 1901.

Trumbull, J. Hammond, and C.J. Hoadly, eds. *Public Records of the Colony of Connecticut.* 15 vols. Hartford, 1850–1890.

Tyler, Lyon Gardiner, ed. *Narratives of Early Virginia, 1606–1625.* New York: Charles Scribner's Sons, 1907.

Upham, William, ed. "Beverly First Church Records." Essex Institute, *Historical Collections,* XXXV, 177–211, XXXVI, 141–160, 297–324 (1899–1900); XLI, 193–226 (1905).

—— "Town Records of Salem, 1634–1659." Essex Institute, *Historical Collections,* IX (second series, vol. I, 1868), 5–232. Salem, 1869.

Van Laer, A.J.F., trans. and ed. *Documents Relating to New Netherland, 1624–1626, in the Henry E. Huntington Library.* San Marino, Calif.: The Henry E. Huntington Library and Art Gallery, 1924.

—— "Early Records of the City and County of Albany and Colony of Rensselaerswyck." New York State Library, *History Bulletin,* IX–XI. Albany: University of the State of New York, 1916–1919.

—— *Minutes of the Court of Albany, Rensselaerswyck and Schenectady.* 3 vols. Albany: University of the State of New York, 1926–1932.

—— *Minutes of the Court of Fort Orange and Beverwyck (1652–1660).* 2 vols. Albany: University of the State of New York, 1920–1923.

—— *Minutes of the Court of Rensselaerswyck, 1648–1652.* Albany: University of the State of New York, 1922.

Wadsworth, Benjamin. *Mutual Love and Peace Among Christians.* Boston, 1701.

—— *The Well-Ordered Family: or Relative Duties.* Boston, 1712.

Wakeman, Samuel. *A Young Man's Legacy to the Rising Generation.* Cambridge, Mass., 1678.

Walley, Thomas. *Balm in Gilead.* Cambridge, Mass., 1670.

Watertown, Mass. *Watertown Records.* 8 vols. Watertown, 1894–1939.

West, Moses. *A Treatise Concerning Marriage.* Philadelphia, 1730.

Whitefield, George. *A Further Account of God's Dealings . . . To Which is Annexed A brief Account of the Rise, Progress, and Present Situation of the Orphan House in Georgia.* Philadelphia, 1746.

—— *The Great Duty of Family Religion.* Boston, 1739.

—— *A Letter to His Excellency Governor Wright, Giving an Account of the Steps Taken Relative to the Converting the Georgia Orphan-House into a College.* Charles-Town, S.C., 1767.

Willard, Samuel. *The Child's Portion.* Boston, 1684.

—— *Useful Instructions for a Professing People in Times of Great Security and Degeneracy.* Cambridge, Mass., 1673.

William, Williams. *The Duty of Parents to Transmit Religion to Their Children.* Boston, 1721.

Wilson, Caroline Price, ed. *Annals of Georgia.* Vol. I: *Liberty County*

Records and a State Revolutionary Pay Roll. New York: Grafton Press, 1928.

Winthrop Papers. 5 vols. Boston: Massachusetts Historical Society, 1929–1949.

Wright, Louis B., ed. Letters of Robert Carter, 1721–1727: The Commercial Interests of a Virginia Gentleman. San Marino, Calif.: The Huntington Library, 1940.

Wright, Louis B., and Marion Tinling, eds. The Secret Diary of William Byrd of Westover, 1709–1712. Richmond: Dietz Press, 1941.

Notes

Introduction

1. For a sampling of the extensive literature on this subject, see Edward Shorter, *The Making of the Modern Family* (New York: Basic Books, 1975); Lawrence Stone, *The Family, Sex and Marriage in England, 1500–1800* (New York: Harper and Row, 1977); Natalie Zemon Davis, *Society and Culture in Early Modern France* (Stanford: Stanford University Press, 1975); Mack Walker, *German Home Towns: Community, State, and General Estate, 1648–1871* (Ithaca: Cornell University Press, 1971); and Keith Thomas, *Religion and the Decline of Magic* (New York: Scribner's, 1971).

2. On these changes in early modern England, see Peter Clark and Paul Slack, eds., *Crisis and Order in English Towns, 1500–1700* (Toronto: University of Toronto Press, 1972); David Underdown, *Revel, Riot and Rebellion: Popular Politics and Culture in England, 1603–1660* (New York: Oxford University Press, 1985); Anthony Fletcher and John Stevenson, eds., *Order and Disorder in Early Modern England* (New York: Cambridge University Press, 1985); and Keith Wrightson, *English Society, 1580–1680* (London: Hutchinson, 1982).

3. *Records and Files of the Quarterly Courts of Essex County, Massachusetts* (Salem: Essex Institute, 1911–1975), IV, 212–213. Hereafter cited *Essex County Court Records*.

For a discussion of the usefulness of court records with special reference to family history, see Lawrence Stone, "Family History in the 1980's: Past Achievements and Future Trends," *Journal of Interdisciplinary History*, 12 (1981), 51–87. Court records have figured most prominently in studies of New England. See e.g. John Demos, *Entertaining Satan: Witchcraft in the Culture of Early New England* (New York: Oxford, 1982); Laurel Thatcher Ulrich, *Good Wives: Image and Reality in the Lives of Women in Northern New England, 1650–1750* (New York: Knopf, 1982); David Konig, *Law and Society in Puritan Massachusetts: Essex County, 1629–1692* (Chapel Hill: University of North Carolina Press, 1979); N.E.H. Hull, *Female Felons: Women and Serious Crime in Colonial Massachusetts* (Urbana: University of Illinois Press, 1987); and Cornelia Hughes Dayton, "Women Before the Bar: Gender, Law, and Society in Connecticut, 1710–1790," diss., Princeton University, 1986. The procedures and assumptions of colonial courts varied both by region and by the nature of the specific court (for example, chancery courts were courts of equity rather than common law); among the best discussions of judicial function and procedure in colonial courts are David Konig, ed., "Introduction," *Plymouth Court Records* (Wilmington: Michael Glazier, 1978), and Robert Wheeler, "The County Court in Colonial Virginia," in Bruce Daniels, ed., *Town and County: Essays on the Structure of Local Government in the American Colonies* (Middletown: Wesleyan University Press, 1978).

4. Edmund Morgan, Lawrence Cremin, James Axtell, and Philip Greven, to name a few, have noted that the shortage of labor and especially skilled labor was a persistent problem in the colonies. It seems likely that colonial apprenticeship began earlier but did not last as long as in England, and Morgan argues that it led to fewer and weaker restraints on servants and apprentices. Greven suggests that "the scarcity of labor fostered the interdependence of families as each obtained goods and services from others and provided them in turn." Axtell also argues that shorter terms of apprenticeship may have joined with more abundant land and other factors to place "men at an earlier age 'very near upon a level' with their parents." This leveling process increased the familiarity between parents and children "even to the point of reversing the roles upon occasion." See Edmund Morgan, *The Puritan Family* (Boston, 1944; rev. ed., New York: Harper and Row, 1966), pp. 124–126; Lawrence Cremin, *American Education: The Colonial Experience, 1607–1783* (New York: Harper and Row, 1970), pp. 132–134; Philip Greven, *Four Generations: Population, Land, and Family in Colonial Andover, Massachusetts* (Ithaca: Cornell University Press, 1970), pp. 68–70; and James Axtell, *The School upon a Hill* (New Haven: Yale University Press, 1974), pp. 93–95. Contemporaries also noted the labor shortage. John Winthrop complained in 1633 that "the scarcity of workmen had caused them to raise their wages to an excessive rate." Among "the evils which were springing, etc., were 1. Many spent time idly, etc., because they could get as much in four days as would keep them a week." J. K. Hosmer, ed., *Winthrop's Journal* (New York: Charles Scribner's Sons, 1908), I, 112. The problem remained forty years later; in 1672 the Massachusetts General Court observed that "there have binn sundry and frequent complaints preferred to this Court of oppression by excessive wages of worke men and labourers, which, notwithstanding the endeavours of this Court to redress such oppressions, continue, and further increase." Nathaniel B. Shurtleff, ed., *Records of the Governor and Company of Massachusetts Bay* Boston: William White, 1853), IV, part 2, 510.

5. Thomas Cobbet, *A Fruitful and Useful Discourse Touching the Honour due from Children to Parents and the Duty of Parents toward their Children* (London, 1656), p. 11.

6. On the social implications of patriarchalism, see Gordon Schochet, *Patriarchalism in Political Thought* (New York: Oxford University Press, 1975); on the implications specifically for women's subordination, see Mary Beth Norton, "The Evolution of White Women's Experience in Early America," *American Historical Review*, 89 (1984), 593–619, esp. pp. 610–612.

7. Barry Levy, *Quakers and the American Family: British Settlement in the Delaware Valley* (New York: Oxford University Press, 1988), pp. 127–128.

8. See Timothy Breen, "Transfer of Culture: Chance and Design in Shaping Massachusetts Bay, 1630–1660," esp. pp. 69, 226n, and "Looking Out for Number One: The Cultural Limits on Public Policy in Early Virginia" (the reference to an aberrant society occurs on p. 109), in Breen, *Puritans and Adventurers: Change and Persistence in Early America* (New York: Oxford University Press, 1980).

9. See, e.g. Rhys Isaac, *The Transformation of Virginia, 1740–1790* (Chapel Hill: University of North Carolina Press, 1982); and Rutman and Rutman, *A Place in Time*. For a discussion that places a greater emphasis on the elements of individualism in some of these customs, see Timothy Breen, "Horses and Gentlemen: The Cultural Significance of Gambling Among the Gentry of Virginia," in *Puritans and Adventurers*.

10. Darrett Rutman and Anita Rutman, *A Place in Time: Middlesex County, Virginia, 1650–1750* (New York: Norton, 1984), p. 59.

11. Gloria Main, *Tobacco Colony* (Princeton: Princeton University Press, 1982), p.46.

12. Lois Green Carr, "The Foundations of Social Order: Local Government in Colonial Maryland," in Bruce Daniels, ed., *Town and County: Essays on the Structure of Local Government in the American Colonies* (Middletown: Wesleyan University Press, 1978), p. 74. See these other essays on the Chesapeake in the same volume: Wheeler, "The County Court in Colonial Virginia," and William Seiler, "The Anglican Church: A Basic Institution of Local Government in Colonial Virginia."

13. Cambridge, Mass., *The Records of the Town of Cambridge, 1630–1703* (Cambridge, 1901), II, 226; Watertown, Mass., *Watertown Records, 1634–1820* (Watertown, 1894–1939), II, 18; *Province and Court Records of Maine* (Portland: Maine Historical Society, 1928–1975), II, 261.

14. William Hand Browne et al., eds., *Archives of Maryland* (Baltimore: Maryland Historical Society, 1883–1972), XLI, 528. Hereafter cited *Archives of Maryland*.

15. Prince George's County Court Records, liber D, f. 235, Maryland Hall of Records.

16. Ibid., liber B, f. 270.

17. William Shewen, *A Brief Testimony Against Tale-Bearers, Whisperers, and Back-biters* (Philadelphia, 1701), pp. 11–12.

18. Berthold Fernow, ed., *The Records of New Amsterdam, 1653–1674* (New York: Knickerbocker Press, 1897), I, 33–34. In a similar case, Massachusetts Bay stopped plans underway to build a brothel in 1672 not only to prevent "such land defiling evils" but also because "the encrease of which evil, if not timely prevented, may tend to the debauching multitudes of persons, and tend to the utter ruine of their estates, soule and body." See *Records of the Governor and Company of Massachusetts Bay*, IV, part 2, 513.

19. *Essex County Court Records*, IX, 221–222.

20. Court of General Quarter Sessions, New York City, bk. 2, f. 190, microfilm CMS1, Historical Documents Collection, Queens College, City University of New York; C.G. Chamberlayne, ed., *The Vestry Book of Petsworth Parish, Gloucester County, Virginia, 1677–1793* (Richmond: Library Board, 1933), p. 71.

21. *Archives of Maryland*, XLI, 528; *Essex County Court Records*, IV, 269.

22. Colonial Society of Pennsylvania, *Records of the Court of New Castle of Delaware, 1676–1681* (Lancaster: Wickersham Printing Company, 1904), p. 215.

23. *Essex County Court Records*, IV, 269.

24. Ibid., I, 23.

25. Benjamin Wadsworth, *The Well-Ordered Family* (Boston, 1712), pp. 29–30.

26. Nathaniel B. Shurtleff, ed., *Records of the Colony of New Plymouth* (Boston: William White, 1855), III, 159. Hereafter cited *Plymouth Colony Records*.

27. *Records of New Amsterdam*, I, 286–87.

28. *Records of the Governor and Company of Massachusetts Bay*, V, 63.

29. *Records of the Court of New Castle of Delaware, 1676–1681*, p. 289.

30. *Records of the Governor and Company of Massachusetts Bay*, V, 4, and II, 217.

31. Cobbet, *A Fruitful and Useful Discourse*, p. 11. Axtell, *The School upon a Hill*, pp. 160–165, discusses the "New England imbroglio over long hair."

32. *Records of the Governor and Company of Massachusetts Bay*, IV, part 2, 41–42. On the themes and possible meanings of jeremiads, see Perry Miller, "Declension in a Bible Commonwealth," in *Nature's Nation* (Cambridge: Harvard University Press, 1967); Miller, "Errand into the Wilderness," in *Errand into the Wilderness* (New York: Harper and Row, 1956); and Sacvan Bercovitch, *The American Jeremiad* (Madison: University of Wisconsin Press, 1978).

33. Franklin Bowditch Dexter and Zara Jane Powers, eds., *New Haven Town Records, 1649–1769* (New Haven, 1917–1919, 1962), I, 448–449.

34. *Watertown Records,* II, 13.

35. *Essex County Court Records,* V, 306.

36. *New Haven Town Records,* II, 379–80. For similar complaints, see ibid., I, 176–177; *Records of the Governor and Company of Massachusetts Bay,* IV, part 1, 200-201 and V, 60–61; *Cambridge Town Records,* II, 164; Lynn, Mass., *Records of the Town Meeting of Lynn, 1691–1742* (Lynn: Lynn Historical Society, 1949–1964), III, 33; and J. Hammond Trumbull and C.J. Hoadly, eds., *Public Records of the Colony of Connecticut* (Hartford, 1850–1890), VI, 277–278.

37. Cotton Mather, *A Family Well-Ordered* (Boston, 1699), pp. 3–4.

38. William Gouge, *Of Domesticall Duties* (London, 1622), p. 18.

39. John Dod and Robert Clever, *A Godly Forme of Household Government* (London, 1612), p. 14.

40. Eleazer Mather, *A Serious Exhortation to the Present and Succeeding Generation in New England* (Cambridge, 1671), p. 20.

41. Mather, *A Family Well-Ordered,* pp. 3–4.

42. Society of Friends, *Advice and Caution from our Monthly Meeting in Philadelphia Concerning Children and Servants* (Philadelphia, 1732), p. 2.

43. Dod and Clever, *A Godly Forme of Household Government,* p. 255; Mather, *A Family Well-Ordered,* p.17.

44. Dod and Clever, *A Godly Forme of Household Government,* p. 18.

45. Wadsworth, *The Well-Ordered Family,* p. 12; Cotton Mather, *Family Religion Excited and Assisted* (Boston, 1714), p. 4.

46. Cotton Mather, *Cares About the Nurseries* (Boston, 1702), p. 41; Mather, *Family Religion Excited and Assisted,* p. 4.

47. Cotton Mather, *Corderius Americanus: An Essay Upon the Good Education of Children* (Boston, 1708), p. 1.

48. Gouge, *Of Domesticall Duties,* pp. 532, 491.

49. Dod and Clever, *A Godly Forme of Household Government,* p. 338. Note the equivalence here of "parents" and "fathers," a common assumption in seventeenth-century childrearing advice books. For the shift in emphasis to mothers as the primary parents in the late eighteenth century, see below, Chapter 5.

50. Levy, *Quakers and the American Family,* pp. 76–78. Levy's book also demonstrates, in fascinating detail, the centrality of familialism and domesticity to Delaware Valley Quakers. In this respect, the Quakers formed a distinctive and, Levy argues, "precociously modern" culture in seventeenth-century America. Though I find Levy's book extremely suggestive and persuasive on most counts, I do think he understates the degree to which Quaker domesticity was reinforced by—in some ways, even imposed by—the Quaker meeting.

51. Society of Friends, *Advice and Caution from our Monthly Meeting in Philadelphia Concerning Children and Servants,* p. 7.

52. *Records of New Amsterdam,* I, 33.

53. *Records of the Governor and Company of Massachusetts Bay,* V, 241. For a fuller discussion of this social ethic in New England, see Stephen Foster, *Their Solitary Way: The Puritan Social Ethic in the First Century of Settlement in New England* (New Haven: Yale University Press, 1971); Timothy Breen and Stephen Foster, "The Puritans' Greatest Achievement: A Study of Social Cohesion in Seventeenth-Century Massachusetts," *Journal of American History,* 60 (1973), 5–22; and Michael Zuckerman, *Peaceable Kingdoms: New England Towns in the Eighteenth Century* (New York: Knopf, 1970).

54. Wadsworth, *The Well-Ordered Family,* p. 24.

55. Gouge, *Of Domesticall Duties,* p. 225.

56. Wadsworth, *The Well-Ordered Family,* pp. 25–26.

57. Wrightson, p. 91.

58. Shewen, *A Brief Testimony Against Tale-Bearers,* pp. 5–6.

59. Joseph Morgan, *Love to Our Neighbors Recommended* (New London, 1727), p. 8.

60. *Province and Court Records of Maine,* I, 137.

61. Dod and Clever, *A Godly Forme of Household Government,* pp. 82–83.

1. The Force of Community

1. On housing arrangements and settlement patterns, see David H. Flaherty, *Privacy in Colonial New England* (Charlottesville: University Press of Virginia, 1967), esp. chs. 1–3; David H. Flaherty, "Crime and Social Control in Provincial Massachusetts," *Historical Journal,* 24 (1981), 339–360; Anthony N. B. Garvan, *Architecture and Town Planning in Colonial Connecticut* (New Haven: Yale University Press, 1951); John R. Stilgoe, *Common Landscape of America, 1580–1845* (New Haven: Yale University Press, 1972); Kevin P. Kelley, 'In dispers'd Country Plantations': Settlement Patterns," in Tate and Ammerman, eds., *The Chesapeake in the Seventeenth Century;* Rhys Isaac, *The Transformation of Virginia, 1740–1790* (Chapel Hill: University of North Carolina Press, 1982); Darrett Rutman and Anita Rutman, *A Place in Time: Middlesex County, Virginia, 1650–1750* (New York: Norton, 1984); Stephanie Grauman Wolf, *Urban Village: Population, Community, and Family Structure in Germantown, Pennsylvania, 1683–1800* (Princeton: Princeton University Press, 1976); and James Lemon, *The Best Poor Man's Country: A Geographical Study of Early Southeastern Pennsylvania* (New York: Norton, 1972).

2. *Essex County Court Records,* V, 291.

3. Shurtleff, ed., *Plymouth Colony Records,* V, 83.

4. Browne et al., eds., *Archives of Maryland,* LIV, 534.

5. Chancery Court Proceedings, VII, f. 109, Maryland Hall of Records.

6. *Essex County Court Records,* III, 209.

7. A.J.F. Van Laer, trans. and ed., *Minutes of the Court of Albany, Rensselaerswyck and Schenectady* (Albany: University of the State of New York, 1926–1932), III, 306-07.

8. Prince George's County Court Records, liber S, ff. 482–83, and liber W, ff. 1 and 581, Maryland Hall of Records.

9. See David Rothman, *The Discovery of the Asylum: Social Order and Disorder in the New Republic* (Boston: Little, Brown, 1971), esp. chs. 1–2. For some specific examples of household care, see Susie Ames, ed., *County Court Records of Accomack-Northampton, Virginia, 1632–1640* (Washington, D.C.: American Historical Association, 1954), p. 133; Chamberlayne, ed., *The Vestry Book of St. Paul's Parish, Hanover County, Virginia, 1706–1786*, p. 117; *Archives of Maryland*, X, 215; Richard B. Morris, ed., *Select Cases of the Mayor's Court of New York City, 1674–1784* (Washington, D.C.: American Historical Association, 1935), p.68.

10. *Plymouth Colony Records*, II, 174.

11. H. Clay Reed and George J. Miller, eds., *The Burlington Court Book: A Record of Quaker Jurisprudence in West New Jersey, 1680–1709* (Washington, D.C.: American Historical Association, 1944), p. 76; *Essex County Court Records*, III, 48.

12. Chancery Court Proceedings, VII, f. 307, Maryland Hall of Records.

13. C. J. Hoadly, ed., *Records of the Colony and Plantation of New Haven, 1638–1649 and 1653–1664* (Hartford, 1857–1858), II, 171. See similar examples in "Records of the Particular Court of Connecticut, 1639–1663," Conn. Hist. Soc., *Colls.*, XXII, 30–31, and *Essex County Court Records*, I, 408.

14. Colonial Society of Pennsylvania, *Records of the Court of New Castle of Delaware, 1676–1681* (Lancaster: Wickersham Printing Company, 1904), p. 389.

15. *Pennsylvania Archives* (Philadelphia and Harrisburg, 1852–1935), I, 192.

16. For instance, Naomi Sylvester's neighbors persuaded the Plymouth court in 1663 that she was a "frugall and laborious woman" who needed some help, and nearly a century later in Maryland, George Harrison was granted relief after referring to his neighbors for proof that "his Calamity" did not result from "an Idle or dissolute Course of Life." See *Plymouth Colony Records*, IV, 46; Prince George's County Court Records, Liber MM, f. 152, Maryland Hall of Records.

17. "Records of the Suffolk County Court, 1671–1680," Colonial Society of Massachusetts, *Collections* (Boston, 1933), XXIX, 222; *Plymouth Colony Records*, VI, 175–76.

18. Chancery Court Proceedings, V, f. 557, Maryland Hall of Records.

19. *Plymouth Colony Records*, XI, 18 and 91.

20. Franklin Bowditch Dexter and Zara Jane Powers, eds., *New Haven*

Town Records, 1648–1684 and 1684–1769 (New Haven, 1917–1919, 1962), I, 445–446.

21. *Plymouth Colony Records,* III, 102.

22. *Essex County Court Records,* V, 104. On the distrust of all "solitary livers" in New England, especially young men, see also Arthur Calhoun, *A Social History of the American Family from Colonial Times to the Present* (repr., 3 vols., New York: Barnes and Noble, 1960), I, 67–68, and George Haskins, *Law and Authority in Early Massachusetts: A Study in Tradition and Design* (New York: Macmillan, 1960), p. 80.

23. *Province and Court Records of Maine* (Portland: Maine Historical Society, 1928–1975), II, 53, 261.

24. *Records of the Court of New Castle of Delaware, 1676–1681,* p. 330.

25. *Essex County Court Records,* I, 174, and VI, 193.

26. "Charles City County Court Orders, 1655–1658," in Beverly Fleet, ed., *Virginia Colonial Abstracts* (Richmond, 1937–1949), X, 7–8.

27. Norfolk County Wills and Deeds, 1656–1666, liber D, f. 137, microfilm 45, Virginia State Library.

28. *Essex County Court Records,* VIII, 98.

29. A.J.F. Van Laer, trans. and ed., "Early Records of the City and County of Albany and the Colony of Rensselaerswyck," New York State Library, *History Bulletin* (Albany: University of the State of New York, 1916–1919), X, 341.

30. Cf. Flaherty, *Privacy in Colonial New England.* I believe Flaherty overstates the degree to which colonial New Englanders valued privacy. On this point, see Nancy Cott, "Eighteenth-Century Family and Social Life Revealed in the Massachusetts Divorce Records," *Journal of Social History,* 10 (1976), 20–43.

31. *Province and Court Records of Maine,* II, 171, 269; *Essex County Court Records,* I, 174; *New Haven Town Records,* I, 245. For an excellent analysis of speech crimes in colonial Massachusetts, see Robert St. George, "'Heated' Speech and Literacy in Seventeenth-Century New England," in *Seventeenth-Century New England: A Conference Held by The Colonial Society of Massachusetts,* Publications, vol. 63 (Boston, 1984), pp. 275–322.

32. Quoted in David Konig, *Law and Society in Puritan Massachusetts: Essex County, 1629–1692* (Chapel Hill: University of North Carolina Press, 1979), p. 117.

33. *Essex County Court Records,* IV, 428–29.

34. See Philip Gura, *A Glimpse of Sion's Glory: Puritan Radicalism in New England, 1620–1660* (Middletown: Wesleyan University Press, 1984), esp. ch. 6.

35. Paul Lucas, *Valley of Discord: Church and Society along the Connecticut River, 1636–1725* (Hanover, N.H.: University Press of New England, 1976), p. 205. On ministers as a focus of hostility, see, e.g. Gregory Nobles,

Divisions Throughout the Whole: Politics and Society in Hampshire County, Massachusetts, 1740–1775 (New York: Cambridge University Press, 1982), pp. 14–15, for problems in the 1650s; Paul Boyer and Steven Nissenbaum, *Salem Possessed* (Cambridge: Harvard University Press, 1974), ch. 2; Konig, *Law and Society in Puritan Massachusetts*, pp. 98–107. On development of the New England ministry in general and problems in the late seventeenth century in particular, see David Hall, *The Faithful Shepherd: A History of the New England Ministry in the Seventeenth Century* (Chapel Hill: University of North Carolina Press, 1972), esp. chs. 8, 10–11.

36. *Essex County Court Records,* IV, 353.

37. Shurtleff, ed., *Records of the Governor and Company of Massachusetts Bay,* V, 180–81. For similar cases, see also IV, part 1, pp. 160–66, V, 149, and V, 231.

38. Boyer and Nissenbaum, *Salem Possessed;* Konig, *Law and Society in Puritan Massachusetts,* p. 105.

39. Konig, *Law and Society in Puritan Massachusetts,* pp. 98–107. In eighteenth-century Plymouth County, William Nelson has found that in disputes involving towns, conflicts between towns and ministers were one of the two most common types of disputes. See his *Dispute and Conflict Resolution in Plymouth County, Massachusetts, 1725–1825* (Chapel Hill: University of North Carolina Press, 1981), p. 17; see also pp. 19–21 for a couple of such cases.

40. William H. Seiler, "The Anglican Parish in Virginia," in James Morton Smith, ed., *Seventeenth Century America: Essays in Colonial History* (New York: Norton, 1959); Isaac, *The Transformation of Virginia.* Cf. Deborah Gough on the Anglican church in Philadelphia, "The Roots of Episcopalian Authority Structures: The Church of England in Colonial Philadelphia," in Michael Zuckerman, ed., *Friends and Neighbors: Group Life in America's First Plural Society* (Philadelphia: Temple University Press, 1982).

41. Michael Kammen, *Colonial New York: A History* (New York: Scribner's, 1975), p. 216.

42. Thomas Walley, *Balm in Gilead* (Cambridge, 1670), pp. 18–19.

43. Boyer and Nissenbaum, *Salem Possessed;* Konig, *Law and Society in Puritan Massachusetts;* Stephen Innes, *Labor in a New Land: Economy and Society in Seventeenth-Century Springfield* (Princeton: Princeton University Press, 1983), pp. 136–137; Christine Heyrman, *Commerce and Culture: The Maritime Communities of Colonial Massachusetts, 1690–1750* (New York: Norton, 1984), pp. 108–124, on religious heterodoxy in general, and pp. 112–117 on Salem in particular. On Salem, see also Richard Weisman, *Witchcraft, Magic, and Religion in 17th-Century Massachusetts* (Amherst: University of Massachusetts Press, 1984). For discussions of the social context of witchcraft in Europe, see Alan Macfarlane, *Witchcraft in Tudor and Stuart England* (London: Routledge and Kegan Paul, 1970); Keith Thomas, *Religion and the*

Decline of Magic (New York: Scribner's, 1971); H. C. Erik Midelfort, *Witch Hunting in Southwestern Germany, 1562–1684: The Social and Intellectual Foundations* (Stanford: Stanford University Press, 1972); and Christina Larner, *Enemies of God: The Witch-hunt in Scotland* (Baltimore: Johns Hopkins University Press, 1981).

44. See John Demos, *Entertaining Satan: Witchcraft and the Culture of Early New England* (New York: Oxford University Press, 1982),and his earlier article, "Underlying Themes in the Witchcraft of Seventeenth-Century New England," *American Historical Review,* 75 (1970), 1311–1326; Carol Karlsen, *The Devil in the Shape of a Woman: Witchcraft in Colonial New England* (New York: Norton, 1987).

45. *Records of the Governor and Company of Massachusetts Bay,* IV, part 1, p. 269; "Records of the First Church in Boston, 1630–1868," Col. Soc. Mass., *Colls., XXXIX, 32–33.* See also the discussions in Demos, *Entertaining Satan,* pp. 87–88, and Karlsen, *The Devil in the Shape of a Woman,* pp. 1–2, 150–152.

46. *Essex County Court Records,* VII, 148. See also Konig, *Law and Society in Puritan Massachusetts,* pp. 146–147.

47. "Charles City County Order Book, 1655–1665," in Fleet, ed., *Virginia Colonial Abstracts,* XIII, 2.

48. Haskins, *Law and Authority in Early Massachusetts,* p. 213.

49. *Oxford English Dictionary.*

50. *Essex County Court Records,* V, 376.

51. Browne et al., eds., *Archives of Maryland,* LVII, 605.

52. Some time after writing this chapter, I read Bruce Mann's interesting and important book, *Neighbors and Strangers: Law and Community in Early Connecticut* (Chapel Hill: University of North Carolina Press, 1987), which includes a chapter on arbitration. Our discussions of arbitration address many of the same issues, and it is fair to say that we agree on most major points. One small difference arises from the different sources we used. Mann based his discussion on petitions from the "Private Controversies Series of the Connecticut Archives." He notes that the only petitions that appear in this file are for arbitrations that failed and he goes on to say that "Successful arbitrations did not leave tracks" (pp. 104-105n). This is not true of the records, primarily county court records, that I rely on here; the county courts discussed and recorded both successful and unsuccessful arbitrations.

53. Essex County Quarterly Papers, XV, f. 106, Essex County Courthouse, Salem, Mass.

54. On the Boston town meeting, see Jerold S. Auerbach, *Justice Without Law?* (New York: Oxford University Press, 1983), p. 23; on Providence, see *Records of the Colony of Rhode Island and Providence Plantations* (Providence: J.R. Bartlett, 1856–1865; repr. New York: AMS Press, 1968), I, 28–29. The order was reaffirmed in 1640; see Providence, R.I., *Early Records of*

the Town of Providence (Providence: Snow and Farnham, 1892–1915), XV, 2–3.

55. See e.g. Thomas Lechford, "Note-Book Kept by Thomas Lechford, Esq., Lawyer, in Boston, Massachusetts Bay, From June 27, 1638, to July 29, 1641," American Antiquarian Society, *Transactions and Collections* (1885), VII, 213; Josephine Frost, ed., *Records of the Town of Jamaica, Long Island, New York, 1656–1751* (Brooklyn: Long Island Historical Society, 1914), I, 54; *Abstracts of the Wills of the State of South Carolina, 1670–1740*, I, 62; "Abstracts of the Wills on File in the Surrogate's Office, City of New York, 1665–1800," *Collections of the New-York Historical Society*, XXV, 385–86; and *Records of the Court of New Castle of Delaware, 1676–1681*, p. 348.

56. *Archives of Maryland*, X, 69.

57. Arbitration cases were often referred to as "private hearings" or "private references." See e.g. Joseph H. Smith, ed., *Colonial Justice in Western Massachusetts, 1639–1702: The Pynchon Court Record* (Cambridge: Harvard University Press, 1961), p. 205, and *New Haven Town Records*, I, 29–30, and I, 41–43.

58. See e.g. the Maryland Chancery Court's action in Tilley versus Parker in Chancery Court Proceedings, II, f. 174, Maryland Hall of Records.

59. William Saunders, ed., *The Colonial Records of North Carolina* (Raleigh, 1886–1890), II, 574; Susie Ames, ed., *County Court Records of Accomack-Northampton, Virginia, 1640–1645* (Charlottesville: University Press of Virginia, 1973), p. 137; John Cox Jr., ed., *Oyster Bay Town Records, 1653–1763* (New York: Tobias Wright, 1916–1931), I, 138.

60. Chancery Court Proceedings, III, f. 302, Maryland Hall of Records.

61. *Minutes of the Common Council of the City of New York, 1665–1776* (New York: Dodd, Mead and Company, 1905), II, 123; *Calendar of Virginia State Papers and Other Manuscripts* (Richmond, 1875–1893), I, 120–21; Charles R. Street, ed., *Huntington Town Records, 1653–1873* (Huntington, New York: 1887–1889), II, 324–325.

62. Victor Hugo Paltsits, ed., *Minutes of the Executive Council of the Province of New York: Administration of Francis Lovelace, 1668–1673* (Albany, 1910), I, 327–31; *Archives of Maryland*, X, 449.

63. J. Hammond Trumbull and C. J. Hoadly, eds., *Public Records of the Colony of Connecticut* (Hartford, 1850–1890), I, 117; *Records of the Court of New Castle of Delaware, 1676–1681*, pp. 7–8.

64. *Plymouth Colony Records*, III, 169; Howard M. Chapin, ed., *The Early Records of the Town of Warwick* [Rhode Island] (Providence: E.A. Johnson, 1926), p. 175.

65. *Plymouth Colony Records*, I, 44; *Archives of Maryland*, X, 25. For some other cases that focused on problems of evidence, see Berthold Fernow, ed., *The Records of New Amsterdam, 1653–1674* (New York: Knickerbocker Press, 1897), III, 161; *Plymouth Colony Records*, IV, 183; *New Haven Col-*

ony Records, I, 169–70; and *New Haven Town Records,* I, 222, 300, and II, 25.

66. *New Haven Town Records,* I, 165; *Minutes of the Court of Albany, Rensselaerswyck and Schenectady,* I, 224–225.

67. Henrico County Record Book No. 2, Orders and Wills, 1678–1693, transcript, p. 99, microfilm 53, Virginia State Library; "Journal of William Stephens," *Colonial Records of the State of Georgia* (Atlanta and Athens, 1904–1979), IV, 22.

68. Watts quoted in Morton J. Horwitz, *The Transformation of American Law, 1780–1860* (Cambridge: Harvard University Press, 1977), p. 146.

69. Essex County Quarterly Papers, XXIX, f. 147, Essex County Courthouse; Testamentary Proceedings, XIII, ff. 156–157, Maryland Hall of Records; *Province and Court Records of Maine,* VI, 253.

70. Samuel Arnold, *David serving his Generation* (Cambridge, Mass., 1674), pp. 17–18.

71. Byrd quoted in Daniel J. Boorstin, *The Americans: The Colonial Experience* (New York: Random House, 1958), p. 189. On evangelical attitudes toward the law, see Alan Heimert, *Religion and the American Mind from the Great Awakening to the Revolution* (Cambridge: Harvard University Press, 1966), pp.179–182.

72. Alexis de Tocqueville, *Democracy in America,* rev. ed., Phillips Bradley (New York: Vintage, 1945), I, 288. De Tocqueville argued that American and English lawyers owed much of their preeminence to the difficulty of the law; in a legal system based on precedent, the lawyer became "the sole interpreter of an occult science" (I, 287). On the problems of the legal profession in colonial America, see Boorstin, *The Americans: The Colonial Experience,* pp. 195–205; Lawrence M. Friedman, *A History of American Law* (New York: Simon and Schuster, 1973), pp. 81–88; Edwin Powers, *Crime and Punishment in Early Massachusetts, 1620–1692* (Boston: Beacon Press, 1966), pp. 432–39; Milton M. Klein, "The Rise of the New York Bar: The Legal Career of William Livingstone," in David H. Flaherty, ed., *Essays in the History of Early American Law* (Chapel Hill: University of North Carolina Press, 1969), pp. 392–417; Stephen Botein, "The Legal Profession in Colonial North America," in Wilfred Prest, ed., *Lawyers in Early Modern Europe and America* (New York: Holmes and Meier, 1981); and A.G. Roeber, *Faithful Magistrates and Republican Lawyers: Creators of Virginia Legal Culture, 1680–1810* (Chapel Hill: University of North Carolina Press, 1981), esp. chs. 4–5. For a personal, and acerbic, account of colonial attitudes toward lawyers, see the "Note-Book Kept by Thomas Lechford," (note 55 above).

73. On Quakers, see Minutes of the Virginia Yearly Meeting of the Society of Friends, 1702–1805, microfilm M810, f. 1, and Minutes of the Baltimore Yearly and Half Yearly Meetings of the Society of Friends, 1677–1758, microfilm M547, f. 100, Maryland Hall of Records. On Quakers' use of arbitration

specifically, see Auerbach, *Justice Without Law?* pp. 28–31. On Quaker attitudes and behavior generally, see Barry Levy, *Quakers and the American Family* (New York: Oxford University Press, 1988); Jack Marietta, *The Reformation of American Quakerism, 1748–1783* (Philadelphia: University of Pennsylvania Press, 1984); Sydney V. James, *A People Among Peoples: Quaker Benevolence in Eighteenth-Century America* (Cambridge: Harvard University Press, 1963); Gary Nash, *Quakers and Politics: Pennsylvania, 1681–1726* (Princeton: Princeton University Press, 1968); Mary Maples Dunn, *William Penn: Politics and Conscience* (Princeton: Princeton University Press, 1967); and Wolf, *Urban Village*. The Maryland case refers to the will of Luke Gardner in Testamentary Proceedings, VI–A, f. 267, Maryland Hall of Records. Gardner apparently set high standards of behavior for his relations: his children would also forfeit their inheritance if they left the Roman Catholic faith or if they proved "Irreverant and Stubborne."

74. *Collections of the Rhode Island Historical Society* (Providence, 1902), X, 53.

75. Dod and Clever, *A Godly Forme of Household Government* (London, 1612), p. 83.

76. *Early Records of the Town of Providence*, IV, 236.

77. "Early Records of the City and County of Albany and the Colony of Rensselaerswyck," New York State Library, *History Bulletin*, X, 347.

78. "Records of the Particular Court of Connecticut, 1639–1663," Conn. Hist. Soc., *Colls.*, XXII, 9; "Salem Town Records, 1659–1680," Essex Institute, *Historical Collections* (vols. XL–XLIII, XLVIII–XLIX, 1904–1907, 1912–1913), XLI, 119; *Minutes of the Executive Council of the Province of New York: Administration of Francis Lovelace, 1669–1673*, II, 749–750.

79. *Early Records of the Town of Warwick*, p. 174; *New Haven Colony Records*, I, 473; *Records of the Governor and Company of Massachusetts Bay*, IV, part 1, p. 20.

80. Walley, *Balm in Gilead*, p. 19.

81. Auerbach, *Justice Without Law?* p. 6, uses the phrase "community of profit" in discussing how arbitration could advance principles of community whether they were defined in religious terms or in secular, commercial terms.

82. Susan Kingsbury, ed., *The Records of the Virginia Company of London* (Washington, D.C.: Government Printing Office, 1906, 1933, 1935), I, 260.

83. Prince George's County Court Records, liber N, f. 248, Maryland Hall of Records.

84. *Public Records of the Colony of Connecticut*, IV, 72; *Records of New Amsterdam*, VI, 5; *Minutes of the Court of Albany, Rensselaerswyck and Schenectady*, II, 165.

85. See e.g. Anne King Gregorie and J. Nelson Frierson, eds., *Records of the Court of Chancery of South Carolina, 1671–1779* (Washington, D.C.: American Historical Association, 1950), p. 127; *Archives of Maryland*, XLI, 452–

453; Chancery Court Proceedings, VIII, ff. 119–120, Maryland Hall of Records; *Records of New Amsterdam,* III, 385; "Early Records of the City and County of Albany and the Colony of Rensselaerswyck," New York State Library, *History Bulletin,* X, 329; *Essex County Court Records,* II, 27; and "Note-Book Kept by Thomas Lechford," VII, 343.

86. Chancery Court Proceedings, II, f. 427, Maryland Hall of Records.

87. *Public Records of the Colony of Connecticut,* IV, 275; Chester County Orphans' Court Docket, I, f. 20, microfilm 15–16, Pennsylvania State Archives; *Records of New Amsterdam,* III, 132.

88. *Colonial Justice in Western Massachusetts,* pp. 206-207; *Colonial Records of Pennsylvania: Minutes of the Provincial Council* (Harrisburg and Philadelphia, 1838–1853), II, 434; *Public Records of the Colony of Connecticut,* VIII, 152; Chancery Court Proceedings, IV, ff. 1–2, Maryland Hall of Records; *Select Cases of the Mayor's Court of New York City, 1674–1784,* p. 551. In a case in Plymouth in 1763, both parties "prayed" that the referees' report "might not be received"; the case was continued but the court ultimately did accept the report. See *Plymouth Court Records,* ed. David Konig (Wilmington, Del.: Michael Glazier, 1978), VIII, 74; hereafter cited *Plymouth Court Records.*

89. Heyrman, *Commerce and Culture,* p. 214, mentions this incident in discussing ethnic tensions in seventeenth-century Essex County. On this subject, see also David Konig, "A New Look at the Essex 'French': Ethnic Friction and Community Tensions in Seventeenth-Century Essex County, Massachusetts," Essex Institute, *Historical Collections,* CX (1974), 167–180; Konig, *Law and Society in Puritan Massachusetts,* pp. 69–74; and St. George, "'Heated' Speech and Literacy in Seventeenth-Century New England," p. 299.

90. *Essex County Court Records,* II, 443–446; III, 16, 414–419; IV, 108, 114–117, 126, 145–146, 151; V, 49, 129, 181–182.

91. The development of commercial arbitration presents a different, more successful story. See Horwitz, *Transformation of American Law,* ch. 5, and Auerbach, *Justice Without Law?* pp. 32–33. On changes in arbitration in the eighteenth century, see below, Afterword.

2. The Tyranny of Neighbors

1. "Kingston Court Records, 1661–1667," *New York Historical Manuscripts: Dutch* (Baltimore: Genealogical Publishing Company, 1976), XXV, part 1, p. 219.

2. According to the *Oxford English Dictionary,* "The question 'Has your mother sold her mangle?' (quot. 1836–37) was at one time the commonest piece of 'chaff' used by London street-boys."

3. *Essex County Court Records,* VIII, 300. On this incident, see also David

Konig, *Law and Society in Puritan Massachusetts: Essex County, 1629–1692* (Chapel Hill: University of North Carolina Press, 1979), p. 134.

4. Chancery Court Proceedings, VIII, ff. 820–26, Maryland Hall of Records. The Govanes eventually reconciled (VIII, 948).

5. George B. Curtis, "The Colonial Court, Social Forum and Legislative Precedent," *Virginia Magazine of History and Biography,* 85 (1977), p. 284; N.E.H. Hull, *Female Felons: Women and Serious Crime in Colonial Massachusetts* (Urbana: University of Illinois Press, 1987), p. 42.

6. R. H. Helmholz, ed., *Select Cases on Defamation to 1600* (London: Selden Society, 1985), p. xxvi.

7. This summary is based on Colin Rhys Lovell, "The 'Reception' of Defamation By the Common Law," *Vanderbilt Law Review,* 15 (1962), 1051–1071; William S. Holdsworth, "Defamation in the Sixteenth and Seventeenth Centuries," *Law Quarterly Review,* 40 (1924), 302–315; J. A. Sharpe, *Defamation and Sexual Slander in Early Modern England: The Church Courts at York* (Borthwick Papers No. 58, University of York, 1980); and Helmholz, *Select Cases on Defamation to 1600,* pp. xi–cxi. See also William S. Holdsworth, *A History of English Law* (London: Methuen, 1909, 1922–), and Clara Ann Bowler, "Carted Whores and White Shrouded Apologies: Slander in the County Courts of Seventeenth-Century Virginia," *Virginia Magazine of History and Biography,* 85 (1977), 411–426.

8. Helmholz, *Select Cases on Defamation to 1600,* p. xxix.

9. Lovell, "The 'Reception' of Defamation By the Common Law," p. 1065; Holdsworth, *A History of English Law,* V, 210; Leonard Levy, *Legacy of Suppression: Freedom of Speech and Press in Early American History* (Cambridge: Harvard University Press, 1960); James Morton Smith, *Freedom's Fetters: The Alien and Sedition Acts and American Civil Liberties* (Ithaca: Cornell University Press, 1956).

10. Berthold Fernow, ed., *The Records of New Amsterdam, 1653–1674* (New York: Knickerbocker Press, 1897), I, 114, and VI, 17.

11. William Waller Hening, ed., *The Statutes at Large; being A Collection of all the Laws of Virginia from the First Session of the Legislature, in the Year 1619* (repr. Charlottesville: University Press of Virginia, 1969), II, 72–73.

12. Browne et al., eds., *Archives of Maryland,* LIV, 370. For a discussion of reputation and officeholding in England at the same time, see Anthony Fletcher, "Honour, Reputation and Local Officeholding in Elizabethan and Stuart England," in Fletcher and John Stevenson, eds., *Order and Disorder in Early Modern England* (Cambridge: Cambridge University Press, 1985), pp. 92–115.

13. "Council Minutes [of New Netherland], 1638–1649," *New York Historical Manuscripts: Dutch* (Baltimore: Genealogical Publishing Company, 1974), IV, 177.

14. Colonial Society of Pennsylvania, *Records of the Court of New Castle of Delaware, 1676–1681* (Lancaster, 1904), pp. 226–30.

15. *Province and Court Records of Maine* (Portland: Maine Historical Society, 1928–1975), I, 68–69; Shurtleff, ed., *Plymouth Colony Records*, IV, 178.

16. "Kingston Court Records, 1661–1667," *New York Historical Manuscripts: Dutch*, XXV, part 1, p. 72; William Saunders, ed., *Colonial Records of North Carolina* (10 vols., Raleigh, N.C., 1886–1890), II, 766.

17. Lancaster County Orders, no. 1, 1666–1680, f. 102, microfilm 24, Virginia State Library.

18. *Essex County Court Records*, VI, 124–125.

19. Ibid., VI, 328, 335; II, 6; III, 405-406.

20. "Northumberland County Court Orders, 1652–1655," in Beverly Fleet, ed., *Virginia Colonial Abstracts* (Richmond, 1937–1949), II, 20.

21. *Essex County Court Records*, IV, 108, 146, 151. This is of course the same Smith of the contentious Smith-Rowland clan discussed above, Chapter 2.

22. *Essex County Court Records*, I, 14.

23. *Plymouth Colony Records*, VII, 298–299.

24. *Archives of Maryland*, IV, 234; *Colonial Records of North Carolina*, II, 87.

25. *Essex County Court Records*, I, 276, 348.

26. Ibid., I, 78, 81.

27. Ibid., IV, 129, 133.

28. "Records of the Particular Court of Connecticut, 1639–1663," Conn. Hist. Soc., *Colls.* (Hartford, 1928), XXII, 135.

29. *Essex County Court Records*, II, 157.

30. *Records of New Amsterdam*, IV, 1.

31. *Essex County Court Records*, I-IV, passim. For an extended analysis of John Godfrey, see John Demos, "John Godfrey and His Neighbors: Witchcraft and the Social Web in Colonial Massachusetts," *William and Mary Quarterly*, 3d ser., 33 (1976), 242–265, and his *Entertaining Satan: Witchcraft in the Culture of Early New England* (New York: Oxford University Press, 1982), ch. 2. Note also David Konig's suggestion that "John Godfrey" may have been more than one person, in *Law and Society in Puritan Massachusetts*, p. 157n.

32. *Essex County Court Records*, I, 243.

33. Ibid., I, 112; *Records of New Amsterdam*, II, 166.

34. *Essex County Court Records*, I, 332–333 (Beale), I, 392 (Browne), and IV, 66 (Cross).

35. "Charles City County Order Book, 1655–1665," in Fleet, ed., *Virginia Colonial Abstracts*, XIII, 61.

36. *Essex County Court Records*, III, 134.

37. *Archives of Maryland*, LXVIII, 91; *Colonial Records of Pennsylvania:*

Minutes of the Provincial Council (Harrisburg and Philadelphia, 1838–1853), II, 20. In Plymouth County Daniel Hunt complained, as late as 1774, that slanderous remarks had "hindred and prevented him from the Priviledge, Benefit, and Advantage of tending and improving a certain Corn-mill" in Wareham; see Konig, ed., *Plymouth Court Records,* IX, 51–52.

38. Richard B. Morris, ed., *Select Cases of the Mayor's Court of New York City, 1674–1784* (Washington, D.C.: American Historical Association, 1935), p. 355.

39. "Records of the Suffolk County Court, 1671–1680," Col. Soc. Mass., *Colls.* (Boston, 1933), XXX, 880. See also Flood v. Legg, XXX, 858–860, and Legg v. Flood, XXX, 1054–1055.

40. *Calendar of Virginia State Papers, 1790–1792* (Richmond, 1875–1890; repr. New York: Kraus, 1968), I, 5.

41. *Archives of Maryland,* LXVIII, 122.

42. *Select Cases of the Mayor's Court of New York City, 1674–1784,* p. 328.

43. Julian Pitt-Rivers, "Honour and Social Status," in J. G. Peristiany, ed., *Honour and Shame: The Values of Mediterranean Society* (Chicago: University of Chicago Press, 1966), p. 39.

44. *Records of New Amsterdam,* II, 148; *Essex County Court Records,* I, 14; *Plymouth Colony Records,* IV, 111–12; *Records of the Town of East-Hampton* (Sag Harbor, N.Y., 1887–1905), I, 33.

45. *Archives of Maryland,* X, 399; *Records of New Amsterdam,* III, 35–36; *Essex County Court Records,* II, 166.

46. *Essex County Court Records,* III, 106. For other examples of slander suits that answered charges of lying, see ibid., I, 256, I, 257, II, 166, II, 317; *Plymouth Colony Records,* VII, 118; and *Records of the Town of East-Hampton,* I, 33.

47. *Colonial Records of North Carolina,* I, 588.

48. *Records of New Amsterdam,* VI, 33; *Essex County Court Records,* III, 284.

49. For some examples see Susie Ames, ed., *County Court Records of Accomack-Northampton, Virginia, 1640–1645* (Charlottesville: University Press of Virginia, 1973), p. 395; *Archives of Maryland,* IV, 149–150, IV, 258, LIV, 391–392; *Essex County Court Records,* II, 24, III, 182; *Plymouth Court Records,* VI, 275, VII, 423, VIII, 129–133; and Howard M. Chapin, ed., *The Early Records of the Town of Warwick* [Rhode Island] (Providence: E. A. Johnson, 1926), pp. 16–17.

50. Mary Beth Norton, "Gender and Defamation in Seventeenth-Century Maryland," *William and Mary Quarterly,* 3d ser., 44 (1987), 33, 38. Cf. Cornelia Dayton, "Women Before the Bar: Gender, Law, and Society in Connecticut, 1710–1790" (diss., Princeton University, 1986), p. 264, who finds in eighteenth-century New Haven County that in slander cases in general women

claimed to have been slandered by men and women alike, while men almost always accused other men.

51. *Archives of Maryland*, LIII, 319–320.

52. Susie Ames, ed., *County Court Records of Accomack-Northampton, Virginia, 1632–1640*, (Washington, D.C.: American Historical Association, 1954), p. 85.

53. *Province and Court Records of Maine*, I, 174.

54. Roger Thompson, "'Holy Watchfulness' and Communal Conformism: The Functions of Defamation in Early New England Communities," *New England Quarterly*, 56 (1983), 504–522. I am grateful to Roger Thompson for allowing me to read his essay in manuscript. On the effect of slander and gossip on sexual behavior, see also Robert St. George, "'Heated' Speech and Literacy in Seventeenth-Century New England," pp. 275–322; Peter Moogk, "'Thieving Beggars' and 'Stupid Sluts': Insults and Popular Culture in New France," *William and Mary Quarterly*, 3d ser., 36 (1979), 524–547; Sharpe, *Defamation and Sexual Slander in Early Modern England;* Peristiany, ed., *Honour and Shame;* and Greer Litton Fox, "'Nice Girl': Social Control of Women through a Value Construct," *Signs: Journal of Women in Culture and Society*, 2 (1977), 805–817. On the charivari and similar customs, see E. P. Thompson, "'Rough Music': Le charivari anglais," *Annales: Economies, sociétés, civilisations*, 27 (1972), 285–312; Natalie Zemon Davis, "The Reasons of Misrule" and "The Rites of Violence" in her collection of essays, *Society and Culture in Early Modern France* (Stanford: Stanford University Press, 1975); Edward Shorter, *The Making of the Modern Family* (New York: Basic Books, 1975); John Szwed, *Private Cultures and Public Imagery: Interpersonal Relations in a Newfoundland Peasant Society* (Newfoundland Social and Economic Studies, No. 2, Institute of Social and Economic Research, Memorial University of Newfoundland, St. John's, 1966); and J. K. Campbell, *Honour, Family and Patronage* (London: Oxford University Press, 1964).

55. *Archives of Maryland*, LIII, 13; Franklin Bowditch Dexter and Zara Jane Powers, eds., *New Haven Town Records, 1648–1684 and 1684–1769* (New Haven, 1917–1919, 1962), I, 46.

56. "Records of the Particular Court of Connecticut, 1639–1663," Conn. Hist. Soc., *Colls.*, XXII, 253.

57. *Essex County Court Records*, I, 254.

58. *Records of New Amsterdam*, VI, 40; *Essex County Court Records*, IX, 318. On the significance of the term "rogue," see St. George, "'Heated' Speech and Literacy in Seventeenth-Century New England," pp. 295–296.

59. C. J. Hoadly, ed., *Records of the Colony and Plantation of New Haven, 1638–1649 and 1653–1664* (Hartford, 1857–1858), I, 180–181.

60. St. George, "'Heated' Speech and Literacy in Seventeenth-Century New England," pp. 293–295. See also Moogk, "'Thieving Beggars' and 'Stupid Sluts.'"

61. "Kingston Court Records, 1661–1667," *New York Historical Manuscripts: Dutch,* XXV, part 1, p. 21; *Records of New Amsterdam,* I, 221; *Essex County Court Records,* VIII, 103.

62. *Calendar of Virginia State Papers and Other Manuscripts,* I, 37.

63. *Archives of Maryland,* XLIX, 79; Baltimore County Court Proceedings, liber D, ff. 205-06, Maryland Hall of Records.

64. *Records of the Colony of Rhode Island and Providence Plantations* (Providence: J.R. Bartlett, 1856–1865; repr. New York: AMS Press, 1968), I, 184.

65. "Note-Book Kept by Thomas Lechford," American Antiquarian Society, *Transactions and Collections,* VII, 259–260.

66. *Archives of Maryland,* LIV, 576–577. As late as 1796 in Plymouth, Asineth Shurtleff, a "Carver Spinster," argued in a slander suit that after Amos Raymond, a minor, claimed to have committed fornication with her, she had "'lost the company and Friendship of one Cobb Lucas, who courted and had made overtures of marriage' to her." *Plymouth Court Records,* X, 327–328.

67. Dayton, "Women Before the Bar," p. 271.

68. *Essex County Court Records,* VII, 2.

69. Anne Arundel County Court Judgments, liber V.D., no. 1, ff. 141–144, Maryland Hall of Records.

70. *Select Cases of the Mayor's Court of New York City, 1674–1784,* p. 351.

71. *Archives of Maryland,* LIII, 54–55.

72. *Records of the Town of East-Hampton,* I, 34.

73. *Colonial Records of North Carolina,* II, 88.

74. *Records of the Court of New Castle of Delaware, 1676–1681,* pp. 16–17; *Records of New Amsterdam,* V, 146; *Essex County Court Records,* VI, 13; *Calendar of Virginia State Papers and Other Manuscripts,* I, 37.

75. *Archives of Maryland,* LX, 212.

76. *Essex County Court Records,* III, 99; *County Court Records of Accomack-Northampton, Virginia, 1632–1640,* p. 86.

77. Charles County Court Orders, liber I, no. 1, ff. 12–13, Maryland Hall of Records.

78. *Province and Court Records of Maine,* I, 67.

79. *Essex County Court Records,* V, 43.

80. *Archives of Maryland,* LIII, 232.

81. Ibid., XLIX, 117.

82. "Council Minutes [of New Netherland], 1638–1649," *New York Historical Manuscripts: Dutch,* IV, 89.

83. *Essex County Court Records,* VI, 277–278, and VIII, 75.

84. See e.g. *Province and Court Records of Maine,* III, 167–168; *Essex County Court Records,* II, 348; Dixon Ryan Fox, ed., "The Minutes of the Court of Sessions (1657–1696), Westchester County, New York," *Publica-*

tions of the Westchester County Historical Society (White Plains, 1924), II, 33; *Records of the Court of New Castle of Delaware, 1676–1681,* pp. 434–435; and "Northumberland County Court Orders, 1652–1655," in Fleet, ed., *Virginia Colonial Abstracts,* II, 9.

85. *New Haven Colony Records,* I, 473.

86. "Council Minutes [of New Netherland], 1638–1649," *New York Historical Manuscripts: Dutch,* IV, 148.

87. *Essex County Court Records,* I, 210, and VIII, 323; *Records of New Amsterdam,* VI, 40; Accomack County Orders and Wills, 1671–1673, f. 223, microfilm 2, Virginia State Library.

88. *Essex County Court Records,* IV, 36–37. For some other typical acknowledgments, see Charles R. Street, ed., *Huntington Town Records, 1653–1873* (3 vols., Huntington, N.Y., 1887–1889), I, 23–24; *Plymouth Colony Records,* IV, 7; *Essex County Court Records,* IX, 331; Accomack County Orders, 1676–1678, f. 28, microfilm 79, Virginia State Library; *Province and Court Records of Maine,* II, 365; and *Rhode Island Records,* IV, 214–215.

89. H. Clay Reed and George J. Miller, eds., *The Burlington Court Book: A Record of Quaker Jurisprudence in West New Jersey, 1680–1709* (Washington, D.C.: American Historical Association, 1944), p. 86; "Abstracts of Wills on File in the Surrogate's Office, City of New York, 1665–1800," *Collections of the New-York Historical Society,* XXV, 76; *Essex County Court Records,* V, 77; *County Court Records of Accomack-Northampton, Virginia, 1640–1645,* pp. 235–36.

90. *Burlington Court Book of West New Jersey, 1680–1709,* p.86; "Abstracts of Wills on File in the Surrogate's Office, City of New York, 1665–1800," *Collections of the New-York Historical Society,* XXV, 76; *Essex County Court Records,* V, 77; *County Court Records of Accomack-Northampton, Virginia, 1640–1645,* pp. 235–36.

91. *Essex County Court Records,* IV, 36–37, 98–99.

92. Ibid., VIII, 420.

93. "Laws Agreed Upon in England," in *Colonial Records of Pennsylvania: Minutes of the Provincial Council* (Harrisburg and Philadelphia, 1838–1853), I, xxxii; J. Hammond Trumbull and C.J. Hoadly, eds., *Public Records of the Colony of Connecticut* (Hartford, 1850–1890), I, 537–38. For examples of fines and whippings imposed as penalties for slander throughout the colonies, see Lancaster County Court Orders, no. 3, 1681–1696, f. 22, microfilm 24, Virginia State Library; "Northumberland County Court Order Book 2, 1652–1655," in Fleet, ed., *Virginia Colonial Abstracts,* II, 6; *Archives of Maryland,* X, 487, and LIII, 21–22; *Burlington Court Book of West New Jersey, 1680–1709,* pp. 64–65; *Records of New Amsterdam,* VII, 231; and "The Minutes of the Court of Sessions (1657–1696), Westchester County, New York," *Publications of the Westchester County Historical Society,* II, 3.

94. *Burlington Court Book of West New Jersey, 1680–1709,* p. 58; *Essex County Court Records,* I, 380.

95. In Massachusetts in 1641, Charles Turner was fined, whipped, and ordered to stand in the meeting house "with a pap[er] on his head written a false acuser"; and in Boston in 1673, John Veering was given thirty stripes "severely .aide on" and sentenced "to stand in the open market place in Boston, exalted upon a Stoole for an houres time . . . after Lecture; with a paper fastned to his breast, with this inscription in a lardge character A Prophane and Wicked Slanderer and impious Reviler of a minister of the Gosple and Church members." See *Essex County Court Records,* I, 36, and "Records of the Suffolk County Court, 1671–1680," Col. Soc. Mass., *Colls.,* XXIX, 231. For the relative frequency with which men and women were prosecuted for slander in one area, see St. George, " 'Heated' Speech and Literacy in Colonial New England," pp. 305–308. Cf. Dayton, "Women Before the Bar," p. 199, who finds that in eighteenth-century New Haven County, women appeared as defendants in slander suits at only a slightly higher rate than their appearance in all types of civil litigation; Dayton argues from this figure that New Englanders did not see slander as a particularly female crime—unlike gossip, which they clearly did associate with women.

96. Benjamin Wadsworth, *The Well-Ordered Family* (Boston, 1712), pp. 29–30; Hening, *The Statutes at Large,* II, 166–167.

97. Norton, "Gender and Defamation in Seventeenth-Century Maryland," p. 6.

98. F. G. Bailey, "Gifts and Poison," in Bailey, ed., *Gifts and Poison: The Politics of Reputation* (New York: Schocken Books, 1971), p. 1.

99. Hening, *The Statutes at Large,* II, 166–67; *Records of the Court of Assistants of Massachusetts Bay,* II, 64.

100. *New Haven Colony Records,* I, 180–81.

101. Peristiany, ed., *Honour and Shame,* p. 11.

102. On honor and shame, see also Bailey, ed., *Gifts and Poison;* Campbell, *Honour, Family and Patronage;* Szwed, *Private Cultures and Public Imagery;* Ruth Benedict, *The Chrysanthemum and the Sword* (Boston: Houghton Mifflin, 1946); Helen Lynd, *On Shame and the Search for Identity* (New York: Harcourt, Brace and World, 1958); Helen Lewis, *Shame and Guilt in Neurosis* (New York: International Universities Press, 1971); Carl D. Schneider, *Shame, Exposure, and Privacy* (Boston: Beacon Press, 1977); and Bertram Wyatt-Brown, *Southern Honor: Ethics and Behavior in the Old South* (New York: Oxford University Press, 1982). On the functions of gossip, see also Max Gluckman, "Gossip and Scandal," *Current Anthropology,* 4 (1963), 307–316; Gluckman, "Psychological, Sociological and Anthropological Explanations of Witchcraft and Gossip: A Clarification," *Man: The Journal of the Royal Anthropological Institute,* new ser., 3 (1968), 20–34; and Peter J. Wil-

son, "Filcher of Good Names: An Enquiry into Anthropology and Gossip," *Man,* 9 (1974), 93–102. Robert Paine offers a critique of Gluckman in "What Is Gossip About? An Alternative Hypothesis," *Man,* 2 (1967), 278–285.

103. Captain Daniel Patrick to John Winthrop, ca. 1641, *Winthrop Papers* (Boston: Massachusetts Historical Society, 1929–1949), IV, 303.

3. The Contradictions of Family

1. Howard M. Chapin, ed., *The Early Records of the Town of Warwick* (Providence: E. A. Johnson, 1926), p. 31.

2. Charles R. Street, ed., *Huntington Town Records, 1653–1873* (Huntington, N.Y., 1887–1889), II, 78–79.

3. *Essex County Court Records,* VI, 14–15.

4. Ibid., III, 189–190. For other cases in which the court supported a suitor against a parent, see ibid., III, 189–90, and Browne et al., eds., *Archives of Maryland,* X, 532. Courts sometimes supported servants in similar situations. In 1653 Anna Vander Donck forbade her servant to marry, but a New Amsterdam court found "that no lawful reasons exist to refuse the marriage." See Berthold Fernow, ed., *The Records of New Amsterdam, 1653–1674* (New York: Knickerbocker Press, 1897), I, 188–189.

5. See e.g. Philip Greven, *Four Generations: Population, Land, and Family in Colonial Andover, Massachusetts* (Ithaca: Cornell University Press, 1970), esp. chs. 4 and 6, on patriarchalism and inheritance patterns in New England.

6. Lorena S. Walsh, " 'Till Death Us Do Part': Marriage and Family in Seventeenth-Century Maryland," in Thad Tate and David Ammerman, eds., *The Chesapeake in the Seventeenth Century: Essays on Anglo-American Society and Politics* (Chapel Hill: University of North Carolina Press, 1979), pp. 131–133.

7. Minutes of the Baltimore Yearly and Half-Yearly Meetings of the Society of Friends, 1677–1785, ff. 34, 60–61, microfilm M547, Maryland Hall of Records.

8. J. William Frost, *The Quaker Family in Colonial America* (New York: St. Martin's Press, 1973), p. 159. On parental control, see also pp. 154–156; on Quaker marriage customs generally, see chs. 8–9.

9. Walsh, " 'Till Death Us Do Part,' " pp. 129–130.

10. *Plymouth Colony Records,* XI, 29; *Records of the Colony of Rhode Island and Providence Plantations* (Providence: J.R. Bartlett, 1856–1865), I, 174.

11. Arthur W. Calhoun, *A Social History of the American Family* (3 vols., Cleveland: Arthur H. Clarke, 1917–1919), I, 260–263.

12. For several instances of enforcement, see "Records of the Suffolk County Court, 1671–1680," Col. Soc. Mass., *Colls.* (Boston, 1933), XXIX, 221, 559; *Essex County Court Records,* V, 103, IX, 532; *Plymouth Colony*

Records, IV, 140; *Records of the Court of Assistants of the Colony of Massachusetts Bay, 1630–1692* (Boston, 1901–1928), II, 97.

13. *Plymouth Colony Records,* III, 5; "Records of the Particular Court of Connecticut, 1639–1663," Conn. Hist. Soc., *Colls.,* XXII, 124–125. John Winthrop noted that in punishing fornication, which was often the result of unauthorized engagements, "the man was only to marry the maid or pay a sum of money to her father," but in a case involving servants, they were "whipped for the wrong offered to the master in abusing his house, and were not able to make him other satisfaction." See James K. Hosmer, ed., *Winthrop's Journal* (New York: Scribner's, 1908), II, 38.

14. Calhoun, *A Social History of the American Family,* I, 271.

15. See e.g. *Essex County Court Records,* VIII, 216.

16. "Council Minutes [of New Netherland], 1638–1649," *New York Historical Manuscripts: Dutch,* IV, 502.

17. *Essex County Court Records,* I, 50, 137.

18. For two examples of such arrangements, see A.J.F. Van Laer, ed., "Early Records of the City and County of Albany and the Colony of Rensselaerswyck," New York State Library, *History Bulletin* (Albany: State University of the State of New York, 1916–1919), IX, 365–366, and *Essex County Court Records,* V, 57. For arrangements that did not work amicably, see *Records of New Amsterdam,* I, 141–142; "Note-Book Kept by Thomas Lechford," American Antiquarian Society, *Transactions and Collections,* VII, 349–350.

19. "Northumberland County Orders, 1678–1713," in Lindsay O. Duvall, ed., *Virginia Colonial Abstracts* (Washington, D.C., and Wharton Grove, Va., 1952–1961), ser. 2, I, 58.

20. "Abstracts of Wills on File in the Surrogate's Office, City of New York, 1665–1800," *Collections of the New-York Historical Society* (vols. XXV–XLI, New York, 1893–1909), XXIX, 185.

21. A.J.F. Van Laer, trans. and ed., *Minutes of the Court of Albany, Rensselaerswyck and Schenectady,* (Albany: University of the State of New York, 1926–1932), III, 148.

22. Minutes of the Baltimore Yearly and Half Yearly Meetings of the Society of Friends, 1677–1758, f. 40, microfilm M547, Maryland Hall of Records.

23. *Essex County Court Records,* V, 67.

24. Ibid., I, 184; "Kingston Court Records, 1661–1667," *New York Historical Manuscripts: Dutch,* XXV, part 1, p. 251.

25. "Kingston Court Records, 1661–1667," *New York Historical Manuscripts: Dutch,* XXV, part 1, p. 252. Three years later Van Amersfoort's wife, Catrina Matthisen, petitioned successfully for a separation from her husband, charging that he squandered their money and beat her and their children. See below, p. 76, and "Kingston Court Records," XXV, part 2, p. 392.

26. Thomas Lyon to John Winthrop, April 14, 1648, *Winthrop Papers* (Boston: Massachusetts Historical Society, 1929–1949), V, 214.

27. *Essex County Court Records,* V, 381–382.

28. Susie Ames, ed., *County Court Records of Accomack-Northampton, 1632–1640* (Washington, D.C.: American Historical Association, 1954), p. 11.

29. *Essex County Court Records,* V, 401-402.

30. Testamentary Proceedings, IV, part B, ff. 1–5, Maryland Hall of Records.

31. J. Hammond Trumbull and C.J. Hoadly, eds., *Public Records of the Colony of Connecticut* (Hartford, 1850–1890), II, 129.

32. Chancery Court Proceedings, VI, quotes from ff. 215–216 and judgment on f. 239, Maryland Hall of Records.

33. *Archives of Maryland,* XLI, 550–51.

34. Chancery Court Proceedings, VIII, ff. 237–43, Maryland Hall of Records.

35. *Essex County Court Records,* V, 363.

36. *Archives of Maryland,* X, 503.

37. Ibid., LXVII, 226.

38. Chancery Court Proceedings, ff. 237–43, Maryland Hall of Records.

39. E. B. O'Callaghan, ed., *Documents Relative to the Colonial History of the State of New York* (Albany: Weed, Parsons, 1856–1861), I, 515.

40. Chancery Court Proceedings, IV, ff. 275–80, Maryland Hall of Records. For some other examples of neighbors who attempted to mediate between quarreling spouses, see "Records of the Suffolk County Court, 1671–1680," Col. Soc. Mass., *Colls.,* XXX, 754–55, 839–840, and *Essex County Court Records,* IV, 90, and IV, 280. In 1712 Benjamin Wadsworth commented on neighbors' responsibility to help compose such disagreements, in *The Well-Ordered Family,* pp. 41–42.

41. Caroline T. Moore and Agatha Aimar Simmons, eds., *Abstracts of the Wills of the State of South Carolina, 1670–1740* (Columbia: R.L. Bryan, 1960), I, 87.

42. *Abstracts of the Wills of the State of South Carolina,* I, 222–223.

43. *Records of the Governor and Company of Massachusetts Bay,* IV, part 2, pp. 157–157; *Essex County Court Records,* IV, 282.

44. Franklin Bowditch Dexter and Zara Jane Powers, eds., *New Haven Town Records, 1648–1684 and 1684–1769* (New Haven, 1917–1919, 1962), I, 452.

45. *Archives of Maryland,* X, 532.

46. The same order appears in *Records of the Governor and Company of Massachusetts Bay,* I, 311, and *Records of the Court of Assistants of Massachusetts Bay,* II, 100.

47. St. George's [Episcopal] Church, Penyman, Harford Co., Md., Vestry Minutes, liber A, f. 40; St. Paul's [Episcopal] Church, Fairlee, Kent Co., Md., Vestry Minutes, II, f. 94: both in Maryland Hall of Records.

48. *Essex County Court Records*, I, 221.

49. *Minutes of the Court of Albany, Rensselaerswyck and Schenectady*, III, 304.

50. *Documents Relative to the Colonial History of the State of New York*, II, 717.

51. *Records of New Amsterdam*, VI, 309–310, 315.

52. H. Clay Reed and George J. Miller, eds., *The Burlington Court Book: A Record of Quaker Jurisprudence in West New Jersey, 1680–1709* (Washington, D.C.: American Historical Association, 1944), pp. 163–64, 169.

53. For examples of vestry actions, see St. Paul's Church, Centreville, Queen Anne's Co., Md., Vestry Minutes, I, f. 23; St. Paul's Church, Fairlee, Kent Co., Md., Vestry Minutes, II, f. 118; Shrewsbury [Episcopal] Church, Kent Co., Md., Vestry Minutes, II, ff. 83 and 135; St. Anne's Church, Annapolis, Anne Arundel Co., Md., Vestry Minutes, p. 126; St. George's Church, Penyman, Harford Co., Md., Vestry Minutes, A, ff. 40, 78; and Christ Church, St. Peter's Parish, Easton, Talbot Co., Md., Vestry Minutes, ff. 225–26: all in Maryland Hall of Records. For vestry cases referred to the courts, see *County Court Records of Accomack-Northampton, 1632–1640*, pp. 128–129, and Anne Arundel County Court Judgments, 1720–1721, Accession 1422, ff. 244–45, Maryland Hall of Records. For some cases in which the Maryland court acted alone, see *Archives of Maryland*, XLI, 528, and LIII, 560; Kent County Court Proceedings, I, f. 37, Maryland Hall of Records; and Joseph H. Smith and Philip A. Crowl, eds., *Court Records of Prince George's County, Maryland, 1696–1699* (Washington, D.C.: American Historical Association, 1964), p. 435.

54. *Essex County Court Records*, IV, 416.

55. Ibid., I, 191.

56. Ibid., IV, 269.

57. Ibid., V, 37, 312; VI, 137, 344, 374–375; VII, 100. Rachel Clenton (Clinton) went on to receive a divorce in 1681 and eventually was accused of witchcraft during the Salem trials. See John Demos, *Entertaining Satan: Witchcraft in the Culture of Early New England* (New York: Oxford University Press, 1982), ch. 1.

58. *Records of New Amsterdam*, III, 297.

59. In 1664 the Plymouth General Court published a protest "att the request of William Tubbs, against Mercye, his wife, as disowneing all debts that shee shall make." A Providence resident, Daniel Abbott, issued a more spirited warning: "my wife Margrett through her Maddnes of folly and Turbulency of her Corrupt will, hath often Threatened to Ruinate my family, Routeing me (as she saith) of horse and foot, Destroying me Root and Branch, putting out one of her owne Eyes to putt out Both mine, and sett my house on fire: And is since departed from me takeing away my Children without my Consent." In particular, since his wife "as I have been Enformed, is now plotting mischiefe with some, of her Turbulent Spirritt, that when I am absent from home to Rifle

my house and take away my Goodes, to accomplish her Divelish Resolution against me," he advised "all persons upon theire perill to forbare any such illegiall proceedings" and "to forbare Bargaineing with, Contracting of Debts, or Receiving any part of my Estate of my said wife Margrett without my approbation." See *Plymouth Colony Records*, IV, 66; Providence, R.I., *Early Records of the Town of Providence* (Providence: Snow and Farnham, 1892–1915), XVII, 37–38.

60. See e.g. *Records of the Governor and Company of Massachusetts Bay*, III, 232; *Plymouth Colony Records*, V, 253; Accomack County Orders, 1701–1714, f. 59, microfilm 80, Virginia State Library; St. James [Episcopal] Parish (Lothian), Anne Arundel Co., Md., Vestry Minutes, f. 19, Maryland Hall of Records; Prince George's County Court Records, liber B, f. 58a, Maryland Hall of Records; Henrico County Record Book No. 2, Orders and Wills, 1678–1693, transcript, p. 226, microfilm 53, Virginia State Library; Chester County Court of Quarter Sessions, 1733–1742, f. 104, microfilm 558,038, Pennsylvania State Archives.

61. *Records of New Amsterdam*, II, 335.

62. *Essex County Court Records*, VII, 418–19.

63. Accomack County Orders, 1666–1670, f. 21, microfilm 78, Virginia State Library. Despite her gesture, Ann Gray's husband divorced her the following year (f. 60b).

64. *Early Records of the Town of Providence*, V, 9.

65. The agreement appears in the *Ecclesiastical Records of the State of New York* (Albany: J. B. Lyon, 1901–1905), II, 764, and with the full case in the *Minutes of Albany, Rensselaerswyck and Schenectady*, III, 151.

66. See e.g. *Public Records of the Colony of Connecticut*, I, 47–48; *Archives of Maryland*, IV, 25, 192; and Minutes of the Baltimore Yearly and Half Yearly Meetings of the Society of Friends, 1677–1758, f. 5, microfilm M547, Maryland Hall of Records. On Quaker "inquiries", see further Barry Levy, *Quakers and the American Family: British Settlement in the Delaware Valley* (New York: Oxford University Press, 1988), pp. 129–130, 132–135, and Frost, *The Quaker Family in Colonial America*, ch. 9.

67. *Records of New Amsterdam*, I, 192, 197–98, 199–200, quote from 200.

68. *Plymouth Colony Records*, VII, 101, 108–109.

69. "Records of the Particular Court of Connecticut, 1639–1663," Conn. Hist. Soc., *Colls.*, XXII, 91.

70. *Essex County Court Records*, I, 44.

71. Ibid., I, 23.

72. *Records of New Amsterdam*, I, 163–165, 173–174, quote from 165.

73. C. J. Hoadly, ed., *Records of the Colony and Plantation of New Haven* (Hartford, 1857–1858), II, 600.

74. Richard B. Morris, ed., *Select Cases of the Mayor's Court of New York City, 1674–1784* (Washington, D.C.: American Historical Association, 1935), p. 744.

75. *Records of the Governor and Company of Massachusetts Bay,* IV, part 1, p. 295.

76. Colonial Society of Pennsylvania, *Records of the Court of New Castle of Delaware, 1676–1681* (Lancaster: Wickersham Printing, 1904), pp. 114–15.

77. "Records of the Suffolk County Court, 1671–1680," Col. Soc. Mass., *Colls.,* XXX, 943; *Province and Court Records of Maine* (Portland: Maine Historical Society, 1928–1975), I, 169; *Records of the Court of New Castle of Delaware, 1676–1681,* p. 289.

78. *Archives of Maryland,* XLI, 528.

79. Calhoun, *A Social History of the American Family,* I, 60.

80. *Records of Rhode Island and Providence Plantations,* III, 436–437. For similar orders, see also *Archives of Maryland,* LXX, 121, LIV, 638, and *Essex County Court Records,* VII, 271, 272.

81. *Records of New Amsterdam,* I, 159–60.

82. Ibid., I, 37–38.

83. *Plymouth Colony Records,* III, 206; IV, 9.

84. *Burlington Court Book of West New Jersey, 1680–1709,* p. 229.

85. *Archives of Maryland,* XLIX, 85.

86. Ibid., XLI, 150.

87. *Colonial Records of the State of Georgia* (Atlanta and Athens, 1904–1979), V, 80.

88. *Records of the Court of New Castle of Delaware, 1676–1681,* p. 179.

89. For examples of authorities punishing fornication without the evidence of pregnancy, see St. Anne's [Episcopal] Church, Fairlee, Kent Co., Md., Vestry Minutes, II, f. 118, Maryland Hall of Records; *County Court Records of Accomack-Northampton, Virginia, 1632–1640,* p. 151; *Archives of Maryland,* LIII; Kent County Court Proceedings, liber I, f. 37, Maryland Hall of Records; *Essex County Court Records,* II, 151; *Court Records of Prince George's County, Maryland, 1696–1699,* p. 435.

90. See e.g. *Archives of Maryland,* XLI, 528.

91. *Plymouth Colony Records,* V, 260.

92. In Virginia in 1638, Alice Wilson testified that when she urged Olive Eaton "in the instant time of her payne in travell, to declare who was the true father of the child she was then to be delivered of, she answered William Fisher." *County Court Records of Accomack-Northampton, Virginia, 1632–1640,* p. 129. See also Catherine M. Scholten, *Childbearing in American Society: 1650–1850,* ed. Lynn Withey (New York: New York University Press, 1985), p. 25.

93. A.J.F. Van Laer, ed., *Minutes of the Court of Fort Orange and Bever-wyck, 1652–1660* (Albany: University of the State of New York, 1920–1923), I, 188–190, quote from 189.

94. *Archives of Maryland*, LIV, 366;"Plymouth Church Records, 1620–1859," in Col. Soc. Mass., *Colls.*, XXII–XXIII (Boston, 1920, 1923), XXII, 265.

95. On Quakers, see Marietta, *The Transformation of American Quaker-ism*, pp. 13–14. On Plymouth, see e.g. *Plymouth Colony Records,* II, 109–110, 112; IV, 83; VI, 115; VI, 201.

96. "Records of the Suffolk County Court, 1671–1680," Col. Soc. Mass., *Colls.*, XXX, 914.

97. *County Court Records of Accomack-Northampton, Virginia, 1632–1640*, p. 129; "Records of the Suffolk County Court, 1671–1680," Col. Soc. Mass., *Colls.*, XXIX, 90–91.

98. "Plymouth Church Records, 1620–1859," Col. Soc. Mass., *Colls.*, XXII, 256.

99. Joseph H. Smith, ed., *Colonial Justice in Western Massachusetts, 1639–1702: The Pynchon Court Record* (Cambridge: Harvard University Press, 1961), pp. 272–273; William Faulkner, *The Town* (New York: Random House, 1957; Vintage ed., 1961), p. 76.

100. Marylynn Salmon, *Women and the Law of Property in Early America* (Chapel Hill: University of North Carolina Press, 1986), p. 12. See also D. Kelly Weisberg, "Under Great Temptations Heer: Women and Divorce Law in Puritan Massachusetts," in Weisberg, ed., *Women and the Law: The Social Historical Perspective* (Cambridge: Schenkman, 1982), II, 117–131.

101. Norton, "The Evolution of White Women's Experience in Early Amer-ica", *American Historical Review,* 89 (1984), 598.

102. See e.g. *Essex County Court Records*, VI, 172; VII, 150; *Ecclesiastical Records of the State of New York*, I, 288.

103. *Province and Court Records of Maine*, II, 304.

104. Boston Registry Department, *Boston Town Records* (Boston: Rock-well and Churchill, 1876–1909), X, 59; *Essex County Court Records*, VII, 238.

105. *Essex County Court Records*, I, 166, 159.

106. Ibid., I, 157.

107. *Records of the Governor and Company of Massachusetts Bay*, IV, Part 1, p. 32; *Records of the Court of Assistants of Massachusetts Bay*, I, 144. For some other examples, see *Records of the Governor and Company of Massa-chusetts Bay*, III, 277; *Public Records of the Colony of Connecticut*, II, 327; *Records of Rhode Island and Providence Plantations*, III, 11.

108. *Plymouth Colony Records*, IV, 156.

109. *Records of Rhode Island and Providence Plantations*, III, 181–182.

110. Records of the Pennsylvania Supreme Court, Eastern District: Appearance and Continuance Dockets, I, 1740–1751, f. 73, Record Group 33, microfilm 1, Pennsylvania State Archives; *Essex County Court Records*, I, 158.

111. Prince George's County Court Records, liber B, f. 300, Maryland Hall of Records; *Public Records of the Colony of Connecticut*, II, 293; *Records of the Court of Assistants of Massachusetts Bay*, I, 200.

112. See e.g. *Early Records of the Town of Providence*, VIII, 179; *Essex County Court Records*, V, 356; Prince George's County Court Records, liber B, ff. 187–187a, liber O, ff. 409–10, liber FF, ff. 4–5, Maryland Hall of Records; Lancaster County Orders, no. 7, 1721–1729, f. 51, microfilm 27, Virginia State Library; *Public Records of the Colony of Connecticut*, I, 224; *Province and Court Records of Maine*, III, 76; *Archives of Maryland*, LXVI, 315.

113. *Essex County Court Records*, IX, 114.

114. Accomack County Orders, 1710–1714, f. 40a, microfilm 80, Virginia State Library; Records of the Pennsylvania Supreme Court, Eastern District: Appearance and Continuance Dockets, I, 1740–1751, f. 11, Record Group 33, microfilm 1, Pennsylvania State Archives.

115. See e.g. the Accomack County, Virginia, case in which a husband who had abandoned his wife had to reimburse the parish for her support; if necessary the wardens were empowered to take him "up as a vagabond and Bind him out to maintaine himselfe and family." Accomack County Orders, 1676–1678, f. 12, microfilm 79, Virginia State Library.

116. See e.g. *Colonial Records of Pennsylvania: Minutes of the Provincial Council* (Harrisburg and Philadelphia, 1838–1853), I, 504; *Records of the Governor and Company of Massachusetts Bay*, V, 39; *Records of Rhode Island and Providence Plantations*, II, 120.

117. *Early Records of the Town of Providence*, XVII, 139. On this case, see also Calhoun, *A Social History of the American Family*, I, 143.

118. For some examples, see Victor Hugo Paltsits, ed., *Minutes of the Executive Council of the Province of New York: Administration of Francis Lovelace, 1668–1673* (Albany, 1910), II, 751; *Plymouth Colony Records*, III, 186, V, 127; *Burlington Court Book of West New Jersey, 1680–1709*, p. 228; William Saunders, ed., *Colonial Records of North Carolina* (Raleigh, 1886–1890), II, 363; Lancaster County Orders, no. 7, 1721–1729, f. 328, microfilm 27, Virginia State Library.

119. *Records of Rhode Island and Providence Plantations*, II, 293–94; *Essex County Court Records*, V, 308.

120. See Nancy F. Cott, "Divorce and the Changing Status of Women in Eighteenth-Century Massachusetts," *William and Mary Quarterly*, 3d ser., 33 (1976), 586–614.

121. *Records of the Court of Assistants of Massachusetts Bay*, I, 10.

122. Accomack County Orders, 1666–1670, f. 51a, microfilm 78, Virginia State Library.

123. Prince George's County Court Records, liber B, ff. 52–52a, Maryland Hall of Records.

124. *Winthrop's Journal*, II, 257–259. The Adultery Law of 1650 made adultery a capital crime, but juries were so reluctant to apply the death penalty for the crime that, as in this case, they typically convicted on a lesser charge. Only one couple convicted of adultery was executed in Massachusetts Bay: Mary Latham and James Britton, in 1644. See N.E.H. Hull, *Female Felons: Women and Serious Crime in Colonial Massachusetts* (Urbana: University of Illinois Press, 1987), pp. 29, 31, 39n, and Edwin Powers, *Crime and Punishment in Early Massachusetts, 1620–1692* (Boston: Beacon Press, 1966), pp. 279, 291–292.

125. *Plymouth Colony Records*, IV, 42.

126. Ibid., III, 110–12; IV, 116–17.

127. *New Haven Colony Records*, I, 233–35, 239.

128. *Burlington Court Book of West New Jersey, 1680–1709*, p. 136; Prince George's County Court Records, liber B, ff. 13a–14, Maryland Hall of Records; *Archives of Maryland*, X, 558.

129. *Province and Court Records of Maine*, II, 42; Christ [Episcopal] Church, St. Peter's Parish, Easton, Talbot Co., Md., Vestry Minutes, ff. 225–26, Maryland Hall of Records.

130. *Plymouth Colony Records*, II, 163.

131. *Minutes of the Court of Albany, Rensselaerswyck and Schenectady*, III, 298.

132. *Province and Court Records of Maine*, VI, 154.

133. Dixon Ryan Fox, ed., "Minutes of the Court of Sessions (1657–1696), Westchester County, New York," in *Publications of the Westchester County Historical Society* (White Plains, N.Y., 1924), II, 8.

134. *Province and Court Records of Maine*, II, 183; *Records of the Court of Assistants of Massachusetts Bay*, II, 93; "Records of the Suffolk County Court, 1671–1680," Col. Soc. Mass., *Colls*, XXIX, 410.

135. *Minutes of the Court of Albany, Rensselaerswyck and Schenectady*, II, 19–20.

136. Charles County Court Records, liber X, no. 1, f. 150, Maryland Hall of Records.

137. See e.g. "Records of the Suffolk County Court, 1671–1680," Col. Soc. Mass., *Colls.*, XXIX, 307, 410; *Province and Court Records of Maine*, III, 189–90; *Plymouth Colony Records*, III, 6–7; *Minutes of the Court of Albany, Rensselaerswyck and Schenectady*, III, 70; and *Essex County Court Records*, VIII, 344–45.

138. See e.g. *Province and Court Records of Maine*, I, 135, II, 217; *Records*

of the Governor and Company of Massachusetts Bay, I, 246; Richard D. Pierce, ed., *Records of the First Church in Salem, Massachusetts, 1629–1736* (Salem: Essex Institute, 1974), p. 149; *New Haven Town Records,* II, 159–62; *Records of the Court of Assistants of Massachusetts Bay,* II, 108; *Essex County Court Records,* II, 344; and *Plymouth Colony Records,* V, 87. For an excellent discussion of the expectations of women in one region, see Laurel Thatcher Ulrich, *Good Wives: Image and Reality in the Lives of Women in Northern New England, 1650–1750* (New York: Knopf, 1982).

139. *Plymouth Colony Records,* III, 75. For some other presentments of women who used or threatened violence against their husbands, see *Essex County Court Records,* I, 6, 25; "Records of the Suffolk County Court, 1671–1680," Col. Soc. Mass., *Colls.,* XXIX, 116; and *Archives of Maryland,* X, 109.

140. See e.g. *Records of New Amsterdam,* III, 90; *New Haven Town Records,* II, 161; and *Plymouth Colony Records,* V, 29.

141. *New Haven Town Records,* I, 246–47.

142. See e.g. *Province and Court Records of Maine,* II, 63–64; *Essex County Court Records,* I, 59, 158, VI, 386–387, VII, 249, 381.

143. *Minutes of the Court of Albany, Rensselaerswyck and Schenectady,* I, 126–127.

144. *Essex County Court Records,* III, 218; *Plymouth Colony Records,* V, 28.

145. *Essex County Court Records,* III, 192.

146. *Province and Court Records of Maine,* II, 460.

147. Court of General Quarter Sessions, New York City, book 3, f. 55, microfilm CMS1, Historical Documents Collection, Queens College, City University of New York.

148. *Plymouth Colony Records,* IV, 93, 106-08, 125–26.

149. *Archives of Maryland,* X, 109–12.

150. "Kingston Court Records, 1661–1667," *New York Historical Manuscripts: Dutch,* XXV, part 2, p. 392.

151. "Early Records of the City and County of Albany and Colony of Rensselaerswyck," New York State Library, *History Bulletin,* X, 363–364.

152. *Essex County Court Records,* VIII, 356. For a similar complaint, see also *Records of Rhode Island and Providence Plantations,* II, 543. On children as the true end of marriage, see Cotton Mather, *Magnalia Christi Americana* (Hartford, 1820), II, 217–218, and the comments of a New York court in the divorce case of Eleazer and Rebecca Leveridge in 1670, in *Minutes of the Executive Council of the Province of New York: Administration of Francis Lovelace, 1668–1673,* I, 334–335. See also John Demos, *A Little Commonwealth: Family Life in Plymouth Colony* (New York: Oxford University Press, 1970), pp. 95–96.

153. *Plymouth Colony Records,* VI, 190–92.

154. *Records of the Court of Assistants of Massachusetts Bay,* III, 131–32.

155. "Charles City County Order Book, 1655–1665," in Fleet, ed., *Virginia Colonial Abstracts,* ser. 1, XIII, 45. For similar cases, see also Chancery Court Proceedings, VI, ff. 207-208, Maryland Hall of Records; and *Colonial Records of North Carolina,* IV, 1042.

156. *Records of Rhode Island and Providence Plantations,* III, 194.

157. "New Hampshire Province Records and Court Papers, 1680–1692," in *Collections of the New Hampshire Historical Society,* VIII (1866), 68.

158. "Records of the Suffolk County Court, 1671–1680," Col. Soc. Mass., *Colls.,* XXIX, 88, and XXX, 867; *Plymouth Colony Records,* V, 61.

159. See e.g. Lancaster County Orders, no. 1, 1666–1680, f. 118, microfilm 24, Virginia State Library; Chester County Court of Quarter Sessions, 1733–1742, f. 104, microfilm 558,038, Pennsylvania State Archives; *Archives of Maryland,* LXV, 50; *Pennsylvania Colonial Records: Minutes of the Provincial Council,* I, 296.

160. Chancery Court Proceedings, II, ff. 579–80, Maryland Hall of Records. For similar cases across the regions, see *Province and Court Records of Maine,* II, 154–155; *Records of New Amsterdam,* VI, 65; *Records of the Court of Chancery of South Carolina, 1671–1779,* pp. 326–327; *Essex County Court Records,* I, 135.

161. *Province and Court Records of Maine,* II, 403, 263.

162. Prince George's County Court Records, liber K, ff. 558, 664, Maryland Hall of Records.

163. *Essex County Court Records,* V, 377.

164. Elizabeth Pleck, *Domestic Tyranny: The Making of American Social Policy against Family Violence from Colonial Times to the Present* (New York: Oxford University Press, 1987), pp. 30–31. For an excellent study of domestic violence with a narrower focus, Boston in the late nineteenth and twentieth centuries, see Linda Gordon, *Heroes of Their Own Lives* (New York: Viking, 1988).

165. On these points generally, see Salmon, *Women and the Law of Property in Early America;* Mary Beth Norton, "The Evolution of White Women's Experience in Early America," *American Historical Review,* 89 (1984), 593–619; Peter Hoffer and N.E.H. Hull, *Murdering Mothers: Infanticide in England and New England, 1558–1803* (New York: New York University Press, 1981); N.E.H. Hull, *Female Felons: Women and Serious Crime in Colonial Massachusetts;* Emil Oberholzer, *Delinquent Saints: Disciplinary Action in the Early Congregational Churches of Massachusetts* (New York: Columbia University Press, 1963). In addition, Barry Levy has argued that in order to protect the inheritance rights of children, Quaker widows were excluded from control of property and finances even more effectively than New England

women; see his *Quakers and the American Family,* pp. 198–203. On the use-fulness of equity law for women, see Suzanne Lebsock, *The Free Women of Petersburg: Status and Culture in a Southern Town, 1784–1860* (New York: Norton, 1984).

166. Mary Beth Norton suggests both of these points in "The Evolution of White Women's Experience in Early America." For a more detailed discussion of the Chesapeake, see Walsh, "'Till Death Us Do Part.'" On the importance of a spiritual, "ministerial" role for Quaker women, see Levy, *Quakers and the American Family,* pp. 203ff.

167. See Carol Karlsen, *The Devil in the Shape of a Woman* (New York: Norton, 1987). For a discussion of heightened reaction to women's offenses in a period of disordered gender relations in England, see David Underdown, "The Taming of the Scold: The Enforcement of Patriarchal Authority in Early Modern England," in *Order and Disorder in Early Modern England,* ed. Anthony Fletcher and John Stevenson (Cambridge: Cambridge University Press, 1985).

168. Prince George's County Court Records, liber N, f. 497, Maryland Hall of Records.

169. *New Haven Colony Records,* I, 415; *Calendar of Virginia State Papers, 1790–1792* (Richmond, 1875–1890; repr. New York: Kraus Reprint, 1968), I, 53.

170. *Essex County Court Records,* I, 360.

171. *Records of Rhode Island and Providence Plantations,* I, 319; Accomack County Orders and Wills, 1671–1673, f. 59, microfilm 2, Virginia State Library.

172. *Minutes of the Court of Fort Orange and Beverwyck,* I, 248.

173. *Essex County Court Records,* VI, 194–95, 297–99.

174. *Minutes of the Court of Albany, Rensselaerswyck and Schenectady,* III, 133, quote from 149.

175. "Kingston Court Records, 1661–1667," *New York Historical Manuscripts: Dutch,* XXV, part 2, pp. 478–79.

176. *Colonial Justice in Western Massachusetts,* pp. 235–36.

177. *Records of New Amsterdam,* II, 335, 374–75; IV, 304.

178. Ibid., VII, 27.

179. *Records of the Governor and Company of Massachusetts Bay,* IV, part 2, pp. 426–27.

180. Accomack County Orders and Wills, 1671–1673, f. 73, microfilm 2, Virginia State Library. On records of divorce, see Accomack County Orders, 1666–1670, f. 60b, microfilm 78, Virginia State Library.

181. *Records of New Amsterdam,* V, 206-07, 275–76, 282.

182. *Records of Rhode Island and Providence Plantations,* II, 251.

183. *Records of New Amsterdam,* III, 23.

184. *Essex County Court Records,* VIII, 272.

185. Prince George's County Court Records, liber AA, f. 350, Maryland Hall of Records.

186. Accomack County Orders and Wills, 1671–1673, ff. 10. 11, 84, 105; quote from ibid., f. 319: both on microfilm 2, Virginia State Library.

187. *Records of New Amsterdam,* V, 276; *Province and Court Records of Maine,* II, 92.

188. "New Hampshire Province Records and Court Papers, 1680–1692," in *Collections of the New Hampshire Historical Society,* VIII, 100-101.

189. *Province and Court Records of Maine,* I, 264–65, 300; "Kingston Court Records, 1661–1667," *New York Historical Manuscripts: Dutch,* XXV, part 2, p. 487.

190. "Records of the Suffolk County Court, 1671–1680," Col. Soc. Mass., *Colls.,* XXX, 837–41, quote from XXX, 840; *Records of the Court of Assistants of Massachusetts Bay,* I, 91, 101.

4. The Ambiguities of Family

1. Daniel Scott Smith, "The Demographic History of Colonial New England," *Journal of Economic History,* 32 (1972), 165–83; Lorena S. Walsh, "'Till Death Us Do Part,'" in Thad Tate and David Ammerman, eds., *The Chesapeake in the Seventeenth Century: Essays on Anglo-American Society and Politics* (Chapel Hill: University of North Carolina Press, 1979). See also John Demos, *A Little Commonwealth: Family Life in Plymouth Colony* (New York: Oxford University Press, 1970), ch. 4; Philip Greven, *Four Generations: Population, Land and Family in Colonial Andover, Massachusetts* (Ithaca: Cornell University Press, 1970), ch. 2; Susan L. Norton, "Population Growth in Colonial America: A Study of Ipswich, Massachusetts," *Population Studies,* 25 (1971), 433–452; John J. McCusker and Russell Menard, *The Economy of British North America, 1607–1789* (Chapel Hill: University of North Carolina Press, 1985); Russell Menard, "Immigrants and Their Increase: The Process of Population Growth in Early Colonial Maryland," in Aubrey C. Land, Lois Green Carr, and Edward C. Papenfuse, eds., *Law, Society, and Politics in Early Maryland* (Baltimore: Johns Hopkins University Press, 1977); Gloria L. Main, *Tobacco Colony* (Princeton: Princeton University Press, 1982), pp. 11–16; Darrett B. Rutman and Anita H. Rutman, "'Now-Wives and Sons-in-Law': Parental Death in a Seventeenth Century Virginia County," in Tate and Ammerman, eds., *The Chesapeake in the Seventeenth Century.* The Rutmans suggest that, in seventeenth-century Middlesex County, orphanhood was "an event for almost 20 percent of the children before their thirteenth birthday and for over 30 percent before their eighteenth." (p. 162).

2. See e.g. "Abstracts of Wills on File in the Surrogate's Office, City of New York, 1665–1800," *Collections of the New-York Historical Society* (New

York, 1893–1909), XXVI, 276–277, 363–364; Richard B. Morris, ed., *Select Cases of the Mayor's Court of New York City, 1674–1784* (Washington, D.C.: American Historical Association, 1935), p. 188; Colonial Society of Pennsylvania, *Records of the Court of New Castle, Delaware, 1676–1681* (Lancaster: Wickersham Printing Company, 1904), pp. 59–60; Berthold Fernow, ed., *The Records of New Amsterdam, 1653–1674* (New York: Knickerbocker Press, 1897), I, 235.

3. Caroline T. Moore and Agatha Aimar Simmons, eds., *Abstracts of the Wills of the State of South Carolina, 1670–1740* (Columbia: R.L. Bryan, 1960), I, 2.

4. See e.g *Essex County Court Records,* I, 157–158, and IX, 226; Norfolk County Orders, 1746–1750, n.f. [March 1748], microfilm 53, Virginia State Library. For restrictions on Quaker widows in particular, see Barry Levy, *Quakers and the American Family: British Settlement in the Delaware Valley* (New York: Oxford University Press, 1988), pp. 198–203.

5. "Abstracts of Wills on File in the Surrogate's Office, City of New York, 1665–1800," *Collections of the New-York Historical Society,* XXVIII, 341, and XXV, 216. For examples of more specific instructions, see ibid., XXVIII, 198, 419, and Testamentary Proceedings, V-A, f. 37, Maryland Hall of Records.

6. Shurtleff, ed., *Plymouth Colony Records,* V, 212.

7. J. Hammond Trumbull and C.J. Hoadly, eds., *Public Records of the Colony of Connecticut* (Hartford, 1850–1890), I, 446.

8. "Probate Records of New Hampshire, 1635–1771," *New Hampshire State Papers* (Concord, 1907–), XXXI, 167–168.

9. Providence, R.I., *Early Records of the Town of Providence* (Providence: Snow and Farnham, 1892–1915), X, 46–47.

10. *Essex County Court Records,* V, 307-08.

11. Ibid., VI, 299.

12. Prince George's County Court Records, liber LL, f. 131, Maryland Hall of Records.

13. *Plymouth Colony Records,* II, 143; *Essex County Court Records,* I, 382–383.

14. Baltimore County Court Proceedings, liber I.S.No. B [A], f. 93, Maryland Hall of Records.

15. Accomack County Orders, 1710–1714, f. 8, microfilm 80, Virginia State Library.

16. *Colonial Records of the State of Georgia* (Atlanta and Athens, 1904–1979), II, 391.

17. Prince George's County Court Records, liber Z, f. 189, Maryland Hall of Records.

18. "Note-Book Kept by Thomas Lechford," American Antiquarian Society, *Transactions and Collections* (1885), VII, 411.

19. "Journal of William Stephens," in *Colonial Records of Georgia*, IV, 393–395.

20. Franklin Bowditch Dexter and Zara Jane Powers, eds., *New Haven Town Records, 1648–1684 and 1684–1769* (New Haven, 1917–1919, 1962), II, 208–209.

21. Testamentary Proceedings, VI-A, f. 270, Maryland Hall of Records; *Essex County Court Records*, I, 140; Susie Ames, ed., *County Court Records of Accomack-Northampton, Virginia, 1640–1645* (Charlottesville: University Press of Virginia, 1973), p. 247.

22. "Abstracts of Wills on File in the Surrogate's Office, City of New York, 1665–1800," *Collections of the New-York Historical Society*, XXX, 173–174. This view of stepparents accords with the English experience. Peter Laslett observes that "the step-mother and her evil influence is so conspicuous a feature of the fairy tales and of the literature as a whole, that it seems to correspond to something important in the lives of those who repeated them"; he notes further that "it cannot be without significance that 35.5 per cent of all the children alive in Clayworth in May, 1688, were orphans in the sense that one parent or other had died whilst they were still dependent" (*The World We Have Lost* [2d ed., New York: Scribner's, 1973], pp. 95–96). For a broader discussion of the historical and cultural meanings of early modern fairy tales, see Robert Darnton, "Peasants Tell Tales: The Meaning of Mother Goose," in *The Great Cat Massacre* (New York: Basic Books, 1984), pp. 9–72. On a different level of analysis, Bruno Bettelheim discusses the creation of a wicked stepparent as a response to Oedipal conflicts, in *The Uses of Enchantment* (New York: Knopf, 1977).

23. *Archives of Maryland*, LVII, 234; *Plymouth Colony Records*, III, 156.

24. Anne King Gregorie and J. Nelson Frierson, eds., *Records of the Court of Chancery of South Carolina, 1671–1779* (Washington, D.C.: American Historical Association, 1950), p. 152.

25. *Archives of Maryland*, LIV, 386.

26. Prince George's County Court Records, liber L, ff. 562–63, Maryland Hall of Records.

27. Ibid., liber D, ff. 219, 276–77, Maryland Hall of Records.

28. "Abstracts of Wills on File in the Surrogate's Office, City of New York, 1665–1800," *Collections of the New-York Historical Society*, XXXV, 37.

29. *Archives of Maryland*, LXV, 192–193.

30. On legal protections for orphans in Maryland, see Lois Green Carr, "The Development of the Maryland Orphans' Court, 1654–1715," in Land et al., eds., *Law, Society, and Politics in Early Maryland;* on Virginia, see Rutman and Rutman, "'Now-Wives and Sons-in-Law'" in Tate and Ammerman, eds., *The Chesapeake in the Seventeenth Century*, pp. 164–167.

31. A.J.F. Van Laer, trans. and ed., "Early Records of the City and County

of Albany and Colony of Rensselaerswyck," New York State Library, *History Bulletin* (Albany: University of the State of New York, 1916–1919), X, 206–207.

32. Berthold Fernow, ed., *The Minutes of the Orphan-masters of New Amsterdam, 1655–1663* (New York: Francis P. Harper, 1902), pp. 87–89, 95–96, 99–100, 101, 102–103, 106, 111, 118, 122–123, 135, 142–143, 154–155.

33. "Records of the First Church in Boston, 1630–1868," Publications of the Colonial Society of Massachusetts, *Collections* (Boston, 1961), XXXIX, 20.

34. Baltimore County Court Proceedings, liber I.S. No. A [B], f. 11, Maryland Hall of Records; *Essex County Court Records*, I, 258; Lancaster County Orders, no. 1, 1666–1680, f. 124, microfilm 24, Virginia State Library.

35. *Essex County Court Records*, VI, 242–43.

36. Norfolk County Wills and Deeds, liber D, 1656–1666, f. 237, microfilm 45, Virginia State Library.

37. See e.g. *Archives of Maryland*, LXX, 457; Stratton Nottingham, comp. and ed., *Wills and Administrations of Accomack County, Virginia, 1663–1800* (1931; repr. Cottonport, La.: Polyanthos, 1973), p. 47; "Council Minutes [of New Netherland], 1638–1649," *New York Historical Manuscripts: Dutch* (Baltimore: Genealogical Publishing Company, 1974), IV, 302.

38. *Plymouth Colony Records*, VI, 66.

39. See e.g. *Essex County Court Records*, IX, 217; *Records of the Court of Chancery of South Carolina, 1671–1779*, pp. 269–270; *Archives of Maryland*, LIV, 440.

40. On guardians as general protectors, see e.g. Charles R. Street, ed., *Huntington Town Records, 1653–1873* (Huntington, N.Y., 1887–1889), I, 168; *Records of New Amsterdam*, I, 191. For cases of guardians who accepted direct responsibility for the children, see *Plymouth Colony Records*, III, 22; *Records of the Court of New Castle of Delaware, 1676–1681*, p. 180.

41. "Probate Records of New Hampshire, 1635–1771," *New Hampshire State Papers*, XXXI, 535.

42. See e.g. Berks County Orphans' Court Records, I, 45, microfilm 6–22, Pennsylvania State Archives; Accomack County Orders, 1719–1724, f. 26, microfilm 80, Virginia State Library; *Minutes of the Court of the Orphan-masters of New Amsterdam, 1655–1663*, pp. 5–6, 7–8; "Northumberland County Orders, 1678–1713," in Lindsay O. Duvall, ed., *Virginia Colonial Abstracts* (Washington, D.C., and Wharton Grove, Va., 1952–1961), I, 30; *Archives of Maryland*, XLIX, 552; Prince George's County Court Records, liber O, ff. 237–38, Maryland Hall of Records.

43. *Calendar of Virginia State Papers, 1790–1792* (Richmond, 1875–1890; repr. New York: Kraus Reprint, 1968), I, 4; Prince George's County Court Records, liber L, f. 247, Maryland Hall of Records.

44. *Archives of Maryland,* XLI, 417.

45. *Calendar of Virginia State Papers and Other Manuscripts* [1652–1839], (Richmond, 1875–1893), I, 93; Baltimore County Court Proceedings, liber H.W.S. no. 9, f. 306, Maryland Hall of Records.

46. Rutman and Rutman, " 'Now-Wives and Sons-in-Law,' " in Tate and Ammerman, eds., *The Chesapeake in the Seventeenth Century,* pp. 166–167; Bernard Farber, *Guardians of Virtue: Salem Families in 1800* (New York: Basic Books, 1972), pp. 61–62. In committing his children to relatives in Massachusetts in 1653, John Cogswell urged one to "bee Ernest with my sister waldo to be loveinge and tender to my 3 babes for shee knowed not how sowe hers maye be left to the world." See *Essex County Court Records,* VI, 153.

47. *Essex County Court Records,* I, 268.

48. *Archives of Maryland,* XLI, 330.

49. *Essex County Court Records,* VI, 300.

50. Testamentary Proceedings, VIII-A, 248–49, Maryland Hall of Records; *Archives of Maryland,* LXV, 90.

51. "Plymouth Church Records, 1620–1859," Col. Soc. Mass., *Colls.,* XXII, 265–266.

52. A.J.F. Van Laer, trans. and ed., *Minutes of the Court of Albany, Rensselaerswyck and Schenectady* (Albany: The University of the State of New York, 1926–1932), III, 35–36.

53. Howard M. Chapin, ed., *The Early Records of the Town of Warwick* [Rhode Island] (Providence: E.A. Johnson, 1926), pp. 221–223.

54. *Minutes of the Common Council of the City of New York, 1665–1776* (New York: Dodd, Mead, 1905), IV, 113. On childbirth and midwifery in colonial society, see Catherine Scholten, *Childbearing in American Society, 1650–1850* (New York: New York University Press, 1985), as well as her article, "On the Importance of the Obstetrick Art: Changing Customs of Childbirth in America, 1760–1825," *William and Mary Quarterly,* 3d ser., 34 (1977), 426–445. On colonial New England, see also Laurel Thatcher Ulrich, *Good Wives: Image and Reality in the Lives of Women in Northern New England, 1650–1750* (New York: Knopf, 1982), pp. 126–135.

55. See e.g. *Archives of Maryland,* LIV, 314; Lancaster County Miscellaneous Book: Orphans' Court Records, 1742–1767, part I, p. 42, microfilm 36–19, Pennsylvania State Archives.

56. *Minutes of the Orphan-masters of New Amsterdam, 1655–1663,* p. 11.

57. Prince George's County Court Records, liber D, f. 219, Maryland Hall of Records.

58. Lancaster County Orders, no. 1, 1666–1680, f. 102, microfilm 24, Virginia State Library; Prince George's County Court Records, liber G, f. 213, Maryland Hall of Records.

59. See e.g. *Essex County Court Records,* I, 380; "Abstracts of Wills on File in the Surrogate's Office, City of New York, 1665–1800," *Collections of the*

New-York Historical Society, XXV, 14; *Early Records of the Town of Providence,* VIII, 107.

60. *Essex County Court Records,* I, 245.

61. John Cox, Jr., ed., *Oyster Bay Town Records, 1653–1763* (New York: Tobias Wright, 1916–1931), II, 327–328.

62. Anne Arundel County Court Judgments, liber R.C., ff. 560–561, Maryland Hall of Records.

63. The relative prominence of boys in the records of hiring or putting out may be misleading, however. Cornelia Dayton has suggested that the putting out of girls may have been handled more informally. This is not only plausible, but it would also fit with the work of Laurel Thatcher Ulrich and others on the active, complicated, but still somewhat hidden world of women's economic and labor exchanges in the colonial period. See Cornelia Hughes Dayton, "Women Before the Bar: Gender, Law, and Society in Connecticut, 1710–1790" (diss., Princeton University, 1986), pp. 78–80; I must also thank Cornelia Dayton for sending me an earlier unpublished paper and some relevant documents in which she raises this issue. See also Laurel Thatcher Ulrich, "Martha Ballard and Her Girls: Women's Work in Eighteenth-Century Maine," in Stephen Innes, ed., *Work and Labor in Early America* (Chapel Hill: University of North Carolina Press, 1988).

64. Ray Potter, *Memoirs of the Life and Religious Experiences* (Providence, 1829), pp. 18ff; Richard Lee, *A Short Narrative of the Life of Mr. Richard Lee* (Kennebunk, Maine, 1804), p. 3.

65. *Essex County Court Records,* VIII, 249–250.

66. "Early Records of the City and County of Albany and Colony of Rensselaerswyck," New York State Library, *History Bulletin,* X, 477–478.

67. *Public Records of the Colony of Connecticut,* VII, 229.

68. *Essex County Court Records,* VI, 93–95.

69. *Archives of Maryland,* LIII, 193. This two-year term is so long that it may have extended beyond the period of wet nursing into general care. On wet nursing, see also Scholten, *Childbearing in American Society,* pp. 62–63.

70. C. G. Chamberlayne, ed., *The Vestry Book and Register of St. Peter's Parish, New Kent and James City Counties, Virginia, 1684–1786* (Richmond: Library Board, 1937), p. 217.

71. *Essex County Court Records,* II, 229.

72. Cotton Mather, *Memorable Providences, Relating to Witchcrafts and Possessions* (Boston, 1689), p. 18. On this case, see also Demos, *Entertaining Satan,* pp. 7–9.

73. *Plymouth Colony Records,* IV, 39; *Archives of Maryland,* XV, 47. On adoption, see Yasuhida Kawashima, "Adoption in Early America," *Journal of Family Law,* 20 (1982), 677–696.

74. *Essex County Court Records,* VI, 93–97; quotes from Essex County Quarterly Papers, XXIV, f. 53 ("Inventory and other papers Relating to Capt.

Thomas Lathrop, November, 1675"), Essex County Courthouse, Salem, Mass. I am grateful to Jeffrey Adler for this manuscript reference.

75. See e.g. *Records of the Court of Assistants of the Colony of Massachusetts Bay, 1630–1692* (Boston, 1901–1928), II, 17; "Indentures of Apprentices, 1718–1727," *Collections of the New-York Historical Society,* XLII (1909), p. 131.

76. See e.g. Clarence Brigham, ed., *The Early Records of the Town of Portsmouth* [Rhode Island] (Providence: E. L. Freeman, 1901), p. 414; Accomack County Orders, 1666–1670, f. 59, microfilm 78, Virginia State Library; *Early Records of the Town of Providence,* V, 146–48; *Essex County Court Records,* V, 417. For general information on colonial apprenticeship, see Robert Seybolt, *Apprenticeship and Apprenticeship Education in Colonial New England and New York* (New York: Teachers College, Columbia University, 1917); Marcus Jernegan, *Laboring and Dependent Classes in Colonial America, 1607–1783: Studies of the Economic, Educational and Social Significance of Slaves, Servants, Apprentices and Poor Folk* (Chicago, 1931), esp. chs. 6–8; David Galenson, *White Servitude in Colonial America* (New York: Cambridge University Press, 1981); Edmund S. Morgan, *The Puritan Family: Religion and Domestic Relations in Seventeenth-Century New England* (Boston, 1944; rev. ed., New York: Harper and Row, 1966), pp. 68–76; Lawrence Towner, "A Good Master Well Served: A Social History of Servitude in Massachusetts, 1620–1750," (diss., Northwestern University, 1955); Towner, "The Indentures of Boston's Poor Apprentices: 1734–1805," Colonial Society of Massachusetts, *Transactions,* 43 (1956–1963), 417–468; Bernard Bailyn, *Education in the Forming of American Society* (Chapel Hill: University of North Carolina Press, 1960), pp. 29–36; James Axtell, *The School upon a Hill* (New Haven: Yale University Press, 1974), ch. 3.

77. *Essex County Court Records,* I, 111.

78. See e.g. the 1666 indenture of Cornelius Dyckman of Albany in "Early Records of the City and County of Albany and the Colony of Rensselaerswyck," New York State Library, *History Bulletin,* X, 211. For an example of an indenture that uses both terms, see the indenture of Philip Lyon in "Indentures of Apprenticeship, 1694–1708," *Collections of the New-York Historical Society,* XVIII, 608–609.

79. See e.g. C. G. Chamberlayne, ed., *The Vestry Book of Petsworth Parish, Gloucester County, Virginia, 1677–1793* (Richmond: Library Board, 1933), p. 56; "Indentures of Apprenticeship, 1694–1708," *Collections of the New-York Historical Society,* XVIII, 593–94; *Select Cases of the Mayor's Court of New York City, 1674–1784,* p. 184; *Province and Court Records of Maine* (Portland: Maine Historical Society, 1928–1975), II, 499–500; Philadelphia County Orphans' Court Records, Book 1, f. 11, microfilm 51–124, Pennsylvania State Archives; Prince George's County Court Records, liber L, f. 333, Maryland Hall of Records.

80. Accomack County Orders, 1719–1724, f. 3, microfilm 80, Virginia State Library.

81. Anne Arundel County Court Judgments, liber T.B. No. 1, f. 48, Maryland Hall of Records.

82. C. G. Chamberlayne, ed., *The Vestry Book of Blisland (Blissland) Parish: New Kent and James City Counties, 1721–1786* (Richmond: Library Board, 1935), p. 16; *Select Cases of the Mayor's Court of New York City, 1674–1784*, p. 185; *Early Records of the Town of Providence*, VIII, 174; *Public Records of the Colony of Connecticut*, I, 222.

83. "Abstract of the First Wills in the Probate Office, Plymouth," *New England Historic and Genealogical Register*, IV (1850), 33. On this case, see also Morgan, *The Puritan Family*, pp. 76–77.

84. *Essex County Court Records*, V, 38; Joseph H. Smith and Philip A. Crowl, eds., *Court Records of Prince George's County, Maryland, 1696–1699* (Washington, D.C.: American Historical Association, 1964), p. 560.

85. See e.g. *Court Records of Prince George's County, Maryland, 1696–1699*, p. 131; *Vestry Book and Register of Bristol Parish, Virginia, 1720–1789*, p. 6. See also Galenson, *White Servitude in Colonial America*, p. 101.

86. *New Haven Colony Records*, I, 133–134; "Northumberland County Orders, 1678–1713," in Duvall, ed., *Virginia Colonial Abstracts*, ser. 2, I, 93.

87. Prince George's County Court Records, liber C 3, f. 95a, Maryland Hall of Records; Anne Arundel County Court Judgments, liber R.C. no. 1, f. 29, Maryland Hall of Records.

88. *Early Records of the Town of Warwick*, pp. 317–318; Prince George's County Court Records, liber L, f. 644, Maryland Hall of Records.

89. Court of General Quarter Sessions, New York City, book 2, f. 529, microfilm CMS1, Historical Documents Collection, Queens College, City University of New York.

90. Solomon Mack, *Narrative of the Life of Solomon Mack* (Windsor, Conn., 1810 [?]), p. 3. On Mack's relationship to Joseph Smith Jr., see Richard Bushman, *Joseph Smith and the Beginnings of Mormonism* (Urbana: University of Illinois Press, 1984), ch. 1.

91. *Essex County Court Records*, III, 188 (Rogers), and II, 23 (Johnson).

92. *Plymouth Colony Records*, II, 113.

93. *Early Records of the Town of Providence*, XI, 7; *Vestry Book and Register of Bristol Parish, Virginia, 1720–1789*, p. 45; Lancaster County Miscellaneous Book: Orphans' Court Records, 1742–1767, part I, p. 38, microfilm 36–19, Pennsylvania State Archives.

94. Baltimore County Court Proceedings, liber D, f. 75, Maryland Hall of Records.

95. Accomack County Orders, 1710–1714, f. 57a, microfilm 80, Virginia State Library.

96. See e.g. *Plymouth Colony Records*, V, 116; Charles County Court Rec-

ords, liber F, f. 13, Maryland Hall of Records; Bucks County Orphans' Court Docket, Vol. A–1, f. 19, microfilm 9–20, Pennsylvania State Archives; *Vestry Book of Petsworth Parish, Gloucester County, Virginia, 1677–1793,* p. 35; *Colonial Records of North Carolina,* I, 522. See also Orphans' Court Docket No. 1, ff. 18–20, 24, Office of the Register and Recorder of Northumberland County, Northumberland County Court House, Sunbury, Penn.; I am grateful to Peter Mancall for bringing these records to my attention and for providing me with a copy of the docket.

97. *Select Cases of the Mayor's Court of New York City, 1674–1784,* p. 184; *Early Records of the Town of Providence,* XII, 85.

98. *Vestry Book and Register of St. Peter's Parish, New Kent and James City Counties, Virginia, 1684–1786,* p. 58.

99. Joseph H. Smith, ed., *Colonial Justice in Western Massachusetts, 1639–1702: The Pynchon Court Record* (Cambridge: Harvard University Press, 1961), pp. 326–328.

100. "Records of the Particular Court of Connecticut, 1639–1663," *Collections of the Connecticut Historical Society* (Hartford, 1928), XXII, 97.

101. *Public Records of the Colony of Connecticut,* I, 521–22; William Brigham, ed., *The Compact, with the Charter and Laws of New Plymouth* (Boston, 1836), pp. 270–271.

102. *Essex County Court Records,* IV, 212–13.

103. Morgan, *The Puritan Family,* p. 77. Morgan offers this frankly speculative explanation for cases of putting out that do not seem to make sense in practical terms. I am suggesting that evidence of family crisis or disruption appears in almost all cases of putting out, and it is the only explanation explicitly given for the practice. Even one of the cases Morgan cites as inexplicable appears, upon a closer look, to stem from family crisis. Samuel Fuller of Plymouth, as noted above, referred explicitly to his wife's illness in arranging for the placement of his children after his death, and he also provided that they remain under his wife's care if she recovered. ("Abstract of the First Wills on Files in the Probate Office, Plymouth," *New England Historic and Genealogical Register,* IV, 33.) Some cases of putting out, especially when they involved putting out some children but taking in others at the same time, do seem mysterious, and perhaps some may be traced to New Englanders' fears of spoiling children. But family crisis appears to be a far more common, and more easily proven, explanation for the practice of putting out throughout the colonies.

104. "Records of the Suffolk County Court, 1671–1680," Col. Soc. Mass., *Colls.,* XXX, 599.

105. "Dorchester Town Records," in Boston Registry Department, *Boston Town Records* (Boston: Rockwell and Churchill, 1876–1909), IV, 229. Robert Stiles was no stranger to official displeasure. Eight years before they were ordered to put out their children, in 1671, Stiles and his wife were summoned

to appear before the selectmen "to answer for their Idleness, and upon examination it was found that both hee and his wife have not improved their time to the advantag of their famely as they ought and ther upon was advertized [advised] to reforme or elce to be further proceeded with as the law requiers" (IV, 181).

106. Ibid., IV, 236. In another case in Boston, the selectmen agreed in 1656 "upon the complaint against the son of Goodwife Sammon living without a calling, that if shee dispose nott of him in some way of employ before the next meeting, that then the townsemen will dispose of him according to some service according to law" (II, 132–133).

107. William Williams, *The Duty of Parents to Transmit Religion to Their Children* (Boston, 1721), p. 19.

108. *Essex County Court Records,* VI, 26.

109. *New Haven Town Records,* I, 112. On colonial attitudes toward poverty and the poor and important shifts in the eighteenth century, see Gary Nash, "Poverty and Poor Relief in Pre-revolutionary Philadelphia," *William and Mary Quarterly,* 3d ser., 33 (1976), 3–30; Nash, "Urban Wealth and Poverty in Pre-Revolutionary America," *Journal of Interdisciplinary History,* 6 (1975–1976), 547–576; Nash, *The Urban Crucible: Social Change, Political Consciousness, and the Origins of the American Revolution* (Cambridge: Harvard University Press, 1979), esp. chs. 5 and 9; Stephen Foster, *Their Solitary Way: The Puritan Social Ethic in the First Century of Settlement in New England* (New Haven: Yale University Press, 1971), ch. 5; and John K. Alexander, *Render Them Submissive: Responses to Poverty in Philadelphia, 1760–1800* (Amherst: University of Massachusetts Press, 1980). On the eighteenth century, see also Drew McCoy, *The Elusive Republic: Political Economy in Jeffersonian America* (Chapel Hill: University of North Carolina Press, 1980), esp. pp. 114–119, and J.E. Crowley, *This Sheba, Self: The Conceptualization of Economic Life in Eighteenth-Century America* (Baltimore: Johns Hopkins University Press, 1974), chs. 2–3. Cf. Rothman, *The Discovery of the Asylum,* ch. 7, on the timing of these changes.

110. Lancaster County Order Book No. 8, f. 135, microfilm 4, Virginia State Library; Ulster County, Court of General Sessions of the Peace, n.f. (September 1746), microfilm UC–50, Historical Documents Collection, Queens College, City University of New York.

111. *Plymouth Colony Records,* XI, 38; Jernegan, *Laboring and Dependent Classes in Colonial America,* p. 104; Farber, *Guardians of Virtue,* pp. 35–36; Towner, "The Indentures of Boston's Poor Apprentices, 1734–35," Col. Soc. Mass., *Transactions,* 43, pp. 417–68.

112. *Colonial Records of Georgia,* IV, 394.

113. See e.g. "Note-Book Kept by Thomas Lechford," VII, 158; Prince George's County Court Records, liber K, f. 84, Maryland Hall of Records;

Baltimore County Court Proceedings, accession 5023, f. 384, Maryland Hall of Records.

114. *Vestry Book of Blisland (Blissland) Parish: New Kent and James City Counties, Virginia, 1721–1786,* p. 29.

115. See e.g. *Archives of Maryland,* XLI, 112; "Records of the Suffolk County Court, 1671–1680," Col. Soc. Mass., *Colls.,* XXX, 779; *Vestry Book and Register of Bristol Parish, Virginia, 1720–1789,* p. 94; Minutes of the Quarterly Meeting for the Western Shore, Maryland, Society of Friends, 1680–1688, microfilm M571, f. 94, Maryland Hall of Records.

116. *Court Records of Prince George's County, Maryland, 1696–1699,* p. 542; Prince George's County Court Records, liber G, vol. I, f. 69a, liber P, f. 453, Maryland Hall of Records.

117. See e.g. Frederick County Court Judgment Records, accession 6838, ff. 394–95, Maryland Hall of Records; Baltimore County Court Proceedings, liber I.S. no. B [A], f. 662, Maryland Hall of Records; *Essex County Court Records,* VI, 207; Philadelphia County Orphans' Court Records, book 1, f. 16, microfilm 51–124, Pennsylvania State Archives.

118. "Journal of William Stephens," *Colonial Records of Georgia,* IV, 505-506.

119. *Essex County Court Records,* I, 206.

120. *Archives of Maryland,* LX, 417–18.

121. Baltimore County Court Proceedings, liber T.B. no. T.R., f. 8, Maryland Hall of Records.

122. See e.g. "Dorchester Town Records," *Boston Town Records,* IV, 165, and Cambridge, Mass., *The Records of the Town of Cambridge, 1630–1703* (Cambridge, 1901), II, 202.

123. "Indentures of Apprenticeship, 1694–1708," *Collections of the New-York Historical Society,* XVIII, 582.

124. *Province and Court Records of Maine,* II, 432.

125. *Essex County Court Records,* VI, 353.

126. *New Haven Town Records,* I, 312.

127. *Colonial Justice in Western Massachusetts,* p. 210.

128. *New Haven Town Records,* I, 312.

129. Watertown, Mass., *Watertown Records* (Watertown, 1894–1939), V, 318. For similar orders, see also "Records of the Suffolk County Court, 1671–1680," Col. Soc. Mass., *Colls.,* XXX, 647; Samuel A. Bates, ed., *Records of the Town of Braintree, 1640–1793* (Randolph, Mass.: Daniel H. Hoxford, 1886), p. 253; *Vestry Book of Petsworth Parish, Gloucester County, Virginia, 1677–1793,* p. 270.

130. *New Haven Town Records,* II, 59–60.

131. *Early Records of the Town of Providence,* X, 28.

132. Bucks County Orphans' Court Docket, vol. A–1, ff. 4–5, microfilm 9–20, Pennsylvania State Archives.

133. "Journal of William Stephens," *Colonial Records of Georgia,* IV, supplement, p. 58.

134. *New Haven Town Records,* II, 98–99.

135. *Minutes of the Orphan-masters of New Amsterdam, 1655–1663,* p. 212; Bucks County Orphans' Court Docket, vol. A–1, f. 21, Pennsylvania State Archives. For similar cases, see also *Archives of Maryland,* LIII, 182; H. Clay Reed and George J. Miller, eds., *The Burlington Court Book: A Record of Quaker Jurisprudence in West New Jersey, 1680–1709* (Washington, D.C.: American Historical Association, 1944), p. 215; Anne Arundel County Court Judgments, liber G, ff. 618–19, Maryland Hall of Records; *Minutes of the Orphan-masters of New Amsterdam, 1655–1663,* p. 154.

136. "Abstracts of Wills on File in the Surrogate's Office, City of New York, 1665–1800," *Collections of the New-York Historical Society,* XXVII, 3; Prince George's County Court Records, liber L, f. 368, Maryland Hall of Records.

137. *New Haven Colony Records,* II, 318, 319.

138. "Northumberland County Orders, 1678–1713," in Duvall, ed., *Virginia Colonial Abstracts,* I, 30; "Indentures of Apprentices, 1718–1727," *Collections of the New-York Historical Society,* XLII, 179–80; Prince George's County Court Records, liber P, f. 454, Maryland Hall of Records.

139. *Essex County Court Records,* IX, 595; *Colonial Records of Georgia,* I, 471.

140. Testamentary Proceedings, X, ff. 312–13, Maryland Hall of Records.

141. See e.g. *Early Records of the Town of Warwick,* pp. 289–290; *Colonial Records of North Carolina,* I, 566; *Province and Court Records of Maine,* II, 517; Anne Arundel County Court Judgments, liber G, ff. 278–79, Maryland Hall of Records; Lancaster County Court Orders, No. 7, 1721–1729, f. 271, microfilm 27, Virginia State Library.

142. *Colonial Records of Georgia,* II, 35.

143. "Early Records of the City and County of Albany and Colony of Rensselaerswyck," New York State Library, *History Bulletin,* X, 485; "Indentures of Apprenticeship, 1694–1708," *Collections of the New-York Historical Society,* XVIII, 591–92.

144. Prince George's County Court Records, accession 5747, liber B, f. 289, Maryland Hall of Records.

145. *New Haven Town Records,* I, 192.

146. Kent County Court Proceedings, liber I, f. 585, Maryland Hall of Records; Baltimore County Court Proceedings, liber I.S. no. B [A], ff. 182, 137, Maryland Hall of Records; Lancaster County Court Orders, no. 9, 1743–1752, f. 62, microfilm 28, Virginia State Library; Charles County Court Records, Liber G, no. 1, f. 1, Maryland Hall of Records.

147. Prince George's County Court Orders, liber D, f. 172, Maryland Hall of Records.

148. Charles County Court Records, liber H, no. 1, f. 124, Maryland Hall of Records; "Indentures of Apprenticeship, 1694–1708," *Collections of the New-York Historical Society,* XVIII, 604–605.

149. See e.g. Accomack County Orders, 1676–1678, f. 71, microfilm 79, Virginia State Library; Prince George's County Court Records, liber D, f. 216, Maryland Hall of Records; Norfolk County Orders, 1746–1750, f. 88, microfilm 53, Virginia State Library.

150. "Town Records of Salem, 1634–1659," Essex Institute, *Historical Collections,* IX (1868), 218–219.

151. See e.g. the case of Thomas Fender in *Plymouth Records,* V, 267, and that of Charles Hodge in Prince George's County Court Records, liber G, vol. I, f. 78, Maryland Hall of Records.

152. See e.g. John Symonds' estate inventory (1671), *Essex County Court Records,* IV, 445, and John Tooker's will (1750), "Abstracts of Wills on File in the Surrogate's Office, City of New York, 1665–1800," *Collections of the New-York Historical Society,* XXVIII, 379.

153. "Records of the Particular Court of Connecticut, 1639–1663," Conn. Hist. Soc., *Colls.,* XXII, 243.

154. *Records of the Court of Assistants of Massachusetts Bay, 1630–1692,* II, 67; *Burlington Court Book of West New Jersey, 1680–1709,* p. 186.

155. "Early Records of the City and County of Albany and the Colony of Rensselaerswyck," New York State Library, *History Bulletin,* X, 287; Bucks County Orphans' Court Docket, vol. A–1, f. 53, microfilm 9–20, Pennsylvania State Archives; York County Orphans' Court Docket, vol. A, f. 196, microfilm 67–111, Pennsylvania State Archives.

156. Prince George's County Court Records, liber S, ff. 125–126, Maryland Hall of Records.

157. *Essex County Court Records,* VII, 14–15.

158. "Salem Town Records, 1659–1680," Essex Institute, *Historical Collections,* XL, 123, 125, 288; XLII, 258–59; XLIII, 34, 41, 147, 151, 156, 262, 263, 265, 272; XLVIII, 27; XLIX, 76, 158.

159. Frederick County Court Judgment Record, accession 6838, ff. 18–19, Maryland Hall of Records.

160. See e.g. Baltimore County Court Proceedings, liber D, f. 212, and liber G, no. 1, f. 398, Maryland Hall of Records; *Select Cases of the Mayor's Court of New York City, 1674–1784,* p. 185; Norfolk County Orders, 1742–1746, n.f., microfilm 53, Virginia State Library; Lucy Downing to John Winthrop, ca. January 1649, *Winthrop Papers* (Boston: Massachusetts Historical Society, 1929–1949), V, 296; "Records of the Suffolk County Court, 1671–1680," Col. Soc. Mass., *Colls.,* XXIX, 555–556; "Northumberland County Orders, 1678–1713," in Duvall, ed., *Virginia Colonial Abstracts,* I, 63; Lancaster County Miscellaneous Book: Orphans' Court Records, 1742–1767,

part I, pp. 54–55, microfilm 36–19, Pennsylvania State Archives; *Plymouth Colony Records,* III, 4–5.

161. See e.g. *Essex County Court Records,* VIII, 249–250; *Burlington Court Book of West New Jersey, 1680–1709,* pp. 229–230; Chester County Court of Quarter Sessions Docket, 1733–1742, f. 190, microfilm 558,038, Pennsylvania State Archives; *Boston Town Records,* II, 156–57; *New Haven Town Records,* I, 361; Baltimore County Court Proceedings, liber T.B., no. T.R., f. 9, Maryland Hall of Records; Prince George's County Court Records, liber S, f. 124, and liber DD, f. 405, Maryland Hall of Records; Court of General Quarter Sessions, New York City, book 3, n.f. (1751), microfilm CMS1, Historical Documents Collection, Queens College.

162. Kent County Court Proceedings, liber I, f. 587; Prince George's County Court Records, box 5747, liber B, f. 196: Maryland Hall of Records.

163. George Whitefield, *A Further Account of God's Dealings . . .* (Philadelphia, 1746), p. 53; Dorothy Flute to John Winthrop, May 5,1640, *Winthrop Papers,* IV, 236–237.

164. Lancaster County Court Orders, no. 1, 1666–1680, f. 470, microfilm 24, Virginia State Library; Charles County Court Records, liber S, no. 1, f. 212, Maryland Hall of Records; *Select Cases of the Mayor's Court of New York City, 1674–1784,* p. 184; Chancery Court Records, II, f. 430, Maryland Hall of Records.

165. *Records of New Amsterdam,* IV, 184–185; *Records of the Towns of North and South Hempstead, Long Island, New York* (Jamaica, N.Y., 1896–1904), III, 219–21.

166. Charles County Court Records, liber S, ff. 283–84, Maryland Hall of Records.

167. Chester County Court of Quarter Sessions Docket, 1723–1733, f. 273, microfilm 558,038, Pennsylvania State Archives; Accomack County Orders, 1714–1717, f. 15, microfilm 80, Virginia State Library; Prince George's County Court Records, liber V, f. 294, Maryland Hall of Records.

168. *Archives of Maryland,* LXV, 95; Chester County Court of Quarter Sessions, 1742–1759, f. 5, microfilm 558,038, Pennsylvania State Archives.

169. *County Court Records of Accomack-Northampton, Virginia, 1640–1645,* p. 266; *Essex County Court Records,* I, 84; Kent County Court Proceedings, liber J.D., no. 3, ff. 58–58 [59], Maryland Hall of Records.

170. The jury had found, "upon due serch and examination, that the body of John Walker was blackish and blew, and the skin broken in divers places from the middle to the haire of his head, viz, all his backe with stripes given him by his master, Robert Latham, as Robert himself did testify; and alsoe was found a bruise of his left arme, and one of his left hipp, and one great bruise of his brest; and there was the knuckles of one hand and one of his fingers frozen, and alsoe both his heeles frozen . . . and alsoe wee find that the said John was

forced to carry a logg which was beyond his strength, which hee indeavoring to doe, the logg fell upon him, and hee, being downe, had a stripe or two, as Joseph Beadle doth testify; and wee find that it was some daies before his death; and wee find, by the testimony of John Howland and John Adams, that heard Robert Latham say that hee gave John Walker some stripes that morning before his death; and alsoe wee find the flesh much broken of the knees of John Walker, and that hee did want sufficient food and cloathing and lodging, and that the said John did constantly wett his bedd and his cloathes, lying in them, and soe suffered by it, his clothes being frozen about him; and that the said John was put forth in extremity of cold, though thus unabled by lameness and sorenes to performe what was required; and therefore in respect of crewelty and hard usuage hee died." See *Plymouth Colony Records*, III, 71–73, III, 82, and VII, 75, on charges against Susanne Latham.

171. Chester County Court of Quarter Sessions Docket, 1714–1723, n.f., microfilm 558,038, Pennsylvania State Archives. For other examples, see also Court of General Quarter Sessions, New York City, book 2, f. 343, microfilm CMS1, Historical Documents Collection, Queens College; *Select Cases of the Mayor's Court of New York City, 1674–1784*, p. 185.

172. See e.g. Norfolk County Deed Book 5, part 2, n.f. [1689], microfilm 2, Virginia State Library; Baltimore County Court Proceedings, liber I.S., no. C, f. 2, Maryland Hall of Records.

173. *Essex County Court Records*, VIII, 302-303. Philip Fowler's sister, Martha Neland, testified that this "was not the first time that Philippe had done this." See ibid., VIII, 314.

174. Court of General Quarter Sessions, New York City, book 2, f. 535, microfilm CMS1, Historical Documents Collection, Queens College; Prince George's County Court Records, liber MM, f. 510, Maryland Hall of Records; "Note-Book Kept by Thomas Lechford," VII, 230.

175. *Essex County Court Records*, VIII, 295–96.

176. See Elizabeth Pleck, *Domestic Tyranny: The Making of American Social Policy against Family Violence from Colonial Times to the Present* (New York: Oxford University Press, 1987), ch. 1.

177. Peter Hoffer and N.E.H. Hull, *Murdering Mothers: Infanticide in England and New England, 1558–1803* (New York: New York University Press, 1981), p. 46. Elizabeth Pleck has suggested that the revolutionary generation may have been even harsher than its predecessors in using corporal punishment on children; this observation, however, is based on relatively few, socially skewed reminiscences and is not entirely persuasive. See Pleck, *Domestic Tyranny*, p. 45.

178. *Essex County Court Records*, VII, 421–22.

179. *Archives of Maryland*, LIV, 29; *Records of the Town of East-Hampton* (Sag Harbor, New York, 1887–1905), I, 288–89; "Early Records of the City

and County of Albany and the Colony of Rensselaerswyck," New York State Library, *History Bulletin*, X, 415.

180. Prince George's County Court Records, liber H, f. 1031, Maryland Hall of Records.

181. *Essex County Court Records*, VI, 97.

182. *Records of New Amsterdam*, II, 247; *Essex County Court Records*, II, 27; *Archives of Maryland*, XLI, 515.

183. *Essex County Court Records*, IV, 261.

184. Ibid., II, 176. The letter, or rather a fragment of it, appears on the reverse side of a deposition. The style of the letter as well as the reference to instruction in algebra strongly suggest that it was written by an adolescent boy.

185. *Early Records of the Town of Warwick*, pp. 235–236; *Early Records of the Town of Providence*, IV, 213.

186. Charles R. Street, ed., *Huntington Town Records, 1653–1873* (Huntington, N.Y., 1887–1889), I, 275.

187. *Early Records of the Town of Portsmouth*, p. 409; Henrico County Record Book No. 2, Orders and Wills, 1678–1693, transcript, p. 115, microfilm 53, Virginia State Library; "Indentures of Apprenticeship, 1694–1708," *Collections of the New-York Historical Society*, XVIII, 606.

188. *County Court Records of Accomack-Northampton, Virginia, 1640–1645*, pp. 436–437.

189. *County Court Records of Accomack-Northampton, Virginia, 1640–1645*, p. 368.

190. *Records of the Towns of North and South Hempstead, Long Island, New York* (Jamaica, N.Y., 1896–1904), I, 128–129; Norfolk County Deed Book 5, part 2, n.f., microfilm 2, Virginia State Library. In some cases, of course, masters were forced to sue parents for compensation; see e.g. David Konig, ed., *Plymouth Court Records* (Wilmington, Del.: Michael Glazier, 1978), VII, 226.

191. Charles County Court Records, liber X, no. 1, f. 251, Maryland Hall of Records; *Plymouth Colony Records*, II, 82–83.

192. *Essex County Court Records*, IV, 219–220; "Kingston Court Records," *New York Historical Manuscripts: Dutch*, XXV, part 1, p. 308.

193. *Colonial Records of Georgia*, I, 471. This would fit with the English servant experience, at least for the eighteenth century. Using evidence from the town of Cardington, Roger Schofield found that "most servants (about two-thirds of the boys, and almost three quarters of the girls) were employed either within the parish, or in neighboring parishes within 8 kilometers (5 miles) of home." See "Age-Specific Mobility in an Eighteenth Century Rural English Parish," *Annales de demographie historique* (1970), p. 271. On the movement of Boston apprentices in the eighteenth century, see Towner, "The Indentures of Boston's Poor Apprentices: 1734–1805," Col. Soc. Mass., *Transactions*, 43, pp. 417–468.

194. *Essex County Court Records,* VII, 264.

195. *Records of New Amsterdam,* VI, 152.

196. "Indentures of Apprentices, 1718–1727," *Collections of the New-York Historical Society,* XLII, 117.

197. "Early Records of the City and County of Albany and the Colony of Rensselaerswyck," New York State Library, *History Bulletin,* X, 422–423.

198. *New Haven Colony Records,* II, 137–39.

199. *Records of New Amsterdam,* V, 243; A.J.F. Van Laer, trans. and ed., *Minutes of the Court of Fort Orange and Beverwyck* (Albany: University of the State of New York, 1920–1923), II, 17.

200. *Essex County Court Records,* II, 46; "Note-Book Kept by Thomas Lechford," VII, 251; William Piggott to John Winthrop, May 4, 1647, *Winthrop Papers,* V, 154–155.

201. *Essex County Court Records,* II, 403; *Minutes of the Court of Albany, Rensselaerswyck and Schenectady,* II, 216–217.

202. *Province and Court Records of Maine,* V, 185.

203. *Plymouth Colony Records,* II, 58–59. John Demos, "Notes on Life in Plymouth Colony," *William and Mary Quarterly,* 3d ser., 22 (1965), 286, gives Billington's age.

204. Prince George's County Court Records, liber P, ff. 596–97, Maryland Hall of Records.

205. *Essex County Court Records,* II, 275–276.

Afterword

1. The theme of provincialism runs through much of American cultural history. For an interesting discussion of the problem in the life of one early American, see Kenneth Silverman, *The Life and Times of Cotton Mather* (New York: Harper and Row, 1984).

2. See the works cited above, Introduction, notes 1–2.

3. See Lawrence Stone, *The Family, Sex and Marriage in England, 1500–1800* (New York: Harper and Row, 1977). On timing, cf. Randolph Trumbach, *The Rise of the Egalitarian Family: Aristocratic Kinship and Domestic Relations in Eighteenth-Century England* (New York: Academic Press, 1978). See also Edward Shorter, *The Making of the Modern Family* (New York: Basic Books, 1973); Joan W. Scott, "Review Essay: The History of the Family as an Affective Unit," *Social History,* 4 (1979), 509–516; Jean-Louis Flandrin, *Families in Former Times: Kinship, Household, and Sexuality* (New York: Cambridge University Press, 1979); and Philippe Ariès, *Centuries of Childhood,* trans. Robert Baldick (New York: Knopf, 1961). For a discussion of seventeenth-century Dutch family history that raises some questions about the timing and class boundaries of Stone's argument, see Simon Schama, *The Embarrassment of Riches* (New York: Knopf, 1987). On the medieval family, see

Barbara Hanawalt, *The Ties That Bound: Peasant Families in Medieval England* (New York: Oxford University Press, 1986).

4. See Jacqueline Reinier, "Rearing the Republican Child: Attitudes and Practices in Post-Revolutionary Philadelphia," *William and Mary Quarterly*, 3d ser., 39 (1982), 150–165.

5. Jay Fliegelman, *Prodigals and Pilgrims: The American Revolution Against Patriarchal Authority, 1750–1800* (New York: Cambridge University Press, 1982). I am grateful to Janet Riesman for first suggesting Fliegelman's work to me.

6. Philip Greven, *The Protestant Temperament: Patterns of Childrearing, Religious Experience, and the Self in Early America* (New York: Knopf, 1977). See also the review essay on Fliegelman, *Prodigals and Pilgrims*, by Thomas Slaughter, "Family Politics in Revolutionary America," *American Quarterly*, 36 (1984), 598–606.

7. Ariès, *Centuries of Childhood*, p. 413, quoted in Fliegelman, *Prodigals and Pilgrims*, p. 263.

8. See Philip Greven, *Four Generations: Population, Land and Family in Colonial Andover, Massachusetts* (Ithaca: Cornell University Press, 1970). See also Christopher Jedrey, *The World of John Cleaveland: Family and Community in Eighteenth-Century New England* (New York: Norton, 1979) and Robert Gross, *The Minutemen and Their World* (New York: Hill and Wang, 1976). Cf. John Demos, *A Little Commonwealth: Family Life in Plymouth Colony* (New York: Oxford University Press, 1970).

9. On New England, see Jedrey, *The World of John Cleaveland*, and David Jaffee, "The People of the Wachusett: Founding and Village Culture in New England, 1630–1764," (diss., Harvard University, 1982); on other regions, see Daniel Blake Smith, *Inside the Great House: Planter Family Life in Eighteenth-Century Chesapeake Society* (Ithaca: Cornell University Press, 1980); Allan Kulikoff, *Tobacco and Slaves: The Development of Southern Cultures in the Chesapeake, 1680–1800* (Chapel Hill: University of North Carolina Press, 1986); Stephanie Grauman Wolf, *Urban Village: Population, Community, and Family Structure in Germantown, Pennsylvania, 1683–1800* (Princeton: Princeton University Press, 1976); and James Lemon, *The Best Poor Man's Country: A Geographical Study of Southeastern Pennsylvania* (Baltimore: Johns Hopkins University Pess, 1972). On sharper divergences between women in north and south, see Mary Beth Norton, "The Evolution of White Women's Experience in Early America," *American Historical Review*, 89 (1984), 593–619.

10. Gordon Schochet, *Patriarchalism in Political Thought* (New York: Oxford University Press, 1975), p. 273 and passim.

11. On the effects of the Great Awakening on established authority, see Richard Bushman, *From Puritan to Yankee: Character and the Social Order in Connecticut, 1690–1765* (New York: Norton, 1970); Patricia Tracy, *Jon-*

athan Edwards, Pastor: Religion and Society in Eighteenth-Century North-ampton (New York: Hill and Wang, 1980); Alan Heimert, *Religion and the American Mind, from the Great Awakening to the Revolution* (Cambridge: Harvard University Press, 1966); and Gary Nash, *The Urban Crucible: Social Change, Political Consciousness, and the Origins of the American Revolution* (Cambridge: Harvard University Press, 1979).

12. See Schochet, *Patriarchalism and Political Thought.*

13. Melvin Yazawa, *From Colonies to Commonwealth: Familial Ideology and the Beginnings of the American Revolution* (Baltimore: Johns Hopkins University Press, 1985), p. 87.

14. Quoted in Fliegelman, *Prodigals and Pilgrims,* p. 89.

15. Ibid., p. 5.

16. For the specific implications of this for women, see Norton, "The Evolution of White Women's Experience in Early America," pp. 612–613.

17. Quoted in Fliegelman, *Prodigals and Pilgrims,* p. 124.

18. Daniel Scott Smith, "Parental Power and Marriage Patterns: An Analysis of Historical Trends in Hingham, Massachusetts," *Journal of Marriage and the Family,* 35 (1973), 419–439; Daniel Scott Smith and Michael Hindus, "Premarital Pregnancy in America, 1640–1971: An Overview and Interpretation," *Journal of Interdisciplinary History,* 5 (1975), 537–570; the Bristol figure is cited in James Henretta, *The Evolution of American Society, 1700–1815* (Lexington, Mass.: D. C. Heath, 1973), p. 133.

19. Nancy Cott, "Divorce and the Changing Status of Women in Eighteenth-Century Massachusetts," *William and Mary Quarterly,* 3d ser., 33 (1976), 592. Cf. Mary Beth Norton, *Liberty's Daughters* (Boston: Little, Brown, 1980), pp. 47–51, who stresses women's continuing reluctance to seek divorce and their difficulties in obtaining it. On p. 234, however, Norton cites Cott's evidence as well as studies that find a similar pattern in Connecticut divorce petitions in the same period.

20. Cott, "Divorce and the Changing Status of Women," p. 593.

21. Marylynn Salmon, *Women and the Law of Property in Early America* (Chapel Hill: University of North Carolina Press, 1986), p. 59.

22. Linda Kerber takes a slightly more cautious view than Cott; she argues persuasively that women's gains in this period were slower and the results more ambiguous. See *Women of the Republic* (Chapel Hill: University of North Carolina Press, 1980), esp. ch. 6. Norton takes a similar view in *Liberty's Daughters.* See also the excellent review essay by Norma Basch, "The Emerging Legal History of Women in the United States: Property, Divorce, and the Constitution," *Signs: Journal of Women in Culture and Society,* 12 (1986), 97–117.

23. Smith, *Inside the Great House,* p. 286.

24. John Barnard, *A Present for an Apprentice* (Boston, 1747), p. 21.

25. Robert Irwin v. Catherine Irwin, Records of the Supreme Court, Eastern

District, Record Group 33: Divorce Papers, 1786–1815, carton 2, folder "I–J", Pennsylvania State Archives.

26. For some figures on the incidence of slander by the late eighteenth century, see William Nelson, *Dispute and Conflict Resolution in Plymouth County, Massachusetts, 1725–1825* (Chapel Hill: University of North Carolina Press, 1981), pp. 23, 159n64, and Cornelia Hughes Dayton, "Women Before the Bar: Gender, Law, and Society in Connecticut, 1710–1790" (diss., Princeton University, 1986), p. 208. Dayton (pp. 209, 223) also notes the increasing emphasis of business concerns to the exclusion of more general community concerns in slander cases after 1760.

27. David Konig, ed., *Plymouth Court Records* (Wilmington, Del.: Michael Glazier, 1978), X, 296.

28. Quoted in Michael Rogin, *Fathers and Children: Andrew Jackson and the Subjugation of the American Indian* (New York: Knopf, 1975), pp. 43–44.

29. See John J. McCusker and Russell R. Menard, *The Economy of British North America, 1607–1789* (Chapel Hill: University of North Carolina Press, 1985), ch. 10, for an excellent summary and critical review of the extensive literature on colonial population and migration history. Among the more important specific works are, on New England: Daniel Scott Smith, "The Demographic History of Colonial New England," *Journal of Economic History,* 32 (1972), 165–183; Daniel Scott Smith, "Population, Family, and Society in Hingham, Massachusetts, 1635–1880" (Ph.D. diss., University of California at Berkeley, 1973); Greven, *Four Generations;* Kenneth Lockridge, *A New England Town: The First Hundred Years* (New York: Norton, 1970); Lockridge, "Land, Population, and the Evolution of New England Society, 1636–1790," *Past and Present,* 39 (1968), 62–80; Lockridge, "The Population of Dedham, Massachusetts, 1636–1736," *Economic History Review,* 2d ser., 19 (1966), 318–344; Demos, *A Little Commonwealth;* Demos, "Families in Colonial Bristol, Rhode Island: An Exercise in Historical Demography," *William and Mary Quarterly,* 3d ser., 25 (1968), 40–57; Susan L. Norton, "Population Growth in Colonial America: A Study of Ipswich, Massachusetts," *Population Studies,* 25 (1971), 433–452; Maris Vinovskis, "American Historical Demography: A Review Essay," *Historical Methods Newsletter,* 4 (1971), 141–148; Edward Byers, "Fertility Transition in a New England Commercial Center: Nantucket, Massachusetts, 1680–1840," *Journal of Interdisciplinary History,* 13 (1982), 17–40; Byers, *The Nation of Nantucket: Society and Politics in an Early American Commercial Center, 1660–1820* (Boston: Northeastern University Press, 1987); Douglas Jones, "The Strolling Poor: Transiency in Eighteenth-Century Massachusetts," *Journal of Social History,* 8 (1975), 28–54; and Jones, *Village and Seaport: Migration and Society in Eighteenth-Century Massachusetts* (Hanover: University Press of New England, 1981). On the Middle Colonies: Billy G. Smith, "Death and Life in a Colonial

Immigrant City: A Demographic Analysis of Philadelphia," *Journal of Economic History,* 37 (1977), 863–889; Robert V. Wells, "Quaker Marriage Patterns in a Colonial Perspective," *William and Mary Quarterly,* 3d ser., 29 (1972), 415–442; Lemon, *The Best Poor Man's Country;* Wolf, *Urban Village.* On the Chesapeake: Gloria Main, *Tobacco Colony* (Princeton: Princeton University Press, 1982); Darrett Rutman and Anita Rutman, *A Place in Time: Middlesex County, Virginia, 1650–1750* (New York: Norton, 1984); Rutman and Rutman, "Of Agues and Fevers: Malaria in the Early Chesapeake," *William and Mary Quarterly,* 3d ser., 33 (1976), 31–60; Rutman and Rutman, "'Now-Wives and Sons-in-Law': Parental Death in a Seventeenth-Century Virginia County," in Tate and Ammerman, eds., *The Chesapeake in the Seventeenth Century;* Russell Menard, "Immigrants and Their Increase: The Process of Population Growth in Early Colonial Maryland," in Aubrey Land et al., eds., *Law, Society and Politics in Early Maryland* (Baltimore: Johns Hopkins University Press, 1977); Lorena Walsh, "'Till Death Us Do Part': Marriage and the Family in Seventeenth-Century Maryland," in Tate and Ammerman, eds., *The Chesapeake in the Seventeenth Century.* On the deep South: Peter Wood, *Black Majority* (New York: Knopf, 1974). See also David Galenson, *White Servitude in Colonial America* (New York: Cambridge University Press, 1981).

30. On New England migration and its sources, see e.g. Greven, *Four Generations;* Jaffee, "The People of the Wachusett"; Gross, *The Minutemen and Their World;* Lockridge, "Land, Population and the Evolution of New England Society, 1630–1790"; and Jedrey, *The World of John Cleaveland.* On the trans-Appalachian frontier in the revolutionary period, see Jack M. Sosin, *Whitehall and the Wilderness* (Lincoln: University of Nebraska Press, 1961); Malcolm Rohrbaugh, *The Trans-Appalachian Frontier: People, Societies, and Institutions, 1775–1850* (New York: Oxford University Press, 1978); Ray Allen Billington, *Westward Expansion: A History of the American Frontier* (New York: Macmillan, 1949). The figures on the growth of the northern New England frontier come from David P. Jaffee, "One of the Primitive Sort: Portrait Makers of the Rural North, 1760–1860," in Steven Hahn and Jonathan Prude, eds., *The Countryside in the Age of Capitalist Transformation* (Chapel Hill: University of North Carolina Press, 1985), p. 133n12.

31. See Bernard Bailyn, *The Peopling of British North America: An Introduction* (New York: Knopf, 1986), and his *Voyagers to the West: A Passage in the Peopling of America on the Eve of the Revolution* (New York: Knopf, 1986).

32. St. John's [Episcopal] Church (Hillsboro), Vestry Minutes, f. 60, Maryland Hall of Records.

33. William Bentley, *The Diary of William Bentley* (Salem, Mass.: Essex Institute, 1905–1914; repr. 1962), I, 255.

34. *Records of the First Church of Rockingham, Vermont, 1773–1839* (copied by Thomas Bellows Peck, Boston: David Clapp, 1902), p. 17.

35. See e.g. Michael Grossberg, *Governing the Hearth: Law and the Family in Nineteenth-Century America* (Chapel Hill: University of North Carolina Press, 1985), and Norton, *Liberty's Daughters.*

36. Catherine Sedgwick, *Home* (Boston, 1845), ch. 2.

37. Quoted in Norton, *Liberty's Daughters.*

38. Grossberg, *Governing the Hearth,* p. 17.

39. Ibid., pp. 18–20; quote from 19.

40. This paragraph draws on Salmon, *Women and the Law of Property,* pp. 63–64, 71, 78, 80, and Grossberg, *Governing the Hearth,* p. 238. See also Kerber, *Women of the Republic,* ch. 6.

41. Grossberg, *Governing the Hearth,* pp. 18–24; Salmon, *Women and the Law of Property,* p. 80.

42. The fullest discussion of this is Ruth H. Bloch, "American Feminine Ideals in Transition: The Rise of the Moral Mother, 1785–1815," *Feminist Studies,* 4 (1978), 101–126. See also Nancy Cott, *The Bonds of Womanhood* (New Haven: Yale University Press, 1977), esp. chs. 2–3; and Kerber, *Women of the Republic,* esp. ch. 7.

43. Mather, *Help for Distressed Parents* (Boston, 1695), pp. 8–9.

44. Bloch, "American Feminine Ideals in Transition," pp. 106, 109ff. See also Cott, *The Bonds of Womanhood,* ch. 2; Kathryn Kish Sklar, *Catharine Beecher: A Study in American Domesticity* (New Haven: Yale University Press, 1973); and Ann Douglas, *The Feminization of American Culture* (New York: Knopf, 1977), ch. 2.

45. See e.g. Cott, *The Bonds of Womanhood,* esp. chs. 1–2; Mary Ryan, *The Cradle of the Middle Class* (New York: Cambridge University Press, 1981); and Anthony F. C. Wallace, *Rockdale* (New York: Knopf, 1978).

46. Quoted in Bloch, "American Feminine Ideals in Transition," pp. 113–114.

47. Quoted in ibid., p. 117.

48. Quoted in Cott, *The Bonds of Womanhood,* p. 85.

49. Quoted in Kerber, *Women of the Republic,* p. 229. On women's improving literacy, see Kenneth Lockridge, *Literacy in Colonial New England* (New York: Norton, 1974), pp. 57–58, and Cott, *The Bonds of Womanhood,* p. 15. On women's education in this period, see Cott, *The Bonds of Womanhood,* chs. 2–3; Kerber, *Women of the Republic,* ch. 7; and Sklar, *Catharine Beecher.* See also Bernard Wishy, *The Child and the Republic* (Philadelphia: University of Pennsylvania Press, 1968).

50. Quoted in Grossberg, *Governing the Hearth,* p. 264.

51. Ibid., p. 242.

52. See Grossberg, *Governing the Hearth,* ch. 7.

53. Ibid., pp. 259–261. See also Marcus Jernegan, *Laboring and Dependent Classes in Colonial America, 1607–1783: Studies of the Economic, Educational and Social Significance of Slaves, Servants, Apprentices and Poor Folk* (Chicago, 1931); Paul Johnson, *A Shopkeeper's Millennium* (New York: Hill and Wang, 1978; Alan Dawley, *Class and Community* (Cambridge: Harvard University Press, 1976); Ryan, *Cradle of the Middle Class;* and Wallace, *Rockdale.*

54. "Journal of William Stephens," *Colonial Records of the State of Georgia* (Atlanta and Athens, 1904–1979), IV, 543. For similar cases in the late eighteenth century, see Charles County Orphans' Court Proceedings, in Wills, liber A.F. No. 7, f. 229, Maryland Hall of Records (1778); *Records of the Town of East-Hampton* (Sag Harbor, N.Y., 1887–1905), IV, 250 (1786); and *Laws of Maryland* (Rev. Virgil Maxcy, Baltimore: Philip Nicklin, 1811), II, 203-205 (1794).

55. Grossberg, *Governing the Hearth,* pp. 263–266.

56. Ibid., p. 265.

57. Ibid., p. 265.

58. Allegany County Orphans' Court Proceedings, liber A, ff. 125–26, Maryland Hall of Records.

59. Quoted in Grossberg, *Governing the Hearth,* p. 267. On the children's asylum movement, see David Rothman, *The Discovery of the Asylum* (Boston: Little, Brown, 1971); Paul Boyer, *Urban Masses and Moral Order in America* (Cambridge: Harvard University Press, 1978), esp. ch. 6; and Miriam Langsam, *Children West: A History of the Placing Out System of the New York Children's Aid Society* (Madison, Wisc., 1964).

60. Grossberg, *Governing the Hearth,* p. 267.

61. Catherine Sedgwick, *Home,* ch. 2.

62. William G. McLoughlin, "Evangelical Child-Rearing in the Age of Jackson: Francis Wayland's Views on When and How to Subdue the Willfulness of Children," *Journal of Social History,* 9 (1975), 20–43. Greven discusses Wayland's case in *The Protestant Temperament,* pp. 38–42.

63. Quoted in Kirk Jeffrey, "The Family as Utopian Retreat from the City," *Soundings,* 55 (1972), p. 28.

64. Demos, *A Little Commonwealth,* p. 186. For a fuller discussion of this theme, see also Jeffrey, "The Family as Utopian Retreat from the City," pp. 21–41; Demos, "Images of the Family, Then and Now," in Virginia Tufte and Barbara Myerhoff, eds., *Changing Images of the Family* (New Haven: Yale University Press, 1979), pp. 43–60, reprinted in Demos, *Past, Present, and Personal* (New York: Oxford University Press, 1986), pp. 24–40; Barbara Laslett, "The Family as a Public and Private Institution: An Historical Perspective," *Journal of Marriage and the Family,* 35 (1973), 480–492.

65. Quoted in Cott, *The Bonds of Womanhood,* p. 74. There is an extensive literature on the cult of domesticity and its implications. See, in addition to

Cott's book, Barbara Welter, "The Cult of True Womanhood," *American Quarterly*, 18 (1966), 151–174; Sklar, *Catharine Beecher;* Ann Douglas, *The Feminization of American Culture* (New York: Knopf, 1977); Ellen K. Rothman, *Hands and Hearts: A History of Courtship in America* (New York: Basic Books, 1984); Ryan, *Cradle of the Middle Class;* and Carroll Smith-Rosenberg, *Disorderly Conduct: Visions of Gender in Victorian America* (New York: Oxford University Press, 1986). See also Suzanne Lebsock's excellent *The Free Women of Petersburg: Status and Culture in a Southern Town, 1784–1860* (New York: Norton, 1984).

66. Jeffrey, "The Family as Utopian Retreat from the Family," p. 38. On domestic architecture, see Clifford E. Clark Jr., "Domestic Architecture as an Index to Social History: The Romantic Revival and the Cult of Domesticity in America, 1840–1870," *Journal of Interdisciplinary History*, 7 (1976), 33–56; Gwendolyn Wright, *Moralism and the Model Home: Domestic Architecture and Cultural Conflict in Chicago, 1873–1913* (Chicago: University of Chicago Press, 1980), pp. 9–10; and Dolores Hayden, *The Domestic Revolution: A History of Feminist Designs for American Homes, Neighborhoods, and Cities* (Cambridge: MIT Press, 1981). On the increasing "privatization" of houses beginning in the eighteenth century, see also Rhys Isaac, *The Transformation of Virginia, 1740–1790* (Chapel Hill: University of North Carolina Press, 1982), pp. 302–305 and James Deetz, *In Small Things Forgotten* (Garden City: Anchor Press/Doubleday, 1977), pp. 115–117.

67. This paragraph draws on A. G. Roeber, *Faithful Magistrates and Republican Lawyers: Creators of Virginia Legal Culture, 1680–1810* (Chapel Hill: University of North Carolina Press, 1981); Grossberg, *Governing the Hearth;* Klein, "The Rise of the New York Bar: The Legal Career of William Livingstone," in Flaherty, ed., *Essays in the History of American Law;* Robert A. Ferguson, *Law and Letters in American Culture* (Cambridge: Harvard University Press, 1984); Lawrence Friedman, *A History of American Law* (New York: Simon and Schuster, 1973); Horwitz, *The Transformation of American Law;* William Nelson, *The Americanization of the Common Law: The Impact of Legal Change on Massachusetts Society, 1760–1830* (Cambridge: Harvard University Press, 1975); Stephen Botein, "The Legal Profession in Colonial North America," in Wilfred Prest, ed., *Lawyers in Early Modern Europe and America* (New York: Holmes and Meier, 1981); Hendrick Hartog, ed., *Law in the American Revolution and the Revolution in the Law* (New York: New York University Press, 1981); Maxwell Bloomfield, *American Lawyers in a Changing Society, 1776–1876* (Cambridge: Harvard University Press, 1976); and John M. Murrin, "The Legal Transformation: The Bench and Bar of Eighteenth-Century Massachusetts," in Stanley Katz and John M. Murrin, eds., *Colonial America: Essays in Politics and Social Development* (3d ed., New York: Knopf, 1983), pp. 540–572.

68. Roeber, *Faithful Magistrates and Republican Lawyers*, p. 126.

69. Quoted in Botein, "The Legal Profession in Colonial North America," in Prest, ed., *Lawyers in Early Modern Europe and America,* p. 139. Robert Ferguson notes that some observers were disturbed by Americans' continued antipathy to the law and legal authority; he discusses the case of Hugh Henry Brackenridge, who expressed his concerns in *Modern Chivalry.* See Ferguson, *Law and Letters in American Culture,* pp. 126–127. For a fuller discussion of the view of lawyers in "country" ideology, see Roeber, *Faithful Magistrates and Republican Lawyers.*

70. Murrin, "The Legal Transformation," in Katz and Murrin, eds., *Colonial America,* p. 555.

71. See John Murrin, "Anglicizing an American Colony: The Transformation of Provinicial Massachusetts" (diss., Yale University, 1966). For a discussion of Anglicization in economic and social life, see Rowland Berthoff and John Murrin, "Feudalism, Communalism, and the Yeoman Freeholder: The American Revolution Considered as a Social Accident," in Stephen G. Kurtz and James H. Hutson, eds., *Essays on the American Revolution* (Chapel Hill: University of North Carolina Press, 1973), pp. 256–288.

72. Grossberg, *Governing the Hearth,* esp. ch. 8.

73. Horwitz, *The Transformation of the American Law.*

74. Roeber, *Faithful Magistrates and Republican Lawyers,* pp. 216–217. Nelson makes the same point in *The Americanization of the Common Law,* pp. 173–174. See also Ferguson, *Law and Letters in American Culture,* pp. 199ff.

75. Chancery Court Proceedings, XVI, ff. 114–16, Maryland Hall of Records; *The Diary of Landon Carter,* ed. Jack P. Greene (Charlottesville: University Press of Virginia, 1965), I, 434.

76. Chancery Court Proceedings, XI, f. 74, Maryland Hall of Records; Grant v. Mayer, Records of the Supreme Court, Eastern District, Record Group 33: Rules of Reference and Reports of Referees, 1765–1837, Carton 1, folder G, 1789–1806, Pennsylvania State Archives.

77. William Falkoner and Roger Morcot, assignees of Guy Bryan, v. John Taylor and William Graham, Records of the Supreme Court, Eastern District, Records Group 33: Miscellaneous Court Papers, 1745–1921, carton 1, 1745–1806, folder marked 1782, 1785–88, 1791, Pennsylvania State Archives.

78. *Dr. Gardiner vs James Flagg, Merchant* (Boston, 1767), p. 25.

79. On the increasing formality of arbitration, see "An Act for the more easy and effectually finishing of Controversies by Arbitration" (1750), in *Public Records of the Colony of Connecticut,* X, 201–202; and "An Act to alter and amend the law in certain cases" (1778), *Laws of Maryland,* I, 611. On the decline of arbitration, see Bruce Mann, *Neighbors and Strangers: Law and Community in Early Connecticut* (Chapel Hill: University of North Carolina Press, 1987), ch. 4, esp. pp. 130–132; Horwitz, *The Transformation of American Law,* ch. 5; Nelson, *Dispute and Conflict Resolution in Plymouth*

County, esp. chs. 4–5; and Auerbach, *Justice Without Law?* Cf. David Konig, *Law and Society in Puritan Massachusetts: Essex County, 1629–1692* (Chapel Hill: University of North Carolina Press, 1979), chs. 4–6, who suggests that litigation supplanted arbitration even earlier, by the end of the seventeenth century.

80. Quoted in Wolf, *Urban Village,* p. 182.

81. See e.g. Oscar and Mary Handlin, *Commonwealth: A Study of the Role of Government in the American Economy, Massachusetts, 1774–1861* (rev. ed., Cambridge: Harvard University Press, 1969), on economy; and Jurgen Herbst, "The First Three American Colleges: Schools of the Reformation," *Perspectives in American History,* 8 (1974), 7–52, on education.

82. See Mack Walker, *German Home Towns: Community, State, and General Estate, 1648–1871* (Ithaca: Cornell University Press, 1971).

83. On this point, see also Thomas Bender, *Community and Social Change in America* (New Brunswick: Rutgers University Press, 1978).

84. See Cathy Davidson, *The Revolution and the Word* (New York: Oxford University Press, 1986). On the problem of race and class in republicanism, see Ronald Takaki, *Iron Cages: Race and Culture in Nineteenth-Century America* (Seattle: University of Washington Press, 1979); Edmund S. Morgan, *American Slavery, American Freedom* (New York: Norton, 1975); Winthrop D. Jordan, *White Over Black: American Attitudes Toward the Negro, 1550–1812* (repr. New York: Norton, 1977); David Brion Davis, *The Problem of Slavery in the Age of Revolution, 1770–1823* (Ithaca: Cornell University Press, 1975); and Michael Rogin, *Fathers and Children: Andrew Jackson and the Subjugation of the American Indian* (New York: Knopf, 1975). On women and republicanism, see Kerber, *Women of the Republic;* and Joan Hoff Wilson, "The Illusion of Change: Women and the Revolution," in Alfred F. Young, ed., *The American Revolution: Explorations in the History of American Radicalism* (DeKalb: Northern Illinois University Press, 1976). For a subtle discussion of the place of lower-class as well as middle-class women in republican society, see Christine Stansell's excellent *City of Women: Sex and Class in New York, 1789–1860* (New York: Knopf, 1986). On the problem of commerce and the republican ideal, see Drew McCoy, *The Elusive Republic: Political Economy in Jeffersonian America* (Chapel Hill: University of North Carolina Press, 1980); J. E. Crowley, *This Sheba, Self: The Conceptualization of Economic Life in Eighteenth-Century America* (Baltimore: Johns Hopkins University Press, 1974); Joyce Appleby, *Economic Thought and Ideology in Seventeenth-Century England* (Princeton: Princeton University Press, 1978); Appleby, *Capitalism and a New Social Order* (New York: New York University Press, 1984); and David Shi, *The Simple Life: Plain Living and High Thinking in American Culture* (New York: Oxford University Press, 1985).

85. See e.g. Elaine Tyler May, *Great Expectations: Marriage and Divorce*

in Post-Victorian America (Chicago: University of Chicago Press, 1980), and Robert Griswold, *Family and Divorce in California, 1850–1890* (Albany: State University of New York Press, 1982). For a different emphasis, see William O'Neill, *Divorce in the Progressive Era* (New Haven: Yale University Press, 1967).

86. Jeffrey, "The Family as Utopian Retreat from the City," p. 35. On this point, see also Demos, "Images of the Family, Then and Now," in Tufte and Myerhoff, eds., *Changing Images of the Family.*

87. Lebsock, *The Free Women of Petersburg,* p. 32. In addition to the works on domesticity cited above in note 65, see also Carl Degler, *At Odds: Women and the Family in America from the Revolution to the Present* (New York: Oxford University Press, 1980), and Sheila Rothman, *Woman's Proper Place* (New York: Basic Books, 1978).

88. On these points, see Grossberg, *Governing the Hearth,* and Stephen J. Morse, "Family Law in Transition: From Traditional Families to Individual Liberty," in Tufte and Myerhoff, eds., *Changing Images of the Family.* See also Jacques Donzelot, *The Policing of Families* (New York: Pantheon Books, 1979).

89. See Jan Lewis, *The Pursuit of Happiness: Family and Values in Jefferson's Virginia* (New York: Cambridge University Press, 1983).

90. Fliegelman, *Prodigals and Pilgrims,* p. 263.

91. Robert N. Bellah et al., *Habits of the Heart: Individualism and Commitment in American Life* (Berkeley: University of California Press, 1985; repr. New York: Harper and Row, 1986).

92. Richard Sennett, *The Fall of Public Man* (New York: Random House, 1978); Christopher Lasch, *The Culture of Narcissism* (New York: Norton, 1978).

Acknowledgments

Russell Jacoby has taken academics to task recently for many things, including padded acknowledgments. I think Jacoby is right about this, and I wish I could follow his advice. Instead I find myself closer to the example of Augustine, who prayed for the grace to reform—but not too soon. I welcome the opportunity to mention, since I cannot hope to repay, the many persons and institutions who have contributed to this project.

I would like to thank Harvard University, Radcliffe College, the Artemus Ward Dissertation Fellowship, the Charles Warren Center, the National Endowment for the Humanities, the Haynes Foundation, the LaFetra Fund, and Pomona College for generous financial support. I would also like to thank the many librarians and archivists who made my research easier, especially the staff of Widener Library at Harvard.

I am especially grateful to six individuals who have helped me while I worked on this project: Bernard Bailyn, who directed my dissertation and whose continued kindness and intellectual example have been invaluable to me; John Demos, who bears the blame for my becoming a colonial historian and whose advice and encouragement over the years have made many things easier, including this book; David Jaffee, who has read every draft of this work and whose comments were often considerably more interesting than the material I showed him; Patty Limerick, who gave the manuscript a thorough and uncomfortably sharp-witted reading; Robert Dawidoff, who has given me the benefit of his extraordinary mind as well as his extraordinary capacity for friendship; and Bob Woods, who has displayed sainted patience in teaching me to use a computer and keep my temper at the same time.

I have always been fortunate in my friends and teachers. Most of them have been spared the details of my research and writing, but I am profoundly in their debt nonetheless. I would especially like to thank Deena Aerenson, Fred Anderson, Virginia DeJohn Anderson, Melanie Billings-Yun, Anne Black, Gene Black, Debbie Burke, Mina Carson, Betsy Crighton, Gerry Denault, Pat Denault, Barbara DeWolfe, Audrey Durnan, David Fischer, Judy Fischer, Rena Fraden, Elizabeth Gilmore, John Gilmore, Steve Glaser, Deena Gonzalez, Mary Kennedy, Norine Kiler, Dave King, Jeff Limerick, Ina Malaguti, Kathy McGowan, Marvin Meyers, Chris Miller, Cris Miller, Pat Rafferty, Jon Roberts, Mark Silk, Tema Kaiser Silk, Peggy Waller, and Joanna Worthley. For years these people have borne with my uncertain moods and overly certain opinions, and they have helped me in every conceivable way. To all of them, I am deeply grateful.

H. M. W.
Claremont, California

Index